GETTYSBURG
EDDIE
The Story of EDDIE PLANK

D1572722

Lawrence Knorr

SUNBURY
PRESS
Mechanicsburg, PA USA

Sunbury Press, Inc.
urg, Pennsylvania

www.sunburypress.com

For information about special discounts for bulk purchases, please contact Sunbury Press Orders Dept. at (855) 338-8359 or orders@sunburypress.com.

To request one of our authors for speaking engagements or book signings, please contact Sunbury Press Publicity Dept. at publicity@sunburypress.com.

ISBN: 978-1-62006-170-1 (Trade paperback)

Library of Congress Control Number: 2018940279

FIRST SUNBURY PRESS EDITION: April 2018

Product of the United States of America
0 1 1 2 3 5 8 13 21 34 55

Set in Bookman Old Style
Designed by Crystal Devine
Cover by Lawrence Knorr
Edited by Lawrence Knorr

Continue the Enlightenment!

CONTENTS

Eddie Plank was one of the smartest left-hand pitchers it has been my pleasure to have on my club. He was short and light, as pitchers go, but he made up for the physical defects, if such they were, by his study of the game and his smartness when he was on the pitching peak.
—Connie Mack

I have always been thankful that I was thrown into such intimate contact with so inspiring a man in the days when the majority of ballplayers were of a much lower type than at the present time.
—Jack Coombs

Eddie Plank was not the fastest, not the trickiest, and not the possessor of the most stuff, but just the greatest.
—Eddie Collins

P is for Plank,
The arm of the A's;
When he tangled with Matty
Games lasted for days.

– from the poem "Line-Up for Yesterday: An ABC of
Baseball Immortals" by Ogden Nash

A
MIGHTY BASEBALL
PITCHER

O N JULY 1, 1863, as the forces of Confederate General
Ambrose P. Hill advanced east along the Chambersburg
Pike towards Gettysburg, they met resistance from Union
forces led by General John Fulton Reynolds. The ensu-
ing battle on the first day raged on, around, and over
the John George Plank farm in Cumberland Township, Adams
County, on the west side of Gettysburg. Archer's Brigade, and
later Pettigrew's Brigade, both in Henry Heth's Division, would
have marched across this ground towards Willoughby Run and
later up McPherson's Ridge, near where Reynolds was killed while
placing the Iron Brigade in defense. The Plank farm was situated
by Willoughby Run, where for many years the Gettysburg Country
Club existed until purchased by the National Park Service. Over
the years, the Plank family collected numerous Civil War artifacts
from this property.

In the years before the battle, John George Plank, Jr., had
passed away on September 24, 1852, at the age of 41, leaving a
wife, Mary (Weaver), sons David Luther and John Edward, and
daughter Anna to run the 220-acre farm. Widowed Mary and the
female children moved out to live with her elderly uncle John
Myers within the borough. In 1859, John Edward Plank married
and took over management of the farm along Willoughby Run
with the help of his younger brother David Luther, who lived and
worked there.

On June 30th, 1863, the Planks became aware of the gathering Confederate troops in the area. As the battle started on the
1st of July, Confederate units in Heth's Division under A.P. Hill
were in the area, marching east towards town. Then, on the 2nd
of July, Confederate soldiers arrived at the door and took over
the farm with the intent of setting up a field hospital. Young
David was sent off to live with friends in Maryland. John's family

including his elderly grandparents, John George Plank, Sr., 81, and Elizabeth (Myers), 80, now overwhelmed by the visitors, moved in with a neighbor.

Weeks after the battle was over, the family returned to find their property in disarray. Almost all the furniture was gone and many of the outbuildings and all the fencing had been destroyed for use as firewood. All the chickens, hogs, and cattle were consumed. The crop of grain in the field was completely ruined due to the Confederates turning their horses loose to eat it. In the orchard were found no less than sixty-four confirmed shallow Confederate graves. The floors in the barn and house were strewn with blood-soaked straw and all the sheets and linens were gone, used for bandages. There was an unforgettable pervasive smell of rot and death enjoyed only by the flies and vermin.

Over in nearby Hunterstown, on the opposite side of Gettysburg, Jesse McCreary, the village tailor, and his wife Jane Ann lived in a log home between the Hunterstown Country School and the brick Methodist Church with their daughters Alice, Martha, and Sadie Ann. On July 2nd, 1863, late in the afternoon, shots were heard and Confederate soldiers began arriving in the village, chased by Union cavalry. Then, a line of Union soldiers under General Kilpatrick appeared near the McCreary house, formed a line across the road, and began attacking the rebels. The battle lasted several hours and must have been nerve-wracking for the family.

After the war, and the sacking of the farm near Willoughby Run, the family moved to a farm in Straban Township, just north of Gettysburg close to Hunterstown. Soon after, on April 2, 1867, John George Plank, Sr., passed away at age 85. He had been born just before the end of the American Revolution in 1782, the son of George Plank, who was the son of the immigrant Andrew Plank (Blanck) who arrived in Philadelphia aboard the ship *Andrew* in September of 1752.

In 1870, per the census, young David and Martha (McCreary) Plank were both 21, living with David's mother Mary, aged 57, at the Straban Township farm. The couple had been married earlier that year.

Edward Stewart Plank was born, on August 31, 1875, to David L. and Martha Plank, on their farm in Straban Township, Adams County, Pennsylvania. At the time, the house on the farm was two stories and made of logs situated just west of the barn near a small orchard and other buildings. Per the 1880 census, both David L., a farmer, and Martha E., a housekeeper, were 31 years old. Five children were listed, including daughters Martha "Mattie" Jane, 9, and Grace N., two months old, and sons Luther C., 7, Howard J., 6, and "Steward E.", 4.

The 1900 census listed another son, Ira D., who was 17 at the time. Eddie was listed as "S. Edward," age 23. Sister Grace was still living at home, age 20.

The family Bible also listed Eddie as "Stewart Edward Plank." Thus, the man later known as Edward Stewart Plank was born Stewart Edward Plank.

The years of Eddie's youth were spent on the farm in Straban Township, working with his father and younger brother Ira, and older brothers Luther and Howard. In those days, before tractors, the work was done with horses and mules or by hand. Behind the Plank farm to the west, at the intersection of the farm road and Good Intent Road was the Good Intent one-room schoolhouse where the local children learned the rudiments including Eddie and his siblings. Along the way, there was a creek that was crossed by stepping on a log. When the creek was high, the children were taken on horseback. A familiar sound was the ringing of the school bell by the schoolmaster about five minutes before the day was to begin.

In the one-room schoolhouse, subjects were taught by grade and assignments given while the teacher focused on the next grade. The students had music and recess together.

The teacher at Good Intent in those days was Robert King Major, who was the son of John and Nancy Major. Their log home was on the Harrisburg Road about one mile south of the Plank farm on the way to Gettysburg.

During the Battle of Gettysburg, when Robert was only three, the Major home became the headquarters for Confederate Cavalry General Albert Gallatin Jenkins, who had spent the prior weeks attacking Chambersburg, Carlisle, and Camp Hill at the Battle of Sporting Hill. With her husband gone, Nancy drove the cattle away from the farm so they would not be stolen. She also hid silverware on the rafters and a barrel of flour under the stairs. Young "Robby" was kept amused by the staff officers who would carry him about the place on their shoulders.

Jenkins was wounded on July 2nd and was unable to join the fight. On the 3rd, he had a meeting with his staff officers and passed around a bottle of bitters which was left behind along with a cavalry sword when the rebels retreated.

When Eddie was 9, in 1884, his father was in the newspaper concerning some cattle sold for a good price. This was near the end of the Depression of 1882-85, a tough time economically for most Americans as the railroad boom was cooling off. As the years went by, David Plank became involved in the community politically. For the 1892 election, he was Vice President for the Democratic election committee in Hunterstown, the nearest village. This was the election that Democrat Grover Cleveland won his second, non-contiguous term. Cleveland was the only Democrat to win the Presidency in the post-Civil War era until Woodrow Wilson.

In the spring of 1893, David Plank announced he was the Democratic candidate for Register and Recorder in Adams County. He lost, but he was subsequently a school director for many years. Then, in June of 1896, David was appointed by the court as tax collector for Straban Township, filling the term of J. C. Leivelsperger.

In those days, school teachers were required to be single. Major taught at the school for eleven years, and given that he married Sara E. Gilliland when he was 38 in 1898, he was likely the school teacher from 1886 through 1897, from the time Eddie was 11 until he stopped attending.

All this time, Eddie Plank was growing up, working on the farm. He also worked for Mr. Boyer, a neighboring farmer who owned an adjoining property. Eddie was paid $12 a month. Given that he eventually attended a preparatory academy in his early 20s, he likely had not advanced very far at the Good Intent schoolhouse. This was not uncommon for rural boys in the 19th century.

How and when Eddie Plank picked up a baseball and began pitching is lost to history. There are several apocryphal tales of his youthful origins in the sport. An oft-repeated vignette mentioned that Eddie honed his craft by throwing into hay bales, 'developing speed and curves.'

One thing that is clear is his connection to the Good Intent School, which had a team of local boys and young men. Their slogan was this little ditty, as recalled at a reunion in 1978:

> Rub 'em up the windpipe
> Hit 'em on the lip
> Good Intent Academy
> Rip! Rip! Rip!

George Boyer, an early landowner in the area, donated the grounds for the school. The school operated from 1854 until 1951. There were numerous newspaper accounts of Eddie pitching for the Good Intent team, as early as 1895, when he was 19, going on 20, years of age. However, these are certainly not his earliest games.

Linda K. Cleveland, in her article "From Family Farm to Baseball Hall of Fame," credits Major with encouraging Eddie's improvement as a young pitcher. Eddie would play ball with his brothers, Ira, Luther, and Howard. Eddie would pitch while Luther caught. Howard played shortstop and Ira the outfield. They worked out a system where each got a turn to bat. Eddie also honed his skills tossing pitches against haystacks or rocks through knotholes in the barn siding or at birds. Often these games would start when their father David was expecting them to be working in the fields. A story mentioned in David Plank's obituary (many years later) told of the father scolding both Eddie and Ira for shattering barn doors with their practice pitches.

After Eddie was done as a student at Good Intent, he helped organize a formal baseball team with Major and his brothers. Others from the area joined in. Because there was no village in the immediate vicinity, they called themselves the Good Intent Team. Major managed and played first base. Eddie pitched while Luther caught. Howard Plank played shortstop. Reuben Lower, Robert Cleveland, Emory Cleveland, a Morrison and a Bream also played on the team. Home games were played at Plank's Park, a baseball field located somewhere on the Plank farm, west of the Harrisburg Road.

Regarding his teammates at Good Intent:

Robert King Major (1860–1934), the schoolmaster and first baseman is buried at Evergreen Cemetery.

Brother Luther Calvin Plank (1872–1972) was Eddie's first catcher. He served as the Clerk of Courts in Adams County and was an elder at the Great Conewago Presbyterian Church in Hunterstown. He bought the Table Rock Mill (previously known as Conrad's Mill and Lower's Mill) in 1901 from the Lower family.

Robert Bell and the Major family had also owned it at times in the past. Luther lived nearly 100 years and kept a picture of Eddie in his office at the mill. He often took visitors to the office and talked about his brother. One time a mill worker asked him why he had such "knotty knuckles." Luther explained, "That came from catching Eddie's fastballs all those years." Luther and his wife Bessie had four children, Clyde, born 1902, Doris, born 1904, Gerald, born 1906, and Gladys, born 1909. He is buried in Evergreen Cemetery.

Brother Howard Jessie Plank (born 1874), the shortstop, married Manni R. King in 1910 in Fairfax, Virginia. Howard was a policeman for most of his life in the city of Baltimore. He appeared in the 1940 census, aged 66 and living alone, but nothing more could be found.

Brother Ira David Plank (1882–1951) pitched and played various positions. He was a minor-league ballplayer from 1903 through 1911 and then with the Gettysburg and Hanover teams in the Blue Ridge League from 1915 to 1917. His best season as a pitcher was with New Haven in the Connecticut State League in 1906 when he went 26-10. He also hit over .300 a couple times in professional baseball. He was drafted by the New York Yankees in 1908 but never made it to the majors. Ira was a coach of the Gettysburg College baseball team for 35 seasons compiling a 277-175 record. He is buried at Evergreen Cemetery.

Reuben Ira Lower (1870–1944), the son of George C. and Leah Lower, was a farmer. He is buried at Greenmount Cemetery in Arendtsville.

Robert Calvin Cleveland (1875–1966), the son of John Cleveland and Anna Maria Lower, operated a dairy farm in Straban Township for most of his life. He also operated a campsite, restaurant, and cabins for tourists known as Cleveland Motels. He is buried in Biglerville Cemetery.

John Emory Cleveland (1871–1954), Robert's brother, also had a dairy farm in Straban Township (perhaps the same farm). He also operated a grocery store in Gettysburg for many years. He was laid to rest at Mt. Olivet Cemetery in Hanover.

Researcher David Gulden was ambitious enough to review dozens of old newspaper records for his SABR article "The Forgotten Games of Eddie Plank." He found game records for the Good Intent school from 1896. Gulden missed Eddie's earlier games from 1895, however.

Eddie Plank first showed up in a box score in the *Gettysburg Times* in August of 1895, just before he turned twenty years old. On Friday, August 2, Good Intent defeated Hunterstown 25 to 2 in a game shortened to five innings. "The feature of the game was the pitching and catching of the Plank Brothers."

The following afternoon, Arendtsville, "the Champions of South Mountain," were the next to lose to the Good Intent team, 14 to 13. Fisher, Arendtsville's crack pitcher, was knocked out of the box and forced to retire. The features of the game were a line catch by Daubert that looked good for two bases, and a high fly caught by Ira Plank while on a dead run.

On August 23rd, Good Intent met Arendtsville again, on the Good Intent grounds, and fell 15 to 7. Said the paper, "Plank, Good Intent's pitcher, had the Arendtsville boys completely at his mercy, striking out 13 of their heaviest batters."

On Eddie's 20th birthday, August 31, 1895, Good Intent defeated Hunterstown 13 to 12. While there may have been others, the only remaining games reported were a 12 to 4 victory over New Oxford on October 5, and the team took two of three games from New Oxford on October 19.

Thus, as early as the summer of 1895, Eddie Plank was pitching in the area in organized baseball and was being noticed. It is very likely these were not his first organized baseball games, given he was 19, going on 20.

The following spring, Good Intent was back at it. On May 16, 1896, they played the Gettysburg freshman, winning 14 to 10. Eddie batted second and had a hit. Ira and Luther also played and contributed on offense. The team made 9 errors on defense.

On May 27, Good Intent routed New Oxford 13 to 4. Then, on June 6, they beat Fairfield 17 to 4. They fell 10 to 6 to Idaville on June 13 but beat the same squad 19 to 0 on June 20.

One apocryphal tale, told in 1913, was about the visit of the Idaville team with Good Intent, likely referring to the game on June 20. It is repeated here:

ONE TIME SEVERAL YEARS AGO, Plank was plowing the field at Good Intent, a little village outside of Gettysburg, and the Idaville team was scheduled to play the Good Intent team, of which Eddie was the pitcher.

On the day of the game, the visitors came to Good Intent, and after going through their practice, watched the home team work out. After watching the entire team, and not seeing their pitcher, The Idaville manager asked where their pitcher was.

"Over there in the field, plowing," was the answer of the Good Intent manager, pointing at Plank behind the plow.

At this, the visiting manager laughed, and going back to the teammates, told them about it, and they all had a good laugh, saying what they were going to do to the opposing pitcher that day.

At the time of the game, Plank left the plow and went in to pitch. Not an Idaville player reached first base during the entire nine innings, and many of them were struck out. Eddie did not allow the semblance of a hit, and only two or three balls were hit to the outfield. The final score of the game was Good Intent 13, Idaville 0.

This game, it was said, was the starting of a wonderful career for the veteran southpaw, who yesterday won the world's championship for the Athletics.

A box score was not available to confirm the no-hitter. Good Intent played New Oxford again on June 27, but results were not available.

On July 4th, 1896, Good Intent traveled to York Springs. "Never in the history of York Springs was there so much interest taken in a game of ball as this one," reported the newspaper. The Independence Day festivities began with a grand marshal leading a parade to the northern end of Main Street in York Springs where the Bendersville Band joined. Then, at the Central Hotel, a line was formed which proceeded to the ball field including the grand marshal with six aides on horses, the Bendersville Band, the Good Intent Team, the York Springs team, and a long procession of townspeople.

It was the first time Good Intent traveled—they lost 3 to 1. Eddie struck out 13. Ira and Luther had 2 of only 3 hits.

On August 6th, Gettysburg beat Good Intent 10 to 9 on the college athletic grounds. Eddie struck out 16 and walked 5, yielding 4 earned runs. Ira Plank had a passed ball at catcher. Luther Plank hit a double.

Nine days later, on the 15th, Good Intent combined with Biglerville and other teams to win 6 to 4. Three days afterward, "a jolly party of 24 young ladies and gentlemen enjoyed a hayride and hospitality at the Plank home."

Back on the mound on August 22 against Arendtsville, Eddie lost 4 to 1, striking out 7, walking 2, and hit one batter, in a six-inning game.

Details for 1897 and 1898 are very sketchy. Dave Gulden was also unlucky in uncovering records from these two years. There was one entry in the *Gettysburg Times* regarding the Good Intent team. They lost to Littlestown 16 to 10. Eddie Plank was not mentioned. Gulden stated in his article that Plank continued to play during these years, though "newspaper accounts of the games are rare." Gulden cited an April 20, 1898, game between Gettysburg College and the town team as the earliest box score containing Plank. Eddie struck out six, walked two, and stole two bases in a losing cause. The college team won 6 to 4.

The dearth of reporting regarding local and town baseball teams during this time is puzzling, given the detailed exposure the teams received in 1895 and 1896. Perhaps the Klondike gold rush of 1897, or the Spanish-American War of 1898 were factors in reducing the number of quality players involved or the level of interest.

The stories about Eddie Plank's origins became more embellished over the years. The following item was printed in the *Gettysburg Times* in 1921:

* * *

RECALLS STORY OF EDDIE'S START
Famous Gettysburg Pitcher Gained Fame
First at McSherrystown

From the *Pittsburgh Gazette-Times*.
Teacher—Can any little boy or girl tell me where Adams county is?
Mike—Nevah hoid of it, teacher. Mebbe it's in Africa.
Teacher—Well, does any little girl or boy know who Eddie Plank is?
Mike—Sure thing: he de southpaw bloke wot licked the Giants fer Connie Mack in the world serious.

Few people know the origin of Eddie Plank's nickname, "Farmer," a cognomen which clung to him throughout a long and brilliant career in the American League. To millions of fans, he was familiarly known as "Farmer Eddie," though not one in a thousand knew when or where or why the name was bestowed upon him. The story has never been printed before, but here it is, as told by two prominent Pittsburghers, who were teammates of Plank before he rose to the dizzy heights of eminence as the southpaw pitching ace of Connie Mack's Philadelphia Athletics in World's Series and other notable diamond combats.

It was back in 1899, in Adams County, this state. The two largest towns in that county were Gettysburg, where Lincoln once made an address, and McSherrystown chiefly noted as a cigar manufacturing center. McSherrystown is near Hanover, Pa., the distance between the two being 20 minutes' ride on a street car.

Gettysburg and McSherrystown each had an independent baseball team, and there was a bitter rivalry between the two teams. A series of seven games, to decide the championship of the county, was arranged. The first game was to be played in McSherrystown, whose team was very liberally backed by a wealthy cigar manufacturer. A lot of money was bet on the series and there were numerous sizable wagers on each game.

Speed Stimmel, Gettysburg's star pitcher, being ill, failed to show up on the morning his team boarded a train for McSherrystown to play the first game. Morris Musselman, the Gettysburg manager, was badly worried. Then he happened to remember that there had been a township league for Adams County and that one Edward Plank, who resided in Good Intent township, had gained some laurels as a hurler in that league.

Hasty scanning of Plank's record didn't encourage Musselman much. The last game Plank had pitched, up to that time, had resulted in an ordinary victory for him and his township over the freshman class team of Gettysburg College. Eddie's catcher was his brother Ira, who operated a grist mill, while Eddie, so an excited informant told Musselman, worked on an extensive farm operated by his father.

Not much for a manager to pin hopes on, surely, but Musselman, driven to desperation, decided to drive to Plank's farm, about five miles from Gettysburg, and try to prevail upon Eddie to pitch the game. Arriving at the farm, Musselman found Eddie pitching hay in a field. After a lengthy conference, in which

Eddie's father pointedly expressed his opinion of the foolishness of his son in forsaking his good dollar-a-day job to go gallivanting over the country with 'a possel o' ball throwers.' Eddie was allowed to go with Musselman. They drove in a buggy to McSherrystown, about 20 miles.

Robbin B. Wolf, now a prominent Pittsburgh attorney, was the Gettysburg catcher. It was largely due to his encouragement and his steady handling of the farmer lad's delivery, that Eddie got off to a flying start on his road to fame and fortune. Wolf had been a college catcher and he knew his business. It is no exaggeration to say that Plank, although always a cool customer and unexcitable to the last degree, owed much of his success to Wolf. An authority for this statement, we refer you to W. S. Grenoble, now assistant manager of the William Penn Hotel, Pittsburgh, who played center field for Gettysburg throughout that memorable series.

Gettysburg went first to bat and the first man up was Wolf.

"Play ball!" yelled the ump.

A crowd of spectators watched nervously as Clarence Smith, the McSherrystown twirler, toed the slab, took a signal from his catcher, doubled himself into a bowknot, and grooved the white pill across the rubber.

Crack! The crowd was on its toes as Wolf streaked around the bags. He had pickled the first pitch for a home run. The final score of that game was 13 to 3 in Gettysburg's favor.

The big feature of the game was that Plank struck out either 19 or 21 men, out of 27 who faced him that day, even though the crowd continually yelled "farmer" at him, besides hurling many worse epithets of a derisive and caustic nature.

"I could not be quite sure of it," says Mr. Grenoble, "but my recollection which has always been fairly distinct on that point is that Eddie struck out 21 men in that game. I know it was either 19 or 21."

The unexpected victory gave the Gettysburg rooters more confidence with the result they backed their team to the limit in a betting way.

Then George Winters (sic), a right-hander, joined the Gettysburg team as a pitcher. The series went along until the count stood even, each team having won three games. The final game was played at York, Pa. Winters (sic) pitching and Bill Clay catching for Gettysburg. Gettysburg won that game 7 to 3, thereby taking the series. The game gave Bill Clay his start in baseball. He afterward was a star in the Tri-State League.

During the baseball seasons of 1900 and 1901, Winters (sic) and Plank pitched for Gettysburg College and Gettysburg town teams. The American League was then in its infancy. Connie Mack, heeding the advice of his friend Musselman, gave Plank a tryout with the Athletics at the end of the collegiate year in 1901. At the same time, Winters (sic) was given a tryout with the Boston Americans. Both made good right from the start of their major-league careers.

* * *

The game the article referred to was the July 1st game between Gettysburg and McSherrystown, who was favored after topping Mt. St. Mary's. Gettysburg won 15 to 6, not 13 to 3. Catcher Robbin Wolf did knock the first ball from Smith out for a homer. Eddie struck out 19 (20 per the *Philadelphia Inquirer*) and scattered a few hits. Said the *Gettysburg Times*, "Plank is improving in form and promises to be a sure winner."

The team that day was:

Robbin Wolf, c
E. Plank, p
H. Harper, 1b
G. Griffith, 2b
A. Minnigh, 3b
P. Tate (Capt.), ss
W. F. Dill, lf
E. McCammon, cf
F. McCammon, rf

Prior to that game, on June 24, Eddie struck out 10 as Gettysburg defeated Carlisle 10 to 1. After the game, it was announced there would be a seven-game series with McSherrystown, starting on Saturday the 1st.

Wolf led off another game with a home run on the 4th of July versus a different team—Paxtang. Dill was the winning pitcher, as the game ended after five innings, 17 to 0 in Gettysburg's favor.

In the second game that day, Eddie held the opposition to only two hits. The score was 13 to 1, and the game was well-attended.

After this game, a reporter at the *Hanover Record* poked fun at Eddie in advance of Gettysburg's upcoming series with McSherrystown:

THE GAME WAS FEATURELESS, except for Plank's marvelous pitching. Though speedy, he was steady and had no difficulty in locating the plate. Plank has not pitched more than half a dozen games in his life and is an Adams county rustic. The reporter learned incidentally that he unloaded two huge wagon loads of hay in the morning, and it surely did not seem to affect his arm, for, from appearances, he could have pitched another nine innings.

Eddie Plank pitched the second game of the championship series between Gettysburg and McSherrystown on July 13, 1899, at Gettysburg. He lost 4 to 3 but struck out 17 batters. Yerkes was the opposing pitcher. The series was now tied at one win each. The *Gettysburg Times* described the game:

BEFORE THE LARGEST AND CERTAINLY the most enthusiastic crowd that ever witnessed a ballgame here, the hitherto invincible Gettysburg team was downed by McSherrystown in a contest of the most thrilling nature. The game was nip and tuck from start to finish. McSherrystown scored two runs in the first but were then shut out for six innings. Gettysburg fought hard to tie the score and played a strong uphill game but only tied it at the end of the sixth inning. With the score a tie, the fight became still fiercer, and the fans more excited, and it was anybody's game till the last man was out in the tenth inning, leaving McSherrystown the winner by a narrow margin of one run, in the best game ever played on local grounds.

Two days later, on July 16th, Gettysburg traveled to McSherrystown and lost 2 to 0 in a game in which the visitors complained about their treatment by the umpire. McSherrystown took a 2 to 1 lead in the series.

The July 20th *York Gazette* reported the upcoming game between Gettysburg and the York Athletics. "Plank," said the paper, "will be here to play a game with the Athletics. Plank is the pitcher who, with ease, strikes out from eighteen to twenty-two men in a single game. He is said to be a wonder." The next day, Eddie and Gettysburg won 16 to 0, and Eddie retired 16 of 29 batters via strikeout. An article in the *Gettysburg Times* read:

* * *

A MIGHTY BASEBALL PITCHER
Plank, the Gettysburg Twirler, Struck
Out Sixteen Local Players

Edward Plank, a youth just fresh from an Adams County farm and who but recently aspired to become a baseball pitcher, came to York yesterday to twirl the sphere for the Gettysburg club in a game with manager Webel's Athletics on the local ball field. The newspapers in this vicinity, as well as those in some large cities, have of late been telling stories of young Plank's remarkable pitching abilities and the easy manner in which he disposed of the hard-hitting Athletics in the game yesterday is positive proof that the people, and the newspapers who speak of him as being mighty, did not go wrong in their assertions. The several hundred local enthusiasts who saw him work yesterday are convinced that he is a wonder–about the warmest manipulator of a baseball ever seen in York.

A summary of the game, that is during the time the visitors occupied the field, serves to show exactly how much ability the pitcher has. In all but three innings, the Athletics were retired in one, two, three order, and in two out of the three other innings, only one reached first base in each inning, and but one Athletic player was left on base. Of the twenty-nine batsmen who faced Plank, only one reached third base, and only two reached second base. Three hits, two of which were scratches, were all the home club secured. There was only one fly to the outfield. Sixteen of the twenty-nine were retired on strikes, one was given his base on balls, one was hit by a pitched ball, and the remainder were retired by the infielders, with the exception of the one fly to the outfield.

Barring the ninth inning, the game was an exceptionally good one. Dugan pitched good ball and, although he was not quite as effective as his opponent, the visitors found him hard to hit and the few runs scored in the eight innings were mainly due to errors by his support. In the last inning, however, Dugan lost all control, went away up in the air, and was pounded for eleven safe hits, which netted the visitors ten runs, making the final score 16 to 0.

The fielding of the visitors was perfect, but this is probably accounted for by the fact that few chances were offered them.

The batting of Tate, Wolf, and Sheely, and some clever base running by Dill were other features of the game.

The visitors played a gentlemanly game and were full of ginger throughout the contest.

* * *

On July 27, Gettysburg defeated McSherrystown 5 to 4. Plank allowed only three hits, and Wolf caught an 'elegant' game. Gettysburg now evened the series at two games apiece.

Two days later, on Saturday the 29th, McSherrystown returned the favor 4 to 1. Dill scored the only run after stealing second and then third. Yerkes was the winner. Eddie pitched a 'credible' game as the loser. McSherrystown took the lead, three games to two.

On August 4th, Gettysburg and Eddie lost to Elizabethtown 5 to 2. Per the *Gettysburg Times*, Eddie pitched a strong game against a tough opponent.

August 9th was the sixth game of the series with McSherrystown, who led the series 3 games to 2. They won handily 17 to 4, taking the series 4 games to 2. A second series of five games was agreed to.

On August 19, in the first game of the second series with Gettysburg, McSherrystown blew out Eddie Plank 17 to 4, repeating the horrendous score from twelve days prior. Was something wrong with Eddie? The performances were far out of line with his previous record.

On August 24, McSherrystown shutout Gettysburg 8 to 0 at Nixon Field. The home team was 'bolstered by some new players.' It did not help. It appears there was no third game.

Thus, in the end, the story from 1921 was not completely accurate. While the account of the first game was close regarding its details, except the final score, the entire paragraph about "Winters" and the results of the series was about the 1900 season, the following year. This calls into question the story of coach Musselman traveling to Eddie's farm and pulling him away from his disappointed father. While baseball was not seen as a lucrative way to make a living in those times, Eddie was nearly 24 years old in 1899 and quite capable of making his own decisions. Perhaps the 1921 story was an embellishment of the 1899 teasing by the Hanover paper about Eddie being an 'Adams county rustic' who had just spent the morning throwing hay.

Morris Musselman (1873–1902), the coach mentioned in the story, was not mentioned in the game accounts of 1899 but was mentioned in 1900. Mr. Musselman was a druggist by trade, who passed away from typhoid fever at a very young age. He was buried at Evergreen Cemetery. He likely was not connected to Connie Mack.

The pitcher "Speed" Stimmel was most likely a fabricated name. Per the 1900 census, there was no one with that last name living in Adams County. There were also no newspaper accounts with this person in them.

The article also missed quite a bit of Eddie's prior history when it stated he had only pitched about a half dozen games.

Here is some more information about Eddie's 1899 teammates:

Harry Melville Sheely (1875–1907) was the first baseman that year. Harry became a dentist but succumbed to diabetes at only 32 years of age. His obituary mentioned his baseball prowess, stating, "While attending Gettysburg College, he took high rank in athletics, and was considered an ideal first baseman in baseball, being always cool and ready for any emergency. He never lost interest in athletics, and has umpired dozens of games of Nixon Field, with great credit to himself, for he was looked upon as an authority in the national game." Harry was buried in Evergreen Cemetery.

Preston Smith Tate (1871–1956) was the catcher and captain of the team in 1899. Affectionately known as "Doc," he was the son of Dr. Theodore and Mary (Smith) Tate. Preston was a rural mail carrier for many years and was a former baseball manager and watchmaker. His obituary mentioned he was "Eddie Plank's catcher." He was also buried at Evergreen Cemetery.

Guy Myers Griffith (1878–1955) played second base behind Eddie Plank. In 1912, Guy married Marie A. Stucky in Pittsburgh, where he was a special agent for the Equitable Life Assurance Society. Previously, he had been in the piano business, and then managed a bowling alley in Pittsburgh. Later, he moved to San Francisco, California, where he passed away.

Calvin Keller Gilbert (1872–1959), who pitched and played center field, was born in Chambersburg but moved to the Gettysburg area when he was a teenager. He had been a town mail carrier for many years and was chosen the president of the local postal union in 1932. He was a member of the Odd Fellows. He was buried at Evergreen Cemetery.

Jacob Alfred "Allie" Holtzworth (1874–1958), left fielder, was often mistakenly referred to as "Albert" Holtzworth in the newspapers. "Allie" was a burgess of Gettysburg during the 50th anniversary of the battle, when over 54,000 Civil War veterans camped on the field. He was a coronet player, a liveryman, motorman on the trolley, and deputy county treasurer. He also was a battlefield guide, starting at the age of 15, and quitting only before his final illness, at the age of 83. He was believed to be the oldest such guide at that time. "Allie" was very active in civic organizations, rising to the exalted ruler of the Elks, and worshipful master of the Good Samaritan Lodge of the Masons. Holtzworth's obituary mentioned he had played with Eddie Plank and was an "ardent Philadelphia Athletics rooter."

John Edmond McCammon (1965–1932), known as "Ed," was born in Philadelphia, the son of David C. and Emilie de Crano McCammon, a grandson of General F. M. de Crano, of the Franco-Prussian War. Ed spent his boyhood in Germantown where he attended the Germantown Academy. In his early twenties, the family, including the parents, moved to Gettysburg, where he remained until near his death. He passed away at the York Hotel following a long illness and was buried at Evergreen Cemetery. Ed's brother Frederic C. McCammon was mentioned as surviving him, but no further information could be found except that he was living with his brother in 1900, and was likely born in 1869.

Albert Kuhn Minnigh (also Minnich) (1880 – 1910), right fielder and third baseman, was born in Gettysburg, the son of John and Victoria Kuhn Minnigh. Albert was married to Amanda Minnigh, whom he left a widow when he passed away at 29 years of age from tuberculosis following malaria fever at Mount Holly Springs, Cumberland County, Pennsylvania. He was buried at Mount Holly Springs Cemetery.

Robbin Bayard Wolf (1869–1961), the catcher, was a prominent Pittsburgh attorney who passed away while visiting Daytona Beach, Florida. An article in the *Pittsburgh Post-Gazette* was titled "Robbin Wolf Dies, Plank's Discoverer." It mentioned his younger days in Gettysburg where he was "responsible for discovering Eddie Plank." Wolf had played baseball at the University of Pennsylvania and was the first baseball coach at Carnegie-Mellon

University. He was buried at Chartiers Cemetery in Allegheny County, Pennsylvania.

William Frost Dill (1872–1942), third baseman and pitcher, was born in York Springs, the son of Dr. and Mrs. Armstrong B. Dill. For many years, he was an attorney in Gettysburg, having attended Millersville State Normal School, Phillips Exeter Academy, and the Harvard Law School. The *Gettysburg Times*, in early 1899, mentioned Dill's role as coach of the baseball and track teams at Gettysburg College. The paper touted his training at Harvard, where he had been on the baseball and track teams. However, this was short-lived, as Frank Foreman, a professional player for 15 seasons, was hired to take his place the following year.

For a time, Dill was also in the real estate business in Pittsburgh but resumed his law practice there. William died at the Spangler hospital, in Barnesboro, Pennsylvania, Cambria County, during emergency surgery. He was buried in Dillsburg Cemetery, with his parents.

From this, we can conclude Eddie Plank had been playing organized baseball since at least 1895, through 1899—five seasons with a lot of noteworthy games. He had likely been first influenced by his Good Intent schoolmaster and coach, Robert K. Major. It's not clear how he migrated to the Gettysburg town team, but that might have been the doing of William Dill, who was the coach of the college team, who also played on the town team.

We do know that as the summer of 1899 came to an end, the Gettysburg town team had lost a hotly-contested championship series with McSherrystown following a very strong season. The last three games of the season were terrific defeats, two being by margins of 17 to 4. Was Eddie's arm sore? Why did the team suddenly become so bad? The 1921 article mentioned there was a lot of money being wagered on the championship. If true, could that have been a factor? Regardless of the reason, it was clear, the season ended on a down note.

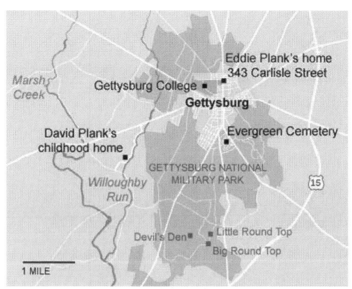

Map of Plank sites around Gettysburg, Pennsylvania.

The John Plank farm as it appears today. (photo by the author)

The David L. Plank farm as it appears today. (photo by the author)

Confederate Brigadier General Albert Gallatin Jenkins.

Luther Plank's Table Rock Mill.

ALMOST
UNHITTABLE

EFORE THE 1900 college baseball season began, Christy Mathewson had dropped out of Bucknell University and was pitching for Norfolk in the Virginia League. He would be called up to the New York Giants later that season, starting his Hall of Fame career.

For the 1899/1900 school year, Eddie Plank, at the age of 24, enrolled in the Gettysburg Academy, the preparatory school run by Gettysburg College on its campus. Given the timing of these two decisions, it is clearly impossible that Mathewson and Plank ever faced each other on a college baseball diamond, as later reported. The later stories, during subsequent World Series in the coming years, were baseball myths.

There have also been numerous reports over the years that Eddie Plank attended Gettysburg College. In fact, he never attended the college—only the academy. However, he was permitted to play on the college's baseball team.

This begs to question, why would a 24-year-old farmer with a sore arm return to school? Based on his subsequent performance, the arm was not sore for long, and reports of his academic results were described as "at best an indifferent student." Preparatory schools are typically meant for teenagers who are preparing to attend a college or university. Usually, they were taking remedial classes to pass the various entrance exams. A 24-year-old would be quite a bit older than the average prep school student. It is very likely, therefore, Eddie Plank was recruited to play for the college team, and enrolling in the Academy was the minimal requirement.

William Dill had been the coach during the 1899 season, and Frank S. Foreman, a pitcher with 15 years of professional, including major league experience, was hired to replace him. Foreman had also played briefly for the Gettysburg town team at the end of their season when their results had been so poor. Perhaps the Harvard-educated Dill had encouraged Eddie to get an education and join the team. Or, perhaps the new coach knew of Eddie's past success and wanted him on the roster. Maybe Robbin Wolf introduced one to the other. Or, some also credit Robert Major, his Good Intent teammate and school teacher with encouraging him. Regardless of the reason, Eddie Plank began pitching for Gettysburg College for the 1900 season, after Christy Mathewson had moved on to the pros.

Saturday, April 7, 1900, Eddie Plank was the pitcher for Gettysburg College in their opening game against Franklin and Marshall at Lancaster. Gettysburg won 14 to 8. The lineup was as follows: Glatfelter at shortstop, Dale at second base, Lantz in center field, Krout at third base, Hoffman at first base, Doty in right field, Moser in left field, White at catcher, and Plank on the mound. Per the *Weekly Gettysburgian,* Plank had eleven strike-outs, four walks, two hits, including a double, a wild pitch, and a hit batter. He gave up only three hits, despite the high score.

Three days later, on the 10th, the team was home to face Syracuse, who won 6 to 5. Per the *Weekly Gettysburgian,* "Plank pitched his usual steady game and with proper support would have won out easily. At critical stages, he showed especial cool-ness, repeatedly retiring the side with men on bases. He struck out seven, walked two, and had one hit, driving in two runs."

On April 12, the *Gettysburg Compiler* reported that coach Frank Foreman had returned to his home in Baltimore, after hav-ing only been in town for six weeks. He left behind many new friends and people were sorry about his departure. The team was only 1–1 at this point and three games coming up in May. Per his minor-league record, Francis Isaiah "Monkey" Foreman, the older brother of former professional pitcher John Davis "Brownie" Foreman, had headed off to Springfield, Massachusetts, to play in the Eastern League at the age of 37. He started 17 games and went 8–7. He spent the second half of the season with the minor-league Buffalo Bisons, going 7-6. The performance was strong enough to get him an opportunity with Boston the next season, in the new American League. Foreman lost that game and was released. He then hooked up with the Baltimore Orioles, also of the new American League, for the remainder of the season, post-ing a respectable 12-6 record as a teammate of Joe McGinnity and John McGraw. Foreman finished his professional career in

Baltimore in 1902, with two losses, ending with a 96-93 record over 11 seasons.

Some sources have credited Frank Foreman with the discovery of Eddie Plank, while he was with the Gettysburg team. Foreman is quoted telling Plank, "If you follow my instructions closely, I'll make you one of the greatest southpaws in the country." Plank had been known for his unorthodox cross-fire motion, that he referred to as "a slant ball," landing his right leg on the first base side of the pitcher's mound and then throwing across his body. Foreman had been credited with Plank's outstanding control, however, this was previously evident in his earliest games back with Good Intent. Thus, the tales of the old major league coach, himself a pitcher, having a great influence on the young hurler, over a period of just six weeks, is likely another fabrication. Instead, it's more likely Foreman recognized Plank's talent and was grateful to have him on the team. The coach was obviously itching to get back into the professional game, and upon his first opportunity, thoughts of developing Eddie Plank into the greatest left-hander of all time went quickly out the window. Foreman couldn't leave town fast enough! However, his brother "Brownie" had played for Connie Mack's Pittsburgh Pirates in 1895 and 1896, a circumstance that would prove important.

On April 20th, the team was home against State College, losing badly 13 to 3. Next, the team began a disastrous road trip starting with a stop in Selinsgrove to play Susquehanna University on Thursday, April 26, followed by stops at Bucknell at Lewisburg on the 27th, and State College on the 28th. The Susquehanna University game was shortened to six innings, with Gettysburg trailing 1 to 0. Apparently, the team walked off the field because the umpire was bad. Plank had two strikeouts and a walk. Bucknell whipped the Gettysburg team 16 to 8. State College also won 13 to 1. Eddie had been hit on his pitching elbow during the game and finished it in right field. He had six strikeouts and two walks. The team came home 1-4.

On May 1st, the *Gettysburg Compiler* announced that Eddie Plank was likely to sign a contract with the Richmond Bluebirds of the Virginia League. Christy Mathewson was amid an 18-2 season with Norfolk in that league, allowing only 15 earned runs in 183 innings. Unfortunately, the troubled Richmond team folded by June, and Eddie never came on board.

On May 5th, the team was back in Selinsgrove for another match, winning 16 to 7 with Eddie on the mound. He had four strikeouts, one walk, and stole a base. The following week, on the 12th, the game against Dickinson in Carlisle, was shortened by rain after 2 1/2 innings. Plank faced nine batters, retired six, including three on strikeouts. There was no score. The game was completed on May 26th in Gettysburg, Eddie striking out 9 en route to a 14 to 8 win.

On May 29th, Gettysburg beat the Carlisle Indians 7 to 2 in Carlisle, followed by a 5 to 4 win on June 2nd against Bucknell. Said the *Gettysburgian*, "Perhaps the largest factor in winning the game was Plank's pitching. He had the men from Bucknell entirely at his mercy. It was one of those hot days that limbers up Eddie's arm and the results were disastrous to 13 of the visitors who failed to find the ball."

On June 11th, the season ended with a defeat to the Carlisle Indians, 11 to 6. Eddie had eight strikeouts, one wild pitch, and gave up 13 hits.

For the season, the team was 5-5, with Eddie going 5-3.

In early July, it was announced that Gettysburg would again field a team in the town league. Morris Musselman was the manager. The team was likely to be: Roberts at catcher, Plank and Pratt at pitcher, Sheely at first, Tate at second, Whitehurst (of Baltimore) at shortstop, Minnigh at third, Holtzworth, David Deatrick and Plank or Pratt in the outfield. The college had permitted the use of Nixon Field, and games were being scheduled with McSherrystown, York, Lancaster, Chambersburg, Hagerstown, Harrisburg, and "other strong teams."

The *Gettysburg Compiler* announced the first game of the season for July 12th against the York YMCA. Gettysburg won this game at Penn Park in York 5 to 2. The team had not played together previously, having little practice. Eddie Plank struck out 19 in a winning effort. Clay, of Baltimore, caught the game and endeared himself to the fans by leading off with a home run over the right-field fence. Pat Whitehurst, also from Baltimore, "played a beautiful fielding game and proved himself a player of no mean ability." The final alignment for the game was Clay at catcher, Plank on the mound, Sheely at first, Stock at second, Minnigh at third, Whitehurst at shortstop, Tate in left, Holtzworth in center, and Deatrick in right. Four of the nine were new to the team.

David Phillip Deatrick (1880-1946), right field, was the son of David and Elizabeth (Eicholtz) Dietrick of Gettysburg. David, Jr., was a dentist by trade, who had attended Gettysburg College. Dietrich was president of the Emaus Orphan's Home, vice president of the Farmer's Bank and Trust Company of Middletown, and owner of a coal company. He died of a heart attack in Middletown, Pennsylvania, and is buried there. In honor of him, Middletown banks closed at 11 AM the Saturday of the service.

Frederick C. "Bill" Clay (1874–1917), catcher, was born in Baltimore, Maryland, and was a long-time minor league ballplayer, who earned a brief stint with the Philadelphia Phillies in 1902. In the pros, he was usually an outfielder and had become a star of the Tri-State League, playing with Reading for a time, where he was a teammate of Home Run Baker. Bill was popular with the fans and earned the moniker "Old Bill" later in his career. He died in York, Pennsylvania, at only 42, from heart valve trouble. He was buried at Prospect Hill Cemetery. He was a veteran of the Spanish-American War.

No more information could be uncovered about "Pat" Whitehurst or Stock.

On July 21st, Gettysburg traveled to York to face Penn Park and lost 6 to 3. Eddie struck out 11 and was not well-supported.

On July 25th, the planned seven-game series with McSherrystown began with a Gettysburg victory, 3 to 2. Eddie yielded only three hits in getting the win. Bill Clay continued to catch, and Wilson was the "new man at shortstop."

The next day, Gettysburg was routed in the second game of the series, 13 to 1. It was unlikely Plank pitched this one.

On August 1st, the team played Biglerville at Nixon Field and won 6 to 3. Allie Holtzworth started at pitcher, throwing the first three innings. Eddie finished the game.

Gettysburg won the third game against McSherrystown, 9 to 0, but details were not available.

The following week, on August 9th, the team again faced Penn Park at Nixon Field, defeating them 12 to 1. Eddie pitched, allowing only four hits while striking out 13.

In the fourth game of the McSherrystown series, played on August 11th, Gettysburg lost big again, 15 to 2. Frank Foreman, the former coach, and major leaguer pitched for Gettysburg and was hit around.

On August 16th, the Actives, of Lancaster, were defeated at Nixon Field, 4 to 3, in ten innings. Eddie scattered six hits and struck out 13.

On the 18th, the game against Chester was postponed after four innings, tied at 3.

In the McSherrystown series, Gettysburg won game five, 3 to 2, but lost game six 14 to 9.

On September 1st, E & H of Harrisburg fell 8 to 1 in an easy victory for Eddie. He struck out 12 and yielded only three hits.

On September 6, 1900, Gettysburg faced McSherrystown for the seventh and deciding game of the championship series. George Winter was to pitch.

George Winter (1878–1951), the pitcher, was born in New Providence, Pennsylvania. He attended Gettysburg College and was a teammate of Eddie Plank in 1901. George pitched eight years in the major leagues, starting with Boston in the new American League in 1901. He had an 83-102 record in the majors, before closing his career with two minor league seasons. Afterward, he briefly coached the University of Vermont team and then opened a sporting goods store in Wilmington, Delaware, where he lived most of his life.

The *Gettysburg Compiler*, quoting a York paper, described the game as follows:

ONE OF THE GREATEST baseball games ever witnessed in this city was played on the baseball field of the County Agricultural Society yesterday afternoon between rival Adams County teams from Gettysburg and McSherrystown. The contest was to decide the championship of Adams County and Gettysburg won. The score was 7 to 3.

The game was a good one principally because both teams gave a clever exhibit of fielding and the brilliant work of both pitchers, which kept the batting down to a minimum and contributed to the enthusiasm which prevailed throughout the contest. It was just the sort of a game that makes the genuine baseball admirer in a city like York wish he could see lots of them.

Gettysburg won the game because of superior playing, both in the field and at the bat. To pitcher Winters (sic), however, belongs the bulk of the credit for the victory. He pitched a remarkable game, allowing the McSherrystown batsmen only two safe hits during the whole nine innings and those two hits came after one out in the last inning. He gave only two bases on balls and as a rule disposed of the side in one, two, three order.

Gettysburg was unable to hit the ball often, but by bunching a few hits, and some clever base running, easily tallied seven runs.

Donald McPherson, of Gettysburg, umpired the game and gave entire satisfaction to both teams. (McPherson was a prominent judge in Adams County.)

The team was given an enthusiastic welcome on their return to Gettysburg, the Gettysburg band and about 500 people were present to greet them.

The article ended with a note about "Wilson, Clay, and probably Plank will play with the Cambridge, Maryland team until the close of their season."

Eddie Plank was a champion. He and the newly acquired George Winter were an unbeatable left-right combination.

Two days later, the great Galveston Hurricane occurred along the Texas coast, ending the golden era of Galveston and resulting in the deaths of between 6,000 t0 12,000 people.

The following month, on October 19, the German physicist Max Planck, perhaps a very distant relation to the Planks of Gettysburg, discovered "Planck's Law" of black-body radiation. This led to Planck's announcement about black body emission in mid-December, resulting in the birth of quantum physics.

On November 8th, 1900, William McKinley was re-elected President of the United States, defeating Democrat William Jennings Bryan.

On January 22nd, 1901, Queen Victoria of England died, ending her reign of 63 years. She was succeeded by her son, Prince Albert, who became King Edward VII.

Less than a week later, on January 28th, 1901, Ban Johnson declared the newly formed American League a major league.

On April 3rd, Connie Mack accused Christy Mathewson of breaking his contract with the Athletics. Mathewson returned to the New York Giants, with whom he had pitched for briefly in 1900.

William Gideon Leisenring (1878–1918) was the manager of the Gettysburg College baseball team for 1901. The prior year, he had secured coach Foreman, but no mention of a coach was made for the current year. Perhaps Leisenring oversaw the team himself. Leisenring had been born in Muncy, Pennsylvania, and attended the Chambersburg Academy and Gettysburg College. He became a bond trader in Chicago, where he passed away.

The season started off well for Gettysburg. On April 4th, Episcopal High School of Alexandria, Virginia, surrendered after six innings, falling behind 18 to 4. Eddie struck out 14 and knocked three hits.

The next day, with George Winter on the hill, Gettysburg lost 14 to 6 to Randolph-Macon, of Ashland, though Winter held them to one hit for the first six innings. Eddie played right field.

At William and Mary, a few days later, Eddie was on top of his game, throwing a two-hitter while striking out nine and walking none. Gettysburg won 8 to 1.

Winter was back on the mound against Franklin and Marshall, defeating them 4 to 0. He struck out 15, with Plank in right field again.

The April 24th *Gettysburgian* had the following item about the baseball team:

Strength in every department is evident, the fielding and batting percentages both standing very high. Along the pitching line, perhaps greater strength was never seen. Plank, the reliable southpaw of last year, and Winter a new man have already shown remarkable ability and seemed almost unhittable.

The team ran into Villa-Nova the next day, on April 25th. Gettysburg dropped their first home game of the season 7 to 3 due to "poor fielding at critical moments." Eddie struck out 12 and allowed only four hits.

The following day, Christy Mathewson won his first major league game, pitching for New York.

Gettysburg easily defeated Dickinson College at Nixon Field on May 1, 9 to 1. Winter dominated the game on the mound while Eddie manned right field and batted fourth.

Plank was back on the hill on May 3rd against Bucknell, striking out nine while allowing only five hits. Gettysburg won 4 to 1. Hess, started for Bucknell.

The next day, Eddie was back in right field as the team dropped a game to State College, 11 to 6.

Plank took the hill on May 8th at Carlisle against the Indians. He won 9 to 3. Said the *Gettysburgian*, "… the principal feature of which was Eddie Plank and his seemingly exhaustless supply of curves and speedy balls. Sixteen of the warriors fell victim to strikeouts and but one scratch hit was made, which came in the ninth inning and which scored two runs."

On May 11th, Gettysburg again faced the Carlisle Indians, tying after ten innings at five apiece. Eddie played right field while Winter pitched. The game ended in a tie because Carlisle had to catch their train. On the field with the Indian School was Charles Chief Bender, who went on to be a teammate with Plank and to the Hall of Fame. It is possible another apocryphal story about a lengthy battle between Plank and Bender in their college days has its origins in this tie game. There is no record yet discovered of the two facing each other in the same game as mound opponents, though Bender did finish the May 8th game in relief.

Around this time, Eddie Plank received a telegram from Connie Mack to come to Baltimore where his Philadelphia Athletics of the newly-formed American League would be playing John McGraw's Baltimore Orioles. Frank Foreman was on the Baltimore roster at that time, but it would seem odd that Foreman, an opposing player, would have suggested to Mack to try out Plank. However, as mentioned previously, Frank's brother Brownie knew Mack from his days in Pittsburgh. Brownie had played his last professional game the prior year, and may have been communicating with Connie Mack. All three were in the Baltimore area at the time.

Per the September 13, 1911, *Gettysburg Compiler*:

ONE NIGHT, WHILE THE Athletics were in Boston (note: was probably Baltimore), Foreman went to the hotel and saw Mack.

"Con," he said, "there's a lefthander down at the college where your humble servant has been coaching that you want to get. His name is Plank. I'm staking you to this information because somebody is going to grab him."

Connie flew downstairs. He grabbed a telegraph blank and wired terms to Plank, telling him if he was willing to accept to join the club in Wilmington.

Per the February 25, 1926, *Philadelphia Inquirer*, Plank had received a request for a tryout in early May, suggesting he come to Baltimore for a trial game. Mack had relayed his message through Morris Musselman, the former town team manager, who was a druggist in Gettysburg. Musselman accompanied him to the tryout.

Per the SABR website, Frank Foreman had recommended Plank to Mack early in 1901. Mack then telegraphed Plank. It's then likely that Musselman, at the pharmacy in town, was notified of the telegraph and then sought out Eddie at the college. At the time, the Western Union telegraph office was at the train station at 35 Carlisle Street, near the college. Charles T. Rose was the operator at the time. Perhaps Charles relayed the message to Musselman, who had been Plank's manager on the town teams. Regardless of how it happened, Eddie got the message and had his tryout in Baltimore.

On Monday, May 14th, Eddie Plank was in Baltimore with the Philadelphia Athletics as they faced the Orioles. Charles "Bock" Baker started the game for the A's against Joe McGinnity. It was Baker's only appearance for Philadelphia. He lasted six innings, yielding 11 runs, 7 earned. Eddie got the call for the last two innings and was roughed up. Said the *Philadelphia Times*, "In the seventh inning, Plank was put in, but was wild at first. A base on balls to Foutz and the outs scored a run. The last two runs were tallied in the eighth off a three-bagger by Keister and a two-bagger by Williams." Eddie also made an error. The A's lost 14 to 6.

May 15th, Eddie picked up the ball and defeated Dickinson College 4 to 2. He yielded only four hits while striking out ten. It was his last appearance for Gettysburg College before signing a professional contract.

*Portrait of Eddie Plank at
Gettysburg College.*

*Close-up of Eddie Plank's
college portrait.*

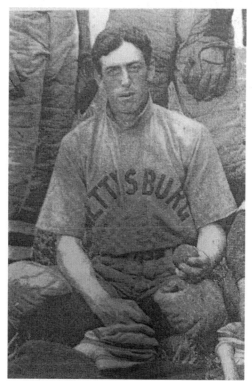

College Eddie sitting with glove and ball.

*Frank Foreman Old Judge card
while with Batlmore.*

*College Eddie ready
to pitch.*

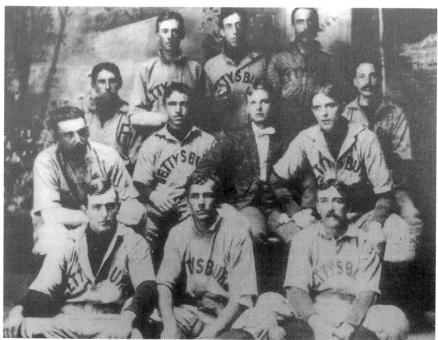

1901 Gettysburg College team. Plank is in the back row in the center.

Informal photo of the Gettysburg College team. Eddie is in the back on the left.

1901:
NEVER IN FINER
FETTLE

THE *PHILADELPHIA INQUIRER* from the morning of Thursday, May 16, 1901, announced the signing by Connie Mack of Edward Plank from Gettysburg College. The deal for $1,500 was likely offered after Eddie pitched that Monday in Baltimore.

Continued the September 13, 1911, *Gettysburg Compiler:* As Eddie explains, "his heart was almost leaping from behind his tongue." Plank packed his trunk that night, was up to take the milk train to Philadelphia at dawn, and went straight to Washington. He introduced himself to Connie and was measured for a uniform.

Eddie headed off to Washington on Friday, arriving to meet the team as it transferred from Baltimore. Mack, the "Tall Tactician," did not wait long to put his young lefty to work. The next day, on Saturday afternoon, May 18, Eddie was tapped to start in Washington against the Senators.

The A's had started the season 5–13, and were near the basement in the American League, in 7th place, when Eddie took the mound. His opponent that afternoon was Dale Gear, back in the major leagues. His last stint had been with the Cleveland Spiders of the National League in 1896.

The Senators lineup was John Farrell in center, Sam Dungan in right, Joe Quinn at second, Pop Foster in left, Bill Everitt at first, Boileryard Clarke behind the plate, Billy Clingman at short, Bill Coughlin at third, and Gear. The team was led by Jim Manning, who would manage only this one season in the major leagues. Quinn, a 17-year veteran, had been playing since 1884 and had amassed over 1,700 hits. Clarke was a veteran platoon catcher for many years, now handling the full-time duty. Coughlin was a young third baseman who would later play with Ty Cobb. In summary, the Senators of 1901 were not a strong team, but found themselves in second place at 11–6 at that point, thanks to a good start.

Connie Mack's lineup that Saturday included: Phil Geier in center, Dave Fultz at second, Jack Hayden in left, Napolean "Larry" Lajoie at short, Ralph Orlando "Socks" Seybold in right, Lafayette Napolean "Lave" Cross at third, Michael Riley "Doc" Powers at first, Morgan Murphy at catcher, and Plank. Lajoie, the future Hall of Famer, had been a star player for the cross-town Phillies before jumping to the new American League. He was having his best season. Seybold was at the beginning of a good run with the A's. Cross, also a former Phillie, was in his 16th season in the big leagues. Powers was usually the catcher, getting a break at first base. Murphy was a veteran utility player, catching Eddie's first start.

Said the *Philadelphia Inquirer* about the game:

THE ATHLETICS WON THEIR first game this week this after-noon, thanks to the excellent delivery of young Plank, the south-paw Manager Mack secured from Gettysburg. One winning game does not stamp a pitcher to be out of the ordinary, but unless all signs fail, the Athletics have secured an A-1 pitcher in this youngster. He has plenty of speed, superb control, and mixes his slow ones with his fast ones in a way that will prove embar-rassing to any set of hitters. He never once left his feet this after-noon despite the efforts of opposing players and the spectators to rattle him.

The *Philadelphia Times* provided the following account:

THE ELONGATED GETTYSBURG BOY, Plank by name, was on the rubber for the Quakers, and the way he twirled the ball, batted and fielded, speaks volumes for his future. His move-ments on the rubber are rather slow, and the crowd got after him, counting off the number as he delivered each ball, but he kept his head in masterful style and made the Senators look like the proverbial thirty cents. But six hits were made off his deliv-ery, and but for his bases on balls getting mixed up with errors, Washington's runs would have been very few.

From the start, Eddie was slow and deliberate on the mound, much to the irritation of the fans, batters, and even umpires.

Eddie would fidget, adjusting his pants, his cap, swatting away bugs real and imagined, swiping the dirt with his hand, rubbing down the ball or asking for a new one, shaking off the signs though actually throwing the first pitch asked for. His goal was always to keep the batter guessing and to disrupt their timing. Often hitters would swing to put the ball in play simply because they were tired of waiting. Fans on the road would get on Plank for these habits and it is said some stayed away because they were concerned they would miss the train home. However, per most of Eddie's box scores, his games were usually over in less than two hours, like almost all the games of that era.

Philadelphia jumped to a 6-to-0 lead in the first two innings, and Eddie took it from there, going the distance and striking out five. His team won easily, 11 to 6. If not for Cross's error in the 6th, the score would have been 11 to 2. At the plate, Plank helped himself with two base hits and two runs scored. Per the paper, Murphy's handling of the young lefty was "a decided help."

The team then headed to Chicago, and then Milwaukee, where Eddie beat the Brewers 8 to 3 for his second career win. The team was next at Cleveland, where they swept a doubleheader. Eddie won the first game 3 to 1, on a four-hitter, defeating veteran Bill Hart, who also gave up only four hits. Plank was "the steadier of the two at the most critical times."

The Athletics finished May at 13-17 by edging Cleveland 15 to 14, now 8–4 since acquiring Eddie. Nearing his 26th birthday, Eddie had now toured several of the major cities in the nation. Attendance at these games was typically in the hundreds to low thousands.

On June 3rd, the A's were in Detroit, where Eddie toiled in a pitchers' duel with Roscoe Miller, the 24-year-old ace of the Tigers. Eddie edged him 2 to 1, giving Philadelphia its 9th straight victory. Said the *Inquirer*, "Young Plank had his nerve tested in the last two innings and proved that he was made of the right kind of stuff and that he is not an aeronaut. The 3,200 spectators tried in every manner possible to rattle the young pitcher, but he finished the game in fine style." The A's were now 16-17, in 5th place.

A few days later, after dropping two games, the A's were in Philadelphia to face the Tigers in what was Eddie Plank's home debut. Over 10,000 spectators, including Robert Rupp and Morris Musselman of Gettysburg, flocked to Columbia Park to see the young left-hander. They were not disappointed. Said the *Inquirer*:

> The pavilion was packed with tastefully attired women and well-groomed men, while the bleachers were unable to hold all the enthusiasts who wanted to be on hand to show the Athletics that they were still with them. From every point of view, the homecoming was a most satisfactory affair. Young Plank made his local debut and he was immediately installed a favorite by the spectators, who lent him all sorts of encouragement as the game progressed. He pitched a superb game, holding the Wolverines down to four hits, one of which was a pure scratch. He struck out five men and nary a base on balls.

The A's jumped out to a 2 to 0 lead. Eddie then cruised to a 6 to 1 win. Fultz and Powers each had two hits. The rookie phenom was now 5–1. The A's improved to 17–19, in sixth place.

Unfortunately, the A's dropped the next two to the Tigers. Milwaukee then came to town and hung a loss on the A's, putting them at 17-22. It seemed the Mackmen were only winning when "Gettysburg Eddie" took the hill. That happened again on June 13th.

Before the game, Lave Cross and other team members complained to Connie Mack about an advertisement in center field, obstructing the batter's eye. "The color of the fence so shades the ball, we are not able to properly sight it," they said. Connie immediately had the advertisement painted over dark green.

The Milwaukee Brewers, managed by future Hall of Famer Hugh Duffy, were worse than the A's, bungling along at 15-24, in 7th place. Only Cleveland was below them in the standings. Duffy, a veteran of fourteen seasons, had been a star with the Boston Beaneaters of the National League. In 1894, Duffy had hit .440. and won the batting title and home run title, but just missed the RBI title. This season, Duffy was playing more than half the time in center field while managing. He was still a .300 hitter, though he went hitless this day.

Eddie retired the Brewers in a scoreless first. The A's then took a 1 to 0 lead, after which Plank cruised to a 6 to 0 victory. It was a two-hit masterpiece for Eddie. Hayden, Cross, and Lajoie each had multiple hit games to lead the offense. Lajoie also turned three double-plays in support. Said the *Inquirer*, "the big southpaw was never in finer fettle." Eddie had ended another losing streak and posted his first shutout.

Said Mack after the game, "If the boys will keep on hitting as well as they did today, I will have the fence painted a different color every day." Suffice to say, the new green coat was of no benefit to Milwaukee.

Two more wins, one against Milwaukee and the other against Cleveland, had the A's at 20–22, creeping up on .500. Unfortunately, Eddie was not able to help this turn, losing 9 to 5.

After splitting two more with Cleveland, the 2nd place Chicago White Sox came to town and defeated the A's in the first game of the series. They then beat Eddie 6 to 4, though the loss was mainly due to poor outfield play. The A's didn't win the rest of the month, ending June at 21–31, in 6th place. The eight-game losing streak included a disappointing debacle in Baltimore where Eddie yielded five first-inning runs to the Orioles in front of hundreds of fans from Gettysburg who had made the trip. The streak ended with Eddie's next start at Washington, which was halted due to the extreme heat with the teams tied 13 to 13 after nine innings. Apparently, all the players were exhausted, and Mack used three pitchers. The team hit rock bottom with another loss on the 2nd of July, now 21– 32.

July 4th, there were to be two games with Washington at Columbia Park. Only one was played in the morning, with rain canceling the afternoon contest. Apparently, over 10,000 fans were turned away due to the weather.

During the early game, Eddie Plank held off the Senators 6 to 5. Washington rallied in the 9th, scoring three runs to narrow the score, but Eddie prevailed.

After an 8 to 7 loss in Baltimore, Eddie's next turn was in Boston, where, on July 11, he faced rookie George Winter, his former Gettysburg teammate. The game was shortened to five innings due to rain, the last two played in a downpour. Winter got the best of Plank, 4 to 1. In was George's 7th consecutive victory. The A's were now 25–36, 14½ games behind the leading Boston Americans.

On July 15th, Boston was in Philadelphia for a rematch of the Plank/Winter Gettysburg confrontation. Eddie got out to a 6 to 0 lead and scattered seven hits. He coughed up a run in the 9th, finishing a 6 to 1 win. Socks Seybold led the offense with three hits, including a triple. The A's improved to 29–37, now nine games back of the White Sox. They would keep pace with the first division the rest of the way. Over in the National League, Christy Mathewson no-hit the St. Louis Cardinals, winning 6 to 0.

Four days later, Eddie was back on the mound in Milwaukee, where he topped the Brewers 3 to 1, scattering seven hits. That day, it was announced that Connie Mack had signed McSherrystown shortstop Robert McKinney, who had also been pursued by Boston. McKinney was touted as "the best ballplayer ever developed in that section of the country." He had been on the opposing side in Eddie Plank's Adams County League confrontations with McSherrystown in 1899 and 1900. It is thought that Frank Foreman may have played a role in Mack's signing. Unfortunately, McKinney would disappoint, clearly not ready for major league ball. He had difficulty making plays in the field and was released after only two frustrating appearances.

In Chicago, on the 22nd, Eddie won a twelve-inning pitchers' duel, 2 to 1, against fellow rookie Roy Patterson. Patterson would go on to a 20-win season and an 81–72 career record. Mack was so happy with Plank's performance; he threw his arms around the young man after the game.

On July 25th, Eddie and the A's were edged by the Tigers 4 to 3 in the second game of a doubleheader, but Plank was back in the winning column with an 11 to 5 victory against Cleveland on the 30th helped by Napolean Lajoie's cycle. After the A's beat Boston 8 to 6 on the 31st, Philadelphia finished July 35–42, in 5th place, 16½ games back of Chicago.

As August began, the McKinnon experiment was over, and William Frederick "Bones" Ely had been signed to take over. Bones had recently been released by the Pittsburgh Pirates, where he had played for six of his previous thirteen seasons. He had been Connie's shortstop when Mack managed the Pirates. Connie hoped old Bones had something left at 38.

Eddie took the mound on August 2nd at home against Boston, with Bones at short. The old infielder came through with three hits and superb play in the field. The headline the next day read "Bones Ely Cleverly Helps the Athletics to Victory." Eddie scattered 12 Boston hits, winning 7 to 4.

After a loss to Washington on the 7th, Eddie beat Boston at home 7 to 1. Plank scattered five hits, while Bones Ely led the offense with three safeties.

On August 14th, in Boston, following Chick Fraser's win over Cy Young in the first game, Plank took the mound against Gettysburg mate George Winter for the third time this season. George won 4 to 2, but Eddie was knocked out of the game in the 6th inning when he was hit while batting. Said the Philadelphia Inquirer, "An unfortunate incident happened in the sixth inning when Plank was at the bat. He was hit by a fast in-shoot of Winters' (sic) and it was feared was badly hurt, but he rallied and walked to the bench." Eddie would miss a few starts.

Throughout the season, the upstart American League led by Ban Johnson was upsetting its National League counterparts. The leagues were battling for players, and things got particularly hot during July. At one point, three teams in the Senior Circuit sought the services of Eddie Plank, offering him as much as $2,400, a $900 increase. Eddie did not bite.

The Athletics ended August with Plank on the bench, recovering from his beaning. Given the duration of the injury, he likely suffered a concussion. The team was still in 5th place but was now 56–52, 10½ games back of Chicago. It had been a stellar 21–10 month.

Eddie was back on the mound in Milwaukee on September 1st. It was his first game in two weeks. The Brewers' Bert Husting kept the A's at bay, and Eddie lost a tough 2 to 1 game. Three days later, on the 4th, the Tigers routed him 9 to 1. On the 7th, in Cleveland, Eddie was tied into the 9th inning, 4 to 4, but Socks Seybold came through with a three-run homer, giving the A's a 7 to 4 win.

During this first week of September, the nation experienced a tragedy when President William McKinley was shot by anarchist Leon Czolgosz in Buffalo, New York. The nation hoped and prayed for McKinley's recovery. He lingered for eight days, before passing on.

On September 12th, in Baltimore, Eddie witnessed "Iron Man" Joe McGinnity throw both ends of a doubleheader, winning the first (over Plank), and losing the second. The A's split the day.

On the 14th, in the second game of a doubleheader against Baltimore, Eddie started and pitched a scoreless 1st. But, in the 2nd inning, after Baltimore scored a run, Eddie was taken ill and had to leave the game. The A's went on to win 3 to 2, Bill Bernhard getting the win in relief.

On this day, Theodore Roosevelt was sworn in as President of the United States, succeeding McKinley and becoming the youngest President ever at 42 years 322 days.

Two days later, on the 16th, the Orioles were in Philadelphia for their final game of the season series. The A's had taken the last three in a row from Baltimore. This day, the former Gettysburg coach Frank Foreman took the mound for Baltimore against Eddie Plank. The Orioles got out to an early two-run lead, but the A's bounced back with three, taking a 3 to 2 advantage by the end of the 6th inning. In the top of the 7th, the Orioles rallied and had men on second and third. Foreman was at the plate and hit a pop into no-man's land behind third base. Napolean Lajoie saved the day. "The big player raced out after the ball, and jumping forward, stuck out his hand and caught the sphere before it touched the ground. It certainly was a great play and deserved all of the applause given," recounted the *Philadelphia Times*. The A's knocked Foreman around for seven runs in the bottom of the 7th and ended with an easy 10 to 2 victory. The A's were now 66–60, in 4th place, 12½ games out with 10 to play.

On September 23rd, Eddie beat the Chicago White Sox, the American League champions 5 to 3. Plank defeated player-manager Clark Griffith, who was wrapping up an excellent 24–7 season on the mound. Griffith had a very effective 20-year career in the major leagues, ending with a 237–146 record. He was later inducted into the Hall of Fame as a baseball executive.

In his last start of the season, on the 26th, Eddie was routed 10 to 3 by the last place Milwaukee Brewers. The A's then won their last three games to finish 74–62, in 4th place, only a half-game behind 3rd place Detroit. The Chicago White Sox won the first American League pennant.

Eddie Plank finished his rookie season 17–13, tied with Bill Bernhard (17–10) for second in wins. Chick Fraser led the club with 22 wins against 15 losses. Boston's Cy Young led the American League with 33 wins.

At the plate, Nap Lajoie won the triple crown, leading the league with a .426 average, 14 home runs, and 125 RBI. Nap's average was the highest ever in major league baseball since 1900.

Socks Seybold hit .334, Lave Cross .328, and Harry Davis, the first baseman, .306.

After hitting bottom at 21–32 in early July, the team finished 53–30, boding well for the future.

The Athletics hit the road for some exhibitions in early October. On the 1st, they were in York to play Penn Park. With Plank on the mound against an old nemesis, the A's easily won 15 to 4. The A's were then off to Chambersburg.

On the 6th, Eddie took the mound at Roxborough, in an exhibition. Plank and a mixture of A's and Brewers won easily, 20 to 5.

In his final start of the season, Eddie pitched for McSherrystown against Penn Park in York. He shut them out on three hits, winning 3 to 0.

Eddie spent the fall and winter at home in Straban Township at his father's farm. In early December, he signed a contract for the 1902 season.

The American League held its annual meeting in Chicago, beginning on December 2nd. Before leaving, Connie Mack and President Ben Shibe, of the Athletics, announced the signing of pitcher Bill Duggleby, outfielders Elmer Flick and Topsy Hartsel, shortstop Monte Cross, and utility player Clyde Robinson. Duggleby, Flick, and Cross were nabbed from the Phillies. Mack said he had completed his team for the 1902 season, and felt they were a stronger club than this past year.

On December 12th, Italian inventor Guglielmo Marconi received the first trans-Atlantic radio signal, sent from Poldhu, England, to Newfoundland.

As the calendar turned to 1902, the first college bowl game was held in Pasadena, California, at the Rose Bowl. Michigan and Stanford faced off on the gridiron.

*Eddie Plank as a rookie with the
Philadelphia Athletics, 1901.*

Connie Mack, owner and general manager of the Philadelphia Athletics.

1902:
A GREATER
TRIBUTE

EDDIE PLANK WAS the first to arrive in Philadelphia for spring training, prior to the March 1 reporting date. The team then traveled to Chapel Hill, North Carolina, where the Athletics were to train with the college varsity. Per the *Philadelphia Times*, "Eddie looked to be in first-class shape, and said that he had been doing light indoor work all winter, and will only have to take off a few pounds to be in good condition."

Meanwhile, on Columbia Avenue, the ballpark was being improved and expanded, permitting more seating in the bleachers.

By March 18th, Mack had decided to move the team to Charlotte due to it being too cold at Chapel Hill. After a couple weeks of workouts at Latta Park, the boys headed north on April 4th. They played an exhibition against Yale College at Columbia Park on the 5th. The next day, tensions with the National League were reaching a crescendo, especially regarding Napolean Lajoie's contract with the Athletics. The Phillies were suing to have him returned, and the American Leaguers were hearing none of it.

On April 12th, Eddie was the starting pitcher in an exhibition against Princeton College. He pitched the first five innings of the 21 to 4 victory. The Athletics played their regular lineup, with Hartsel leading off and playing left, Fultz in center, Davis at first, L. Cross at third, Lajoie at second, Flick in right, M. Cross at shortstop, Steelman at catcher, and Plank.

Around this time, the papers reported Plank was the subject of an effort by the Boston National League club to jump teams and leagues, such was the back and forth between Ban Johnson's group and the Senior Circuit. Eddie ignored the overtures.

On Monday, the 14th, Connie Mack's Athletics hosted the Newark Eastern League club in an exhibition. Eddie pitched the first three innings of a tight contest, ultimately won by the

Athletics 3 to 2 in the 9th inning. Five days later, the Athletics won again, 7 to 5, over the same Newark team, Eddie pitching the last few innings for the save, though he did yield a couple runs.

A few days later, on the 21st, the team ended the exhibition season with an easy win over the Penn Quakers of the University of Pennsylvania. Plank did not play in this one, but Lajoie did. That afternoon, news came that Nap Lajoie, the star second-baseman, would not be allowed to play for the Athletics per a Pennsylvania Supreme Court ruling. Should he play for Connie Mack, he risked going to jail.

On Wednesday, April 23, the Athletics opened their season in Baltimore against John McGraw's Orioles. Nap Lajoie was on the field because he had yet to be served the injunction. During the 9th inning, Mack received a telegram that the restraining order against Lajoie was in effect, and he pulled his star from the game. It would be his only appearance with the A's in 1902, as the team won easily 8 to 1 behind "Strawberry" Bill Bernhard, who had also jumped leagues the prior season.

The next day, with Dave Fultz in for Lajoie and Plank on the mound, the A's fell behind quickly 6 to 0 in the first inning. While Eddie threw shutout ball for the remainder of the game, the Philadelphians managed only two runs against Tom Hughes in a losing cause.

On April 29th, the A's were in Washington to face the Senators. Eddie Plank was on the mound while Lajoie, Bernhard, and Fraser watched from the stands, legally unable to play. Due to some sloppy fielding, the Athletics fell behind and lost 7 to 2, falling to 2-3 on the season. With a win over the Senators the next day, the team ended the month 3-3.

After a win in Washington on May 1, the team headed to Philadelphia for the home opener at Columbia Park on May 2. Pitcher Bert Husting arrived this day, having been purchased from the Boston Americans. He would go on to a strong 14-5 campaign. The festivities opened with a concert by Kendle's First Regiment Band. The music selections that afternoon included:

> March "The Invisible Eagle" by Sousa
> Selections from "Fiodora" by Stuart
> Intermezzo "Vaise Bleue" by Margio
> Medley Overture "Songs of the Day" by Boettger

> Novelette "In a Cozy Corner" by Grace Kimball
> Scenes from "King Dodo" by Luders
> Negro oddity "A Coon Band Contest" by Pryor
> Melodies from "San Toy" by Syd Jones
> Caprice, "The American Patrol" by Meachern
> March Comique "Cotton Blossoms" by Hall

Over 11,000 fans were on hand on a sunny spring afternoon. Per the *Philadelphia Inquirer:*

THE SWAYING MASS OF humanity in the grandstand was rendered conspicuous by the gay dresses of innumerable pretty girls, who lent their beauty and charm to the gay scene ... Kendle's First Regiment Band, stationed on the roof of the grandstand, rendered a program made up of popular music selections. Congratulations are due to the musicians for the efficient manner in which they "sized up" on more than one occasion. When Napolean Lajoie, the "enjoined one," entered the park, neatly attired in a black suit, the leader of the band was "wise" in a minute. Larry had just started towards the players' bench when the soul-stirring strains of "Ain't That a Shame" burst upon the ears of the spectators. The Ethiopian classic in ragtime caught on like wildfire. Immediately the boys in the bleachers took up the refrain and the mighty volume of sound swept over the diamond like a Kansas cyclone. No better evidence of the popularity of the big Frenchman could have possibly been furnished.

Just before the game started, Lajoie was invited out on the field and handed a magnificent bouquet of flowers. He turned and bowed, and headed back to the bench. On the way back, a rooter cried out, "Who's the bouquet from, Larry, Colonel Rogers?" Rogers was the owner of the Phillies who had started the legal proceedings that had tied up Nap. "Don't open dem flowers, Larry, dere's an injuncshun inside."

After Mayor Ashbridge threw out the first pitch, Eddie took the mound but gave up five first-inning runs to fall behind. The A's came back against the Senators, leading 6 to 5 after 6, but lost 7 to 6. Eddie was now 0-3 to start the season, and the A's were 4-4.

Saturday, May 3 was a cold and miserable day. Only 4000 fans braved the weather to watch Bert "Pete" Husting best the

Senators in his Philadelphia debut, 9 to 3. One of those fans was the famous "Ice Man" who was heard bellowing across the ballpark, taunting the enemy players. The next day, it was announced that pitcher Bill Duggleby was the first to jump ship and return to the Phillies of the National League.

After a 7 to 5 win on May 5 thanks to a Harry Davis three-run homer, the A's finished their home series against the Washington club on the 6th. Appeals to try to get Lajoie and the others back on the field failed. Regardless, Eddie took the mound before less than 2000 fans and quickly shut out the Senators on only four hits, 11 to 0. It was Plank's first win of the season. The team improved to 7-4, tied with Detroit for first place.

Over 30,000 people were killed in Martinique on May 8 when Mount Pelée erupted, destroying the town of Saint-Pierre.

The A's then took three of four from Baltimore, including a 13 to 4 thrashing of former Gettysburg coach and teammate Frank Foreman in his final major league game. The former Gettysburg College connections continued May 12 when the Boston Americans came to town. Plank faced off against former teammate George Winter for the first time since being beaned by him the prior season. Winter won this one, 8 to 2. Once again, Eddie was hit hard early, giving up five runs in the first before settling down. Winter only allowed five hits. Plank was now 1-4, but the A's were 10-7, in 4th place in the American League, only a game-and-a-half back from the St. Louis Browns.

After a win against Boston on the 14th, Eddie Plank faced Cy Young on the 15th in Philadelphia. That day, it was announced that Chick Fraser had re-signed with the Phillies. The disposition of Lajoie was still undetermined, but it was expected he would also go back to the Philadelphia National League club. On the mound, the 35-year-old Young was amid one of his best seasons. He scattered seven hits and won 6 to 3. Plank dropped to 1-5. The teams then headed to Boston for a three-game set. Winter won the first one for Boston 4 to 2. Husting returned the favor, winning 7 to 5 in game two. After two offdays, Young and Plank matched up again for the final game. This proved to be a pitchers' duel, eventually won by Young, 2 to 1. The loss dropped Plank to 1-6 on the season, while the team fell to 12-9, in 5th place, but only half a game back of the bunched-up American League.

The A's returned home to face Cleveland. In the first game, the A's won a high-scoring affair 12 to 11. Socks Seybold clinched it with a two-run walk-off homer over the left-field fence in the 9th inning. Husting won the game in relief. In the second game, Wiltse started again against the Bronchos, and this time lost 11 to 9. Eddie pitched the third game against last-place Cleveland, holding them scoreless until the 9th, winning his 2nd victory of the season, 6 to 2. While Cleveland was in town, their owner, Charles Somers, was along to try to negotiate deals with Lajoie and Bernhard. It was reported contracts were signed, making Nap the highest paid player in baseball. At this same time, the Indians released catcher Ossee Schrecongost and their captain, second baseman Frank Bonner. Both were signed by Connie Mack in what was a de facto trade for the loss of the disputed former Phillies. In the final game of the series, the teams tied after nine innings at 9 apiece following a five-run comeback in the bottom of the 9th by the A's. Eddie relieved Husting at that point, and pitched a scoreless tenth, but yielded six runs in the eleventh. His record fell to 2-7. Philadelphia was now 14-11, in fifth place, but still half of a game out.

On May 26, the first-place Detroit Tigers came to town. The A's took this one 8 to 6 behind Snake Wiltse. The next day, the game was rained out, but the A's tied for first thanks to losses by both Chicago and St. Louis. On the 28th, Plank pitched the second game and scattered eleven hits in an easy 11 to 4 win. Eddie improved to 3-7, and the A's kept pace with Chicago and Boston. Wiltse completed the sweep of Detroit, winning the third game 6 to 4. Boston remained tied with the A's, while Chicago slipped a half-game back.

Nearly 12,000 fans showed up for a doubleheader with the St. Louis Browns on May 30th. Eddie pitched the morning game and was knocked around for 11 runs on 17 hits, losing 11 to 7. The A's won the afternoon game 11 to 4 behind Husting.

To close the month, the teams met again the next day. The A's pulled out an exciting win with three runs in the bottom of the 9th, 7 to 6. Wiltse got the win. At the end of May, the A's were alone in first place at 19-12, though Eddie was stumbling along at 3-8.

As June began. Connie Mack was looking for more pitching help. His team resumed play on the 2nd against St. Louis. The A's won 5 to 4 with a run in the 9th thanks to a walk-off single by Topsy Hartsel.

On the 3rd, the Chicago White Sox were in town. Eddie took the mound, and it seemed to be an easy affair until there were two outs in the 9th. With the A's up 9 to 2, Plank proceeded to tire and give up five runs before sealing the deal, 9 to 7. Eddie improved to 4-8.

The next day, Chicago ace Roy Patterson, who had won 20 games in 1901 for the league champions, shutout the Athletics and Snake Wiltse 3 to 0.

Over in Cleveland, Napolean Lajoie made his debut for the Bronchos. Clark Griffith beat Husting easily in the final game 11 to 3. The A's maintained a half-game lead over Boston.

June 7 was the beginning of a road trip with the first stop in Detroit. Wiltse was hit hard in a 9 to 1 loss. In the second game, Eddie Plank defeated Joe Yeager 3 to 2. Eddie was now 5-8. Fred Mitchell, recently acquired from the Boston Americans, was roughed up in the next game 10 to 5. Wiltse dropped the final game of the series 8 to 4. The A's were now a half-game back of Chicago, in second place.

The team next moved to Cleveland to face the rejuvenated Bronchos. With Plank on the mound, Lajoie hit a three-run homer in the 5th to give Cleveland the lead. The A's stayed close, and pulled it out with two runs in the 9th, winning 4 to 3. Eddie's record inched up to 6-8 while the team kept pace with Chicago. The teams split the next two before Bernhard took the hill for Cleveland for the 4th game. He beat Wiltse 6 to 3.

The team then moved on to Chicago to face the league-leading champion White Sox. After a rainout, Rookie James "Odie" Porter was called upon by Connie Mack to pitch his first (and only) major league game. He faced Clark Griffith, and was not a mystery to the Sox sluggers, falling 10 to 5. The A's dropped the next one and were swept by the Sox, who now led by 4 1/2 games.

The team moved on to St. Louis for a series with the Browns on the 19th where they lost 2 of 3. Needing pitching help, Connie Mack coaxed Rube Waddell to join the team, leaving California on the 24th. At the time, the A's were 25-23, 5 1/2 games back in third place.

Waddell was an interesting character, to say the least. The Bradford, Pennsylvania native was known to be unpredictable and prone to distraction, yet a dominant southpaw pitcher when focused. He had bounced around the minor leagues and pitched a few innings for the Louisville Colonels in 1897 which also boasted Fred Clarke and Honus Wagner. Waddell surfaced again with the Colonels in 1899 for ten games, winning seven of them. It was said Waddell had blown his entire signing bonus on a drinking binge. In 1900, Clarke was the manager of the Pittsburgh Pirates and Wagner his shortstop after the Louisville club had folded and been combined with Pittsburgh. Waddell came along as well and led the National League in ERA, though he had a losing record. Rube's erratic behavior led Clarke to suspend him from the team. Connie Mack was the manager of the Milwaukee Brewers of the new American League, formerly the Western League. He obtained permission from Pittsburgh to sign Waddell for the rest of the season. After pitching and hitting the team to a 17-inning victory in mid-August, Mack bribed Rube to pitch the second game of the doubleheader by offering him a three-day fishing trip. The game was shortened to only five innings. Rube agreed and hurled a shutout before heading off to Pewaukee Lake. Soon after, Pittsburgh requested his return, and Mack obliged. Waddell then bounced between the Pirates and the Cubs in 1901, pitching well, but wearing out his welcome once again. By June of 1902, Rube was hurling for Los Angeles in the independent leagues. Hearing of this, and desperate for pitching, Mack sent two Pinkerton detectives to California to retrieve twenty-five-year-old Waddell.

The game that day was in Baltimore against the Orioles. Eddie, who hadn't played in over a week, petitioned to pitch and took the mound against Harry Howell. Trailing 5 to 4 in the 7th, the A's mounted a comeback. Catcher Ossee Schrecongost and pitcher Eddie Plank, batting 8th and 9th, led off the inning with singles. Next up was lead-off batter Topsy Hartsel. He hit a low line drive toward Kip Selbach in left field. It appeared the ball was surely going to drop in for a hit, and Ossee and Eddie took off running. Following is a description of the play from the *Philadelphia Inquirer*: "But Selbach had started promptly, and when the ball was reaching the ground was within six feet of it—a mere detail for such an acrobat. Taking off like a clown who turns somersaults over the elephant, Selbach launched himself into the air with the ball. He grabbed it in the very nick of time, and holding on, slipped a few feet on his face and then springing erect threw to second. Williams caught it, putting out Schrecongost, and then Williams threw to McGann, who caught it, putting out Plank, completing the triple play and saving the game." The Orioles went on to win 6 to 4. Eddie fell to 6-9 on the season.

The next day, Waddell arrived in Baltimore to join the team. Husting started the game and fell behind by four runs in the first. He was replaced by Mitchell. The A's then battled back to ultimately win 8 to 6.

Rube made his American League debut on June 26 to high expectations in Baltimore. Unfortunately, it was not his best performance. The southpaw was wild, and the team lost 7 to 3. The A's had now fallen to 26-25, six games out in 4th place.

Off to Washington, the team opened a series against the Senators with a 4 to 2 win on June 27.

The next day, facing former Phillies ace Al Orth, Plank battled to a 2 to 2 tie through seven innings. The Senators added two in the 8th. The A's only tallied one in the 9th, and Eddie found himself 6-10. The A's finished June at 27-26, 6 1/2 games back of first place Chicago, in 4th place.

July was to be a whole different story for Mack's Men. On the first, Rube Waddell made his home debut in Philadelphia. What a doozy! He held Baltimore to only two singles. Not one got past first base. He struck out thirteen Orioles and walked none. He became the first major league pitcher to strike out the side on only nine pitches. The A's mustered only two runs in support, but Rube held the O's to zero, winning 2 to 0.

The following day, Eddie Plank and Joe McGinnity battled in a 2-to-1 game won by the Orioles. Eddie's record was now 6-11, and the A's were still mired in 4th place at 28-27. However, Plank was beginning to pitch much better.

On the 4th, the Senators were in town to start a series. Before 22,000 fans, the A's swept a doubleheader, winning the first 3 to 1 behind Fred Mitchell, and the second 12 to 9 behind Waddell. Wiltse dropped the final game of the series the next day, 9 to 5.

The team then headed to Boston for a four-game series with the Americans. On July 7, the day John McGraw jumped from the Orioles to become the manager of the Giants, Eddie Plank faced George Winter in Boston. The two battled in a tight 1-1 game until the bottom of the 7th, when Boston tallied three runs. They ultimately won 4 to 2, dropping Eddie to 6-12.

The next day, July 8, Danny Murphy, a young second-base-man who had been hitting .462 for Norwich in the Connecticut League, made his debut for the A's. Backing three A's pitchers, Murphy went 6 for 6 at the plate, leading the A's to a 22 to 9 win. Murphy would prove to be a key player the rest of the way, solidifying the second base situation for Mack.

On the 9th, Murphy went 0 for 7, and the A's found themselves in a tight 2-to-2 contest as Waddell battled Bill Dinneen. Finally, in the 17th inning, the A's scored twice and took the win, 4 to 2.

Cy Young took the mound on the 10th for Boston against Mitchell and won 3 to 1.

Back in Philadelphia, Boston's Winter beat Huston the next day, 8 to 2. Waddell followed with a 3 to 2 over Dinneen. On July 14, young Howard Paul "Highball" Wilson made his debut for Connie Mack against the great Cy Young. The two were tied at three after regulation. The A's won the game with a 10th-inning run.

Up to this point in the season, Plank, who had been the rookie phenom the prior year, was now mired with a 6-12 record while new pitchers were being added to the team. Waddell and Wilson would prove to be very effective the rest of the season. Eddie found himself being skipped on his turn to pitch. How would Eddie fare the rest of the way? The team was only 34-31, seven games back in 4th place. The first-place White Sox were coming to town.

The series opened with Chicago on July 15. Rube Waddell made quick work of them, winning 9 to 3.

The next day, Plank started but was roughed up for five runs in the first two innings. He was pulled for Mitchell, and the A's fell 9 to 4. Clearly, Eddie was not back on his horse yet, losing for the 13th time in less than half a season. But, the A's, behind Wiltse, rebounded for a 7 to 4 win the next day. Waddell was back on the hill for the final game of the series on the 18th. Going into the bottom of the 9th, the A's trailed 6 to 5. That's when Ossee "Schreck" Schrecongost ripped a two-run double that brought in two to win the game. The fans rushed the field and carried the catcher off in a victory celebration. The A's had taken three of four from the league champions and were now five games back at 37-32 in 3rd place.

Cleveland was next in town and was at a disadvantage. Lajoie and Bernhard were forbidden by the court to play in Pennsylvania for any team other than the Phillies. Thus, they were not at the ballpark as they took the field against the A's. Rookie Addie Joss was on the mound for Cleveland against Highball Wilson. The hometown team won easily 9 to 4. On Monday, the 21st, the teams battled in a wild back-and-forth affair. Husting started for the A's but found himself down 7 to 2 in the 3rd. Plank relieved and threw three scoreless innings until being touched for three in the 7th. Waddell then relieved and the A's tied the game at ten in the bottom of the inning. "Schreck" was the hero again with a clutch single in the bottom of the 9th. Waddell got the win in relief.

The next day, Cleveland hit to a 4 to 1 lead over Husting before Mack pulled him in favor of Waddell. The team rallied to a 9 to 4 win, Murphy leading with three base hits. Waddell "vultured" another win in relief. The A's had swept three from Cleveland and were now 40-32, only two games back in third place.

Detroit was next in town. Mack handed the ball to Eddie and was not disappointed. Plank scattered only five hits as the A's edged the Tigers and Win Mercer 5 to 2. Finally, Eddie notched a win, improving to 7-13. The team was only a game out of first, in 2nd place. The next two games with Detroit were rained out.

A series with the St. Louis Browns began on Saturday, July 26th. Rube Waddell twirled a strong game, winning 3 to 1. The next game, on Monday the 28th, Highball Wilson came back to earth losing 9 to 4, ending the A's seven-game winning streak. Waddell dropped the next game, 3 to 1. The A's had slipped to 3rd place, one game out.

The month of July ended in St. Louis with a 4 to 4 tie. The game was called due to darkness with Waddell on the mound for the second straight game. The A's finished the month 42-34, a half-game behind Chicago in 2nd place.

The series continued August 1st in St. Louis. Highball Wilson was hit around, and the A's lost 11 to 5. Eddie took the mound the next day and shut down the Browns 4 to 1, scattering eight hits. At 43-35, the A's were two games back of Chicago, in 2nd place. The White Sox were next on the schedule.

Rube Waddell led off the series with Chicago but lost narrowly 3 to 1. Highball Wilson lost an 11-inning affair the next day, 8 to 7. It was Plank, on August 5th, who saved the series against Chicago by preventing a sweep. Harry Davis, the first baseman, got credit too for a spectacular catch in the last inning. Eddie scattered ten hits to win 4 to 3. His record was now 9-13.

Next, the road trip continued in Cleveland. It would not go well. After Waddell dropped the first game 5 to 4, Mitchell lost the 2nd game by the same score two days later. Eddie was next to lose a close one in Detroit, 4 to 3, on the 9th of August. Finally, the losing streak ended on the 10th with a 9 to 1 win by Husting against the Tigers. Before the final game of the disastrous road trip, Waddell showed up at the park and declared to Connie that "no team on Earth could beat him today feeling as he did." Rube then went out to prove it, holding the Tigers scoreless on only four hits through thirteen innings. Finally, in the 13th, Rube hit a triple and was singled in by Davis, giving the A's a 1 to 0 victory. Heading back home, the A's had slipped to 46-40, 3 1/2 games out in 4th place. Both teams traveled east to Philadelphia.

Back in Philadelphia on the 13th, the A's swept two from the Tigers, taking the doubleheader 8 to 0 behind Waddell and 9 to 0 behind Husting. It was a strange day that saw Harry Davis steal second, with Fultz on third. When the steal did not draw a throw, which would have allowed Fultz to head home, Davis decided to "steal" back to first on the next pitch! He then stole second again. The teams matched up for two more the next day, and the results were similar with Wilson winning the first game, 4 to 3, and Mitchell winning 5 to 1. The A's had won four games in two days and were now 50-40, just a game-and-a-half back in 3rd place. On Friday, the 15th, two more games were played. The A's again swept the doubleheader. Husting won the first game 11 to 3. Eddie won the second game 5 to 2. His record improved to 10-14. At 52-40, the A's took a half-game lead over St. Louis, atop the American League.

Chicago was next in town. Waddell took the mound and held them to a run, winning a tight one 2 to 1. Two days later, Eddie won easily, 12 to 5 to improve his record to 11-14. The team was now 54-40, with a game-and-a-half lead over St. Louis. The White Sox salvaged a win against Waddell, 5 to 2, on August 19th. The second-place Browns were next to come to town.

In the first game against St. Louis, Dan Murphy was the hitting star as Husting held off the Browns 4 to 1. Eddie won the next one 12 to 5. Waddell finished the sweep 12 to 4, holding the Browns after Mitchell gave up three runs in the 1st. The Athletics were now 57-41 and were beginning to pull away to a three-game lead over Chicago.

Cleveland was next into town to face the hot Athletics on August 23rd. Highball Wilson won easily 12 to 1. Mitchell followed with a 7 to 2 win. Eddie finished the sweep the next day with an easy 13 to 2 victory. He was now 13-14, and the A's had won 16 of 17, at 60-41 in 1st place, three games up on Boston.

Heading west on the 27th, the A's dropped a make-up game to Cleveland 2 to 1 despite a fine effort from Wilson.

The following day, they split a doubleheader against Chicago. Husting lost 4 to 1 before Waddell won 5 to 4. Eddie took the next game 10 to 6 to finally reach .500 on the season, 14-14. The teams then split another doubleheader on the 30th, Chicago beating Wilson 4 to 2 in the first game followed by Waddell's win 6 to 5 in the second. The team finished the month in St. Louis, losing a doubleheader. Eddie dropped the first game 1 to 0 on his 27th birthday. Husting lost the second game 3 to 2. The losses dropped the team to 63-46, only one game ahead of Boston. The loss would be Eddie's last of the season as the team came down the stretch.

The month of September did not open well. After an offday, the team played a doubleheader at St. Louis. Waddell lost the first game 5 to 1. Mitchell dropped the second 4 to 3. The Browns had now pulled into second, only a half-game back.

Overnight, on their way to Detroit for a game on the 2nd of September, the team was involved in a train derailment near Peru, Illinois, in the wee hours of the morning. Fortunately, no one on the team was injured, and they completed their journey in time.

Rube Waddell won the game against the Tigers easily, 5 to 1. The next day, Eddie got back to .500 at 15-15 as the A's topped the Tigers again, 5 to 3. Closing out the season series with the Tigers, the Mack Men routed the Bengals 13 to 4 behind Mitchell. The A's were now 66-48, with a game-and-a-half lead over the St. Louis Browns. There were only 24 games to play.

Next up was Cleveland. On the 5th, Lajoie had four hits in an easy 10 to 7 win over Mitchell. Waddell was on the mound the following day, leading the team to a tight 3 to 2 win. After an offday, Waddell was back on the mound for another win, defeating Cleveland 8 to 5. At 68-49, the A's were now two games up on St. Louis.

Baltimore was next in town for four games. On the 10th, the teams played a doubleheader, swept by Philadelphia. Waddell won both games in relief, 9 to 5 and 5 to 4. The A's won another doubleheader the following day, Plank winning the first one with a superior performance, 9 to 1. Wilson won the second game 4 to 3. With the four wins in two days, the A's improved to 72-49, now 3 1/2 games up on St. Louis with 17 to play.

Heading to Boston on the 12th, the A's lost the first game 5 to 4 and then were off for two days due to weather. On the 15th, the teams played a doubleheader, and Plank was on the mound. He held off the Americans and Bill Dinneen 6 to 4. The A's then swept the second game as Waddell topped Cy Young 9 to 2. The A's were now 74-50, ahead 4 games over St. Louis with 14 to play.

Washington was next into town. Highball Wilson knocked them in the first game 7 to 5. Newly signed Andy Coakley, going by the name "Jack McAllister" won the next one 6 to 5. On the 18th, the A's fell behind by 2 in the 1st as Husting was not effective and replaced by Plank. Eddie went the rest of the way for the victory, 6 to 2. The team was now 77-50, maintaining their four-game lead over St. Louis. Eddie had improved to 18-15.

On the 19th, Cy Young and the Boston team were in Philadelphia. Rube Waddell faced old Cy once again, beating him 6 to 4. Eddie was on the hill for the second game and won easily 7 to 2 for his 19th win of the season. The Athletics were now 79-50, five games up over St. Louis with only nine to play.

On the 22nd, the teams split a doubleheader. "McAllister" lost the first game 5 to 1, but Waddell won the 2nd 5 to 3. The team was now 80-51 with a five-game lead over the Browns and only seven to play.

Eddie then took the mound at home against Baltimore and edged them 4 to 3 for his 20th win of the season. Meanwhile, plans for a pennant celebration parade were being made for September 29th, should the Athletics prevail, which seemed almost assured. Mayor Ashbridge was very enthusiastic about the idea, and four players from the 1883 champion Athletics (American Association), Lon Knight, Cub Stricker, Jack O'Brien, and George Bradley were in town.

On September 24th, the A's swept a doubleheader to clinch the pennant. "McAllister" won the first game 7 to 5, followed by a 5-to-3 win by Wilson. The pennant-clincher was a walk-off win thanks to a wild pitch by former Athletic Snake Wiltse, allowing Hartsel to score.

To close the season on the 27th at Washington, the A's rested the regulars. Washington swept the doubleheader, leaving Philadelphia at 83-53, five games ahead of St. Louis.

On Monday, September 29th, the official pennant celebration began. First, an exhibition game was held at Columbia Park before 11,000 adoring fans. Most of the A's players made an appearance against the Wilmington A.A. Team. Fans handed the players flowers to show their gratitude.

The parade that followed was magnificent. Despite a steady rain, the team marched from Broad Street and Girard to Broad and Vine. Said the *Philadelphia Inquirer:* "The parade fairly bustled with features, many of them refreshingly novel. It was when the Second Division appeared, however, that the crowd went wild. And why not? There was Rube Waddell, the mighty Rube, he of the strong arm, surrounded by his colleagues, the pennant-winning Athletics. Seated in a barouche, surrounded on all sides by a sizzling sea of red fire, the champions smilingly responded to the vociferous cheers bestowed upon them by the excited populace. Probably never before, in a demonstration of any character, has a greater tribute been paid to any collection of men in this city."

Socks Seybold was the leading slugger on the team with 16 home runs, which led the American League, and 97 RBI to go with a .316 batting average. Lave Cross led the team with a .342 average, trailing Lajoie's league-leading .378. He also knocked in a team-leading 108 runs. Harry Davis hit .307 and led the team with 43 doubles. Topsy Hartsel hit .283 and led the team with 47 stolen bases, 637 plate appearances, and 109 runs. Dave Fultz hit .302 and scored 109 runs. Danny Murphy hit .313 in a little more than a half-season of play. Catcher Ossee Schrecongost hit a clutch .324. Among the pitchers, Plank hit .292 scoring 15 times and knocking in 16. Waddell hit well too, .286 with a home run and 18 RBI.

On the mound, Rube was superb, going 24-7 with a 2.05 ERA. He struck out 210. Plank went 20-15 with a 3.30 ERA. Despite a slow start, Eddie got better as the season progressed and the pennant race heated up. He went 6-0 in his last six games when it counted most. Bert Husting was a respectable 14-5. Highball Wilson finished at 7-4.

Cy Young again led the American League with 32 wins.

EDWARD S. PLANK
PITCHER OF THE PHILADELPHIA (A. L.) CLUB OF 1902

COMPLIMENTS OF

SPORTING LIFE PHILADELPHIA

"THE PAPER THAT MADE BASE BALL POPULAR"

Eddie Plank in 1902.

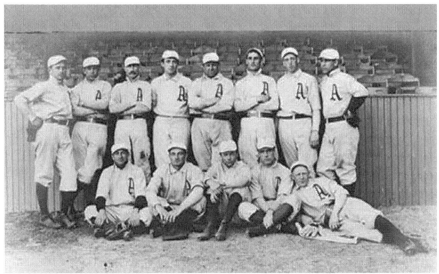

The 1902 Philadelphia Athletics.

MAYOR ASHBRIDGE'S TRIBUTE TO THE NATIONAL GAME
His Honor tossed the ball which opened the American League season in Philadelphia yesterday.

Philadelphia Mayor Ashbridge throws out the first pitch at Columbia Park in 1902.

THE FAMOUS "ICE MAN"

Caught in the act by an Inquirer photographer at Columbia Park, Friday.

Famous and extremely loud fan known as
"The Ice Man."

DAVE FULTZ, OUTFIELDER

Signed a Philadelphia contract in
June, 1898, at the rate of $2400 for
the season. After receiving the usual notice of reservation in the fall
of that year he was offered $1200 for
the year 1899, protested, but that's
all it amounted to.

Speedy center fielder Dave
Fultz.

MONTE CROSS, OF THE ATHLETICS, MAKES A HIT AND STARTS FOR FIRST

Monte Cross knocks a hit on August 25, 1902, against Cleveland.

MURPHY, ATHLETIC'S NEW SECOND BASEMAN

"Murph" has all the earmarks of the real thing and the fans, as well as the club officials, expect that he will make good all along the line.

Teammate Danny Murphy in 1902.

Rube Waddell in 1902.

Cartoon depicting the struggle between the leagues.

Cartoon depicting Connie and the team, victims of the weather.

Connie Mack after winning the 1902 American League pennant.

1903:
FELL LIKE A
LOG

THE JANUARY 18TH *St. Louis Republic* reported an odd story about one of Connie Mack's pitchers from the previous season. Andrew J. Coakley, the star pitcher of the Holy Cross College team had been suspended by the college president for playing professionally the prior season under the assumed name "McAllister." Apparently, Mack had called Coakley when he was desperate for pitching and convinced the young man to help Philadelphia during its pennant race. The young Coakley won two critical games for the A's and held his own despite being only 19 years of age. After each game, "McAllister" made himself scarce, and was not available to photographers or newsmen. Eventually, Mack admitted, after many inquiries, the identity of the young man and that he had noticed him because he had pitched a sixteen-inning tie game against Yale. Coakley had not wanted his real name to become public because his brother was funding his tuition and had threatened to withdraw it if he went professional. Now he was forced into continuing his professional career.

On January 22, 1903, it was announced in the papers that Connie Mack had signed outfielder Irv Waldron, a minor-league veteran who was 31 years old and had previously played for Mack in Milwaukee.

In early February, there were discussions about a seven-game series against Pittsburgh, the champions of the National League, before the regular season. Neither Mack nor Shibe were willing to take Barney Dreyfuss' side wager of $5000. In the end, Dreyfuss withdrew from the idea citing concerns about the weather in Pennsylvania in early April.

Mack planned to start spring training early for the team, cruising on the steamer *Arapahoe* from New York to Jacksonville, Florida, the last week of February. On the cruise, several the players got seasick. Aboard the steamer were young pitchers Weldon Henley, Chief Bender, Tad Quinn, outfielder Danny Hoffman, veteran pitchers Eddie Plank, Rube Waddell, Highball Wilson, catchers Ossee Schrecongost and Doc Powers, second-baseman Danny Murphy, and outfielders Socks Seybold and Everett. The plan was to train at Wolfe's Casino at Jacksonville.

Reports in early March were that Henley and Bender were performing very well, but Eddie Plank was "in the best form." By early April, the team was in Pennsylvania playing exhibition games in preparation for the season.

The Athletics opened the 1903 season with a doubleheader in Boston on April 20th. Rube Waddell started the first game against George Winter. Ollie Pickering, recently from Cleveland, was now manning center field in place of Dave Fultz, who had moved to the New York Highlanders. Unfortunately, Rube was not at his best, losing 9 to 4.

In the second game, Eddie Plank started against Cy Young, but was not sharp, falling behind 3 to 0 by the 3rd. Chief Bender was summoned for his major-league debut and shut down Boston enough the rest of the way while the A's mounted a comeback. Trailing 6 to 0 against Young after the 6th inning, the A's tied the score in the 7th with an outburst against the veteran. Bender earned the victory, 10 to 7.

Charles Albert "Chief" Bender was born May 5, 1884, and had not yet turned 19 when he made his debut. Born in Minnesota to a German father and Native American mother, Bender would spend time at the Carlisle Indian School, playing against Gettysburg College. He had been signed by Mack for $150 a month, provided he performed well.

After an offday to travel to Philadelphia, the two teams met again on the 22nd. Rube Waddell won this one 6 to 1, striking out 10. The next day, 22-year-old Weldon Henley made his debut, beating Boston 7 to 6. On the 24th, Eddie faced Cy Young in a classic pitchers' battle. Both hurlers yielded only six hits, but old Cy had a slight edge, winning 2 to 1. In the final game of the series, Waddell was not able to repeat his earlier performance, losing 4 to 0.

After an offday, the New York Highlanders came to town. Chief Bender was handed the ball and did not disappoint, shutting out New York 6 to 0 on only four hits. Waddell won the next game. The Highlanders took the third game, 5 to 4, defeating Henley.

The final game of April was in Boston and easily won by the Athletics 12 to 2, Eddie Plank defeating George Winter. The team finished April 6-4, only one game behind the first-place Detroit Tigers.

The second game of the series pitted Chief Bender against Bill Dinneen. The veteran got the better in this win, dropping the A's 4 to 2. In the third game, on May 2nd, Eddie faced Cy Young, shutting out the Red Sox 3 to 0. Boston managed only five hits, and Plank hit a home run to help his cause. It was the only run he needed.

The team had a travel day, arriving in New York for a game on the 4th of May. Bender got the call but narrowly lost to Jack Chesbro, 4 to 3. The next day, Henley was roughed up, and the A's fell again, 11 to 3. For the final game of the series, the A's salvaged one thanks to Eddie's fine performance. Plank scattered six hits as the A's won easily, 6 to 1.

The A's were back home on the 7th to host the Senators. They did not treat them kindly, winning 19 to 5, Bender being the beneficiary. Pickering and Monte Cross each had four hits, while four players scored three or more runs.

Waddell was back in the win column the next day with a 5 to 3 victory. Danny Murphy went 4 for 4. In the final game of the series, on the 9th, Eddie won easily, 13 to 4, thanks to four-hit performances from Danny Murphy and Ossee Schrecongost, who was playing first base.

The A's then headed west to Chicago for a game on the 11th. The first game was won by Waddell 4 to 2, thanks to 2 runs in the 9th. In the second game, Bender pitched marvelously but lost 3 to 2 in ten innings. On the 13th, Plank took the ball and was brilliant, yielding only 3 hits as the A's shutout the White Sox 6 to 0. Eddie also added two hits of his own to help the cause. In the final game of the series, Waddell was routed 9 to 3.

The next stop was St. Louis on May 15th. The visiting A's dropped the Browns 4 to 2 behind Rube Waddell. Next up, Chief took the ball against Brown's ace Willie Sudhoff, but the A's couldn't solve the St. Louis native, losing 2 to 0. The series continued with a 12 to 9 shellacking of Eddie Plank, who lasted only five innings before Lave pulled him. Following a rainout on the 18th, the series ended on the 19th. Waddell bested the Browns 7 to 4 to even the series.

The night train then headed to Detroit for a series with the Tigers on the 20th. Eddie was tapped to start, and it was a solid performance. There was drama in the 8th inning when Socks Seybold made a miraculous catch. Per the *Philadelphia Inquirer*: "It was in the eighth with Barrett, Lush, and Crawford on the sacks, one gone, and Elberfield hitting, and the score 2 to 1 in Detroit's favor. Elberfield hit a line fly between Seybold and Hartsel and apparently over the heads of both. It looked like a triple, and Socks running with the ball, pulled it down with his bare hand in the last jump of a mad race. Crawford was so certain that the ball was in a safe spot that he had rounded second, while Lush was at third. Seybold and Murphy relayed the throw to Davis, easily doubling Crawford." Eddie scattered six hits but lost a close one, 3 to 1.

Chief Bender was up next, and was racked for five in the first, but held the Tigers the rest of the way. The A's could only muster three, losing 5 to 3. The game was rained out the next day.

The final stop of the road trip was Cleveland, starting on the 23rd. Waddell beat Joss 4 to 2 in the first game, despite Lajoie's three hits. After an offday, Plank took the mound. It was another tight game and a tough loss for the left-hander. Cleveland bunched some hits in the 2nd, scoring twice. It was all they needed to win 2 to 1. Waddell flipped the series with an 8 to 2 win, ending the road trip on a positive note.

On May 24, the Paris–Madrid automobile race began. Eight people were killed prompting the French government to stop the event at Bordeaux and impound all the competitors' cars.

After a travel day to return to Philadelphia, the A's faced New York at home on the 28th of May. Plank was first up and was nicked by four hits from former National League star Willie Keeler and three hits by former teammate Dave Fultz. The A's fell 5 to 2 in the opener.

The next day, Chief Bender lost another tight one, 3 to 2. Then, on the 30th, the teams played a doubleheader. Henley took the ball in the first game and shut out the Highlanders, 1 to 0 in ten innings. Murphy singled in Seybold for the walk-off win. In the second game, the A's won another behind Waddell, with two clutch runs in the bottom of the 8th. Murphy and Hoffman had the RBIs, winning 4 to 3.

The A's finished May 19-16, in 4th place, only a game back of Chicago. Boston and St. Louis were also ahead of them. The team's pitching was much improved from the prior season, but they were losing close games. The competition seemed to be better. Eddie's record was 4-5 but could have been 8-1 with a little more support.

After an offday on the 31st, the A's started June in Washington against the Senators. Waddell opened the series with a brilliant two-hit shutout, winning 1 to 0. The next game, Chief garnered the following headline from the *Philadelphia Inquirer:* "Bender at Last Captures Scalp." The A's won handily, 12-3. In the 3rd game, Eddie scattered nine hits in topping the Senators 5 to 2, sweeping the series.

The A's headed home for a series against the Tigers starting on the 4th of June. Henley dropped the first game 6 to 4. Waddell edged them 4 to 3 in the 2nd game. Eddie was up next and did not disappoint, winning a close one 3 to 2.

After an offday, Chicago was next in town. Chief picked up another win, 5 to 1. Waddell was masterful in the next game, giving up only four hits en route to a 7 to 1 victory. The final game of the series was postponed due to weather.

The Cleveland Naps were next in town. They took the first game, on June 11th, 3 to 2, defeating Henley. The next game was a classic pitchers' duel between Rube Waddell and Addie Joss. The two were knotted at one through thirteen innings before Ollie Pickering won it with a walk-off home run in the bottom of the 14th. Both teams had only six hits each as Waddell picked up the win for Philadelphia. Bender won the next one easily, 12 to 1.

After an offday, St. Louis came to Philadelphia. Red Donahue, a former Phillie, the Browns' top pitcher the previous season at 22-11, faced off against Eddie Plank. Eddie was masterful, scattering only three hits in a 2-to-1 win. This victory tied the A's for the American League lead. Waddell won the next one easily, 9 to 3, giving the A's a one-game lead. Chief had it easy in the final game, 11 to 1.

The team traveled west for a series at Chicago on June 19th. As they left, the talk about town was how the A's were back atop the American League and likely to win another pennant. Around this time, Rube Waddell married a Massachusetts girl named May Wynne Skinner whom he had met three days earlier. This was his second marriage, and it was to be a very stormy relationship. On the mound in Chicago, Rube was bested 2 to 1, as Chicago scored single runs in the 8th and 9th. Behind Bender in the second game, the A's won 4 to 1. Eddie was next up and pitched a forgettable game, losing 11 to 1.

The team was next off to St. Louis for a series starting on the 23rd. Chief Bender lost a close one, 6 to 5. Waddell dropped another close one, 4 to 3, the following day.

On the 25th, the team was in Detroit, during the three-game losing streak. Eddie was back on his game, winning 3 to 2 in ten innings. Henley fell behind in the next game and was pulled. Eddie relieved him, but the A's couldn't catch up, losing 5 to 3. Rube lost another close one, 2 to 1, in the third game. Chief was the stopper this time, salvaging the tie in a 7 to 3 victory.

Off to Cleveland on the 29th, Eddie took the mound and defeated the Naps 4 to 2. But, Waddell fell again by a run, 4 to 3, to close the month of June.

The A's were now 35-25 on the season, in 2nd place, three games behind Boston. Eddie had improved to 9-6, but Waddell was losing too many close games.

Henley won a wild one, 9 to 8, as the A's overcame a 6 to 3 deficit to win. But, the Naps had the last laugh, as Lajoie had four hits in an 11 to 6 drubbing of the "Chief." Once again the team split a series it could have won.

That evening, while on a train from Detroit back to Washington, star outfielder for the Senators, Ed Delahanty drowned after going over Niagara Falls. He had been kicked off the train by the conductor for being drunk and disorderly, threatening passengers with a straight-razor. He then tried to find his way across an international railroad bridge, between Canada and the US, but either jumped or fell, following a challenge from a security guard. The prior season, at age 34, he had won the American League batting title at .376 and led the league in doubles with 43. He had been a star for the Phillies for many seasons, three times hitting over .400. Delahanty was batting .333 for the Senators when he went over the falls. His body was not found for a week.

After an offday on the 3rd, the team hosted the Tigers for a doubleheader on Independence Day. Eddie was on the mound for the first game and shut out Detroit through seven innings. He was nicked for three runs late, but the A's held on 4 to 3. In the second game, Waddell was hit around, losing 5 to 0.

After an offday, Rube was right back out there, winning narrowly 6 to 5. In the final game of the series, Coakley started, and three other pitchers were called in relief, including Eddie, as the Tigers managed a close 8 to 7 win.

While the French had great difficulty with the automobile race months before, the first Tour de France bicycle race was held from July 1st through the 19th. It was won by Maurice Garin. No one died.

Cleveland was next in town on July 8th. Chief beat them 4 to 3. In the next game, Eddie took the mound and was off to an easy start with a 6 to 0, and then 8 to 4 lead. But, in the 8th, the Naps tied it up at 8. Henley then relieved, and the A's won in ten innings, 9 to 8. In the second game of the series, Addie Joss bested Coakley 4 to 1. Waddell lost the next one 10 to 3.

After a couple offdays, the team was back in Philadelphia. On July 14th, Rube Waddell struck out 14 White Sox, winning 2 to 0. The A's then swept a doubleheader, Bender winning the first 11 to 7, and Eddie winning the second 5 to 2. But, Chicago salvaged the final game against Henley, 11 to 6.

Next up, on the 17th, Waddell fanned a dozen Browns as the A's won 4 to 1. After a rainout and an offday, the teams met again on Monday, the 20th. Plank took the mound and lost a tough one, 3 to 2. The next day, the A's swept a doubleheader, Bender shutting them out 1 to 0 on two hits, Henley winning 11 to 3.

The team was then off to Washington, where Plank faced the Senators on July 22nd, winning a well-pitched game 3 to 1. Waddell made easy work of the Senators the next day, 11 to 3. In the following game, Chief was beaten 5 to 4. The final game of the series was another narrow loss, this one pitched by Waddell, 2 to 1.

The teams shifted to Philadelphia for a series on the 27th. Rube was on the mound and shut out the Senators 3 to 0. Eddie was on the mound in the next one and led 3 to 1 in the 9th when the Senators rallied for two. Henley relieved and picked up the win as the A's walked off in the 10th on a throwing error. The teams tied the following day at 4, Henley on the mound, in a game called after ten innings. The A's then swept a doubleheader the next day, Plank winning 12 to 1 and Waddell winning 6 to 5.

The A's ended the month with a loss in New York to the Highlanders, 3 to 1. Bender did not receive any support.

The loss dropped the Athletics to 52-35, in 2nd place, three games back of Boston. Eddie improved to 13-7 on the season. Despite all their efforts in the month of July, the team did not gain on the Americans.

The A's started August with a loss in New York, Waddell dropping a close one to Chesbro, 3 to 2. In the next one, Eddie scattered 8 hits in beating the Highlanders 5 to 2.

Out in Dakota Territory, Martha Jane Canary, also known as "Calamity Jane," passed away from inflammation of the bowels and pneumonia. Jane had left the *Buffalo Bill's Wild West Show* and had returned to Madame Dora DuFran's brothel at Belle Fourche, Dakota Territory (South Dakota). In late July, she traveled by ore train to the town of Terry, near Deadwood. It was reported she was drinking heavily on the train and became sick to her stomach. The conductor assisted her off the train and she was put up at the Calloway Hotel, where she died. She was buried next to "Wild Bill" Hickok at Mount Moriah Cemetery in Deadwood. Hickok had predeceased her in 1876 when he was shot in the back while playing cards.

The Athletics were back home to face league-leading Boston on August 4th but were rained out. Entering play on the 5th, the Athletics had trimmed a half-game, now trailing by only 2 1/2. Bill Dinneen faced off against Rube Waddell and bested him 3 to 0. The next game was a tight battle between Cy Young and Chief Bender. The A's won narrowly, 4 to 3. In the rubber game, Plank was hit hard, losing 11 to 3.

The teams next moved to Boston. Dinneen was tough again, holding the A's hitless through seven. Despite rallying for six runs in the 9th, the A's fell 11 to 6, Henley taking it on the chin. After an offday, the teams were at it again on the 10th of August, Cy Young facing off against Eddie Plank. The elder Cy proved victorious once again, winning 7 to 2. Waddell failed to solve Boston in the final game, losing 5 to 1.

During this pivotal juncture in the season, the A's had lost five of six from the top team in American League and saw their pennant chances slipping away. Entering the series 2 1/2 games back, they were now 6 1/2 back in second.

The Athletics next hopped a train for Chicago. On the 13th of August, Chief led them to victory against the White Sox, 5 to 1. Waddell dropped the next game, 6 to 0, shut out by Roy Patterson. The following day, the headline for the game results read "Plank's Puzzling Curves Keep the White Sox Squinting ..." Eddie won easily, 5 to 1.

On to St. Louis for a doubleheader on the 16th, the A's were swept by the Browns. Waddell lost the first one 2 to 1, and Bender the second, 6 to 3. Eddie put them back in the winning column with a 3 to 2 gem on the 17th. The team salvaged a split thanks to a 5 to 3 win by Waddell.

After an offday on the 19th, the Athletics were in Detroit for a doubleheader against the Tigers on the 20th. Bender lost the first one, 3 to 0, and Plank the second, 5 to 4. Plank had taken a 4-to-2 lead into the bottom of the 8th, only to give it up. The Tigers then walked-off in the 9th. Another doubleheader followed the next day. Rube Waddell pitched both games, winning the first in masterful fashion, 1 to 0, giving up only three hits. He lost the second game 2 to 1. Trailing 1 to 0 into the 9th, the A's tied the game, but the Tigers won it in the bottom of the inning.

The team moved to Cleveland for a series against the Naps beginning on August 22nd. Chief Bender was hit around, losing 11 to 3. After an offday, the teams went at it again on the 24th. Topsy Hartsel was the only Athletic to register a hit, as Addie Joss shut out Eddie Plank and the A's 3 to 0. Weldon Henley got one back for the A's, winning 9 to 3 the next day. Following the game, Connie Mack announced that Rube Waddell had been "permanently released for misconduct." He was told to hand in his uniform and did not accompany the team home to face Boston.

Bill Dinneen sent a message in the first game against the Athletics in Philadelphia, defeating them 3 to 0, Bender taking the loss. Eddie Plank was the next victim of the Americans, losing

4 to 2. It then rained for a couple days, followed by an offday. The Athletics did not play the rest of the month, finishing August at 63-50, 9 1/2 games back, in second place. They had gone 11-15 during a critical month and had released their most dynamic pitcher due to insubordination. Perhaps Waddell was the distraction leading to the downturn. Eddie was 16-11 on the season, and now 28 years old.

As September began, Connie announced he had signed Waddell to pitch for the team in 1904. New York came to town for two games on the 1st. Eddie dropped the first one, 5 to 1. The second game ended as a 1 to 1 tie, with Bender on the mound.

After an offday, the team traveled to Boston for a game on the 3rd. The Athletics led 5 to 1 into the bottom of the 7th, when Henley was ripped for four runs. Boston won in twelve innings, 6 to 5.

After an offday, the A's were destroyed in the finale, 12 to 1, Coakley taking the loss. Heading home on the 6th, the Athletics were now 60-54, in third place, 14 1/2 games out of first place.

The last place Washington Senators were a welcome sight. The Athletics swept a doubleheader on September 7th. Eddie Plank threw a four-hit shutout, beating Al Orth 6 to 0. In the second game, Henley narrowly won 3 to 2.

Off to New York on the 9th, the team dropped a doubleheader to the Highlanders. Clark Griffith threw a 4 to 0 shutout, beating Bender. Eddie then dropped the second game 6 to 3. The next day, Henley had them back in the win column, 5 to 2. Eddie was back on the mound on the 11th and benefited from a four-run rally in the 9th, giving him a 7-to-4 win. There was a scary moment in the home first when Plank hit the Highlander first baseman in the head with a pitch. Said the *Philadelphia Inquirer*: "He (Plank) came near putting big Ganzel out of business for all time with one of his fast in-shoots. As it was it took ten minutes to bring him to after he got a rap on the head in the first inning. Fortunately, the ball hit where the skull is thickest, for had it hit over or back of the ear it would have been serious. He fell like a log, and the sound of the impact was like that of a solid base hit."

Off to Washington, Bender won the first game 5 to 3 on the 12th. After an offday, Henley won an easy one, 13 to 1. In the final game of the series, Eddie was touched for four runs early, and Al

Orth proved a mystery for the Athletics' batters. The A's dropped this one 4 to 2.

After a couple offdays, the boys were home for two against the St. Louis Browns on September 18th. The Browns jumped out with five runs against Plank in the first, but the A's fought back, and Eddie held them scoreless the rest of the way. Game one went to the A's 7 to 5. St. Louis then jumped on Henley for seven runs in the 1st. Bender took over, but the A's could not recover, losing 9 to 2.

Detroit was next in town on the 19th. Rube Waddell, back in the fold, got the call and lost a close one 2 to 1. Eddie was back on the mound on the 21st, beating the Tigers 5 to 1. Henley lost the finale 7 to 4.

Chicago was in town on the 23rd. Chief Bender won the first game 2 to 1. The A's then swept a doubleheader the next day. Eddie won the first game 4 to 3 in eleven innings. Young Jim Fairbank won his only major league game, 7 to 5, in a five-inning contest. Bender finished the four-game sweep with a 10 to 8 win.

The last team in town for the season was Cleveland. Henley beat them 4 to 2 to move ahead of the Naps into 2nd place. In his final game of 1903, Eddie fell behind 3 to 0 in the second inning. He then rolled off eight shutout innings as the A's climbed back to tie and go into extras. Harry Davis drove in Plank in the bottom of the 10th for the victory. The A's had locked up 2nd place.

In the final game of the season, Ed Pinnance received his only major league start. He was relieved by Fairbank, who took the loss, 7 to 5. In the game, Chief Bender played first base.

The A's finished the season 75-60, 14 1/2 games out, in second place. The Boston Americans had taken the American League crown.

Eddie finished the season 23-16, with a 2.38 ERA. He led the team in starts with 40, and innings, with 336. Waddell was 21-16, while Bender was 17-14. Weldon Henley added 12 wins.

At the plate, only Topsy Hartsel, who had missed over 30 games, batted over .300, hitting .311. Socks Seybold hit .299, and only 8 home runs. Lave Cross led the team with 90 RBI.

While the pitching was strong for the A's, the erratic Waddell proved too much of a distraction. The offense was also quite a bit less productive than the previous season.

In the first World Series in the modern era, the Boston Americans topped the Pittsburgh Pirates 5 games to 3. Bill

Dinneen won three of the games, and Cy Young the other two. Honus Wagner, the Pirate shortstop, was injured during the series and had only 6 hits in 27 at-bats.

In early November, team captain Lave Cross and his wife dropped by Gettysburg to spend some time with Eddie Plank. Eddie took them hunting and shot 39 partridges and many rabbits. The Cross's took the bounty home with them when they left.

In December, when the American League announced its statistics, Lave Cross led the league in fielding percentage at third base. Eddie was the top pitcher for the Athletics.

On December 17th, Orville Wright made his first powered flight at Kitty Hawk, North Carolina.

In Chicago, on the 30th, the deadliest single-building fire in U.S. history at the Iroquois Theater led to the deaths of over 600 people.

OUR OLD FRIEND LAJOIE
Caught in the act by an Inquirer camera.

Napolean Lajoie now with Cleveland.

Cartoon of Plank and Bender at spring training in Jacksonville, Florida.

Cartoon depicting caricature of Chief Bender

Eddie Plank winding-up in 1903.

1904:
A LOATHSOME
BIRD

O N JANUARY 2, 1904, Confederate General James Longstreet passed away in Gainesville, Georgia. Said the *Gettysburg Compiler* on January 12th: "Within a week of each other, two great Confederate Chieftains who participated in the Battle of Gettysburg passed away. General James Longstreet on January 2 and General John B. Gordon on January 9. The troops under Longstreet helped to fight the battle on the evening of the second day which has made the Peach Orchard, Wheatfield, Devil's Den, Valley of Death, and the Round Tops famous in history. It was part of his corps that made the great Pickett's charge. It was Gordon's brigade returning from York who helped to bring about the disaster to the Union Army on the first day. One by one they fall asleep who fought this great battle in history, beholding a united country as the foremost nation on earth."

On the 12th of January, on frozen Lake St. Clair, Henry Ford, driving the Ford 999 racer, set a new land speed record for automobiles at 91.37 mph. The record would stand less than three months.

On February 7th, there was a great fire in Baltimore, Maryland, resulting in the destruction of over 1500 buildings in the town's center. Over 1200 firefighters responded and miraculously, no deaths were directly attributed to the fire. Over 35,000 were unemployed for many months.

On Thursday, March 10, 1904, Eddie received a hearty send-off at the Gettysburg train station as he left for Philadelphia to catch a train to spring training in South Carolina. Many students from Gettysburg College were present to see him off.

Two days later, on the 12th, a large crowd gathered to see Connie Mack and the team head south. Many of the players' wives were also present.

The team arrived in South Carolina on the 13th on a rainy day. It was reported Chief Bender had come down with the mumps.

From Spartanburg, the papers reported Eddie was in fine shape, along with the other Athletics pitchers, Bender and Henley. Plank and Waddell were among the pitchers facing Wofford College in an exhibition on March 25th. The team headed back north on the 29th after little more than two weeks of training.

During the exhibition with the Phillies in early April, Eddie pitched in the game on April 5th. He two-hit the cross-town team, winning 4 to 2.

In the opening game of the season against Washington on April 14th, Eddie shut down the Senators 8 to 3. The next game was called after ten innings because of darkness, tied at six. Henley had pitched for the A's. Rube Waddell was back on the mound for the final game of the series, winning 12 to 2. That same day, April 16th, Eddie's brother Ira Plank, pitching for Gettysburg College, shut out Mt. Saint Mary's 8 to 0. He struck out 10.

The team traveled on the 17th for a series in New York on the 18th. Chief was on top of his game, easily beating Jack Chesbro in the first game, 5 to 1. In the next game, Eddie narrowly lost 5 to 4.

The teams shifted to Philadelphia on the 21st. It was opening day for the Athletics at home. Rube Waddell defeated the Highlanders in 12 innings, 3 to 2.

The World Series champion Boston Americans were next in town. They handed the A's a 3 to 1 loss, Series hero Dinneen beating Henley. In the second game, Plank and Tannehill were tangled in a 1-to-1 game until the 8th when Boston scored twice. They went on to win 3 to 1. On the 25th, the series continued, Rube Waddell beating Cy Young 2 to 0. Boston took the final game, 2 to 1, defeating Henley again.

After a rainy week, the Highlanders were in town on April 30. Eddie took the ball against Jack Chesbro and made easy work of New York, winning 8 to 2.

For the inaugural month of 1904, the A's were 6-4, in second place behind the Boston Americans, three games back. Eddie started the season 2-2.

The Athletics traveled to Boston for a series on May 2nd. Rube Waddell was magnificent, beating Tannehill 3 to 0, allowing but one knock. Bill Dinneen beat Henley 4 to 2 in the second game.

Eddie dropped the next game 3 to 2. The final game of the series, on May 5th, was historic. Cy Young faced Rube Waddell and did not allow anyone to reach base. It was the first perfect game in the modern era. Boston won 3 to 0 and had taken three of four.

Meanwhile, in Panama on May 4th, ground was broken on the Panama Canal.

After not getting a hit, the Athletics were happy to head home to face the Senators on May 6th. Lave Cross led the way with five hits, as the A's tallied 22, winning 16 to 6 in support of Henley. The next day, the A's had 14 more hits in easily winning 11 to 4 behind Waddell. The team tallied 14 more hits two days later, to help Eddie Plank win 6 to 3, completing the three-game sweep.

After a rainout on the 10th, Chicago was in town to play on the 11th. It was a wild affair, with Waddell on the mound. The Athletics tied the game at 4 in the bottom of the 8th. Both teams scored runs in the 11th. Finally, the A's walked-off in the 12th, Danny Murphy, who had five hits on the day, driving in Lave Cross.

Henley won the next game 9 to 3. For Chicago, a rookie pitcher named Ed Walsh made an appearance in relief. He would go on to a Hall of Fame career. Eddie Plank took the mound for the third game and led 2 to 0 through six innings. The Sox scored one in the 7th and two in the 8th to take the lead. The A's could not muster another run, falling 3 to 2. In the final game of the series, Waddell won a close one, 2 to 1 on May 14th.

After an offday on the 15th, the Browns were in town on the 16th. Henley beat them 5 to 4. The next day, Waddell and the team were three-hit, falling 2 to 0.

In Boston, against Cleveland, Cy Young set the modern major league record for pitching 45 consecutive scoreless innings, a streak which began on April 25th and included his perfect game against the Athletics on May 5th. The streak ended when Cleveland scored three runs in the 8th, beating Cy 3 to 1.

Eddie was next up against the Browns on the 18th. He had three hits, including a triple, scoring twice, as the A's beat St. Louis 9 to 4. In the final game of the series, Bender lost 4 to 3.

Cleveland was next in town for a game on the 20th of May. Henley started for the A's and lost 8 to 5. In the second game, Eddie scattered five hits, and shut out the Naps 7 to 0. After an offday, the series continued on the 23rd with Waddell on the mound. The A's led 3 to 1 into the 9th but coughed up three runs to Cleveland, who won 4 to 3.

The Tigers dropped by on the 24th and promptly beat Bender 2 to 1. Eddie took over for game two and easily beat Detroit 10 to 4. Waddell was next, striking out a dozen Tigers en route to a four-hit shutout, 5 to 0.

Next up were the Highlanders, who came to Philadelphia on the 27th. Henley beat Clark Griffith 7 to 5 in the opener. Jack Chesbro returned the favor, four-hitting the A's and winning 1 to 0. Eddie took the loss, allowing four hits to Keeler, who scored the only run of the game in the 8th.

The teams split a doubleheader on the 30th. In the morning game, New York beat Henley 7 to 4. In the afternoon game, Waddell seven-hit the Highlanders, winning 1 to 0. The teams were then off on the 31st.

Philadelphia was now 20-15, in 3rd place, five games back of Boston. Eddie was 6-4 on the season.

June 1st, the A's were in St. Louis to face the Browns. Unfortunately, their bats did not arrive, having been lost somewhere in Ohio. A frantic effort was made to locate the missing equipment while the visitors borrowed sticks from the home team. As expected, the bats favored their owners, the Browns beating Eddie and the A's 3 to 1. The game was not without controversy. In the 3rd inning, when the Browns scored twice, Eddie thought he had a batter struck out, but umpire Connolly called a ball. "Planks face was a picture," reported the *Philadelphia Inquirer*, in response to the disagreeable call.

Rain got in the way of the next game, but Connie took the team down the road to the Louisiana Purchase Exposition World's Fair in St. Louis to see the sights. Rain also interfered with the game on the 3rd. Finally, on the 4th, the teams played, Plank winning 5 to 2.

On June 5th, the team was in Chicago. Waddell and Bender were knocked around in a 14 to 2 loss. Waddell was back out there the next day and won 6 to 3. Rube asked to face the Sox again, and Mack obliged. However, Chicago got the better of him 6 to 1. Eddie took the mound for the final game of the series and lost 8 to 2.

The team next traveled to Cleveland. On the 10th of June, Henley dropped a 3 to 1 game to the Naps. In the next game,

Eddie was masterful, shutting out the Naps on four hits, 1 to 0. After an offday, Waddell fanned 13 Naps to win 9 to 2. Topsy Hartsel broke out of a slump to provide three hits. Rain shortened the final game of the series to 5 innings, Bender pitching a one-hit shutout, 4 to 0.

On June 15th, Detroit hosted the Athletics. Henley lost a tough one, 1 to 0. The big story of the day, though, grabbing all the headlines, was the terrible fire aboard the steamboat *General Slocum* in New York City's East River. The *Philadelphia Inquirer* described the scene: "Men, maddened by fear, trampled down women and children to get to the sides and lean overboard. To most of the terrorized multitude, it was but a choice of death offered. To stay on board meant the awful certainty of being burned alive. To take to the water meant for all but a few the certainty of death by drowning. All the way for the half-mile that the *General Slocum* steamed for North Brother Island beach shore observers were rendered frantic by the pitiable sight which that blazing mass presented. Men and women were seen clinging to the sides like flies and dropping by twos and threes as strength gave out and hope died. They jumped by tens and dozens. Those of them who could swim preferred the desperate possibility of keeping afloat. The most heartrending sight of all was to see the children thrown overboard by those who had them in care." Approximately 1021 of the 1342 people on board died. It was the worst loss of life in New York City prior to September 11, 2001.

Eddie was back on the mound on the 16th and lost a tough one, 6 to 5. Rube won the next game easily, 7 to 1, but Bender lost the final game of the series 7 to 3.

After a travel day on the 19th, the Athletics were home to face last-place Washington on the 20th for a make-up game. The Senators had only won nine games all season. The A's weren't about to let them add to the total. Henley won the first game easily, 11 to 3.

Following a rainout on the 21st, Boston was in town on the 22nd. Cy Young faced Rube Waddell. The Americans got off to a quick start, leading 6 to 0 before the bottom of the 2nd. Rube was pulled in favor of Chief Bender, who allowed only one more run the rest of the way. The A's rallied for six but came up short, 7 to 6. Eddie made the next one look easy, scattering six hits in a 5-to-1 win. Henley benefited from an offensive outburst, including three hits from Hartsel, as the A's won again, 8 to 4.

Washington was back in town on the 25th. The Senators led Waddell 3 to 1 until the bottom of the 7th, when the A's rallied for five, winning 6 to 3.

After an offday, the teams headed to Washington. Chief was on his game in this one, winning 3 to 2. The next day, Plank got no support, losing 2 to 1. It was only Washington's 10th win of the season. In the final game of the series, the A's were ahead 3 to 1, when the game was called because of rain.

In Boston on the final day of June, Young and Waddell battled to a 3-to-3 tie through eight innings. In the 9th, the Americans walked off on a single by Criger.

The Athletics finished June 31-26, 5 1/2 games behind Boston in 4th place. Eddie was now 9-8 on the season.

July 1, the third modern Olympics opened in St. Louis at the Louisiana Purchase Exposition World's Fair. The A's continued their series in Boston. Bender and the A's fell behind 4 to 0 by the 3rd inning, after which the Philadelphia began pecking away. In the 9th inning, trailing 4 to 3, center fielder Danny Hoffman stepped in against Jesse Tannehill, a left-hander with one on and two outs. Said the *Philadelphia Inquirer*, "Hoffman, who had already battled Tannehill for three safe ones, came to bat. Somehow he failed to get out of the way of one of Tannehill's fastest balls. Perhaps he expected the ball would be a curve instead of a straight one, but be that as it may, the ball took him fully in the left eye with a crash that could be heard in all parts of the field. Hoffman sank to the ground and the players gathered around him. Catcher Powers, of the Athletics, attended his comrade, and as soon as he could get to the scene, Dr. T. C. Erb, the physician of the home club, was on the ground. Hoffman was rendered senseless by the concussion, and he was carried to the Athletic bench and after a short interval Waddell shouldered him and carried him limp to the dressing room of the Boston club, where he rallied. It was found that he had sustained a slight concussion. It was all black and blue over his eye and below it was cut and bleeding. He was taken in a carriage to the Quincy House. It will be at least two weeks before he will recover sufficiently from the shock to play again. Manager Connie Mack, at once, wired to Pickering, his spare outfielder, who is in Philadelphia, to report here tomorrow."

Noonan ran for Hoffman, and Lave Cross came to the plate. With two strikes on him, he ripped a ball to right field which got past the fielder. Two runs scored to give the A's the lead. They won 5 to 4.

The next day, Winter defeated Plank 2 to 1. During the game, Seybold had been called out at the plate in a play that most knew was incorrect. Socks had been safe, except in the eyes of umpire Sheridan.

The A's traveled home on the 3rd of July for a doubleheader with the Highlanders on Independence Day. Henley dropped the morning game to Chesbro 9 to 3. Griffith beat Waddell 5 to 2 in the afternoon.

The teams then moved to New York. Bender dropped the first one 6 to 3. Plank lost the next game 7 to 1.

The A's traveled home to face the Senators on July 8th. Eddie won an unusual game 2 to 1, giving up only one hit to Jake Stahl, a bunt single. The teams split a doubleheader the next day. Waddell threw a three-hit shutout in the morning game, winning 3 to 0. Henley and Bender were hit hard in the afternoon game, losing 11 to 3. Danny Hoffman arrived back from New York during the offday on Sunday and the series continued Monday the 11th with Plank on the mound. He won 3 to 1.

Chicago came to Philadelphia for a game on the 12th. Henley won the day, 6 to 4. Chief Bender fanned 13 en route to a three-hit shutout, 3 to 0 the next day. Waddell then struck-out 11 while winning 2 to 1. Eddie scattered six hits to win 6 to 1, finishing the series.

The Browns were next in town on the 16th. Henley and the A's opened with an easy 8 to 1 win. Following an offday on Sunday, Bender edged them 5 to 4 in the next one. Fred Glade, during his best season, got one back for the Browns, winning 1 to 0 against Waddell. Eddie completed the series with a stellar five-hit shutout, winning 2 to 0.

On the 21st of July, Lajoie's Naps were in Philadelphia at Columbia Park. Henley was hit around, the A's falling behind 14 to 1 before rallying late, only to fizzle, 14 to 8. Former teammate Bill Bernhard shut out the A's in the second game, defeating Bender 4 to 0. A doubleheader on the 23rd went just as badly. The Naps won the first game 3 to 2, edging Waddell. Plank dropped the second game 4 to 1, Lajoie knocking out three hits, and the Naps had swept all four games.

After an offday and a rainout, Detroit was in town on the 26th. Eddie was on the mound to try to stop the losing streak, but lost 2 to 1, the go-ahead run scoring on a wild pitch. Finally, Rube provided relief, striking-out eleven Tigers while hurling a three-hit shutout, 5 to 0. Harry Davis hit two home runs in support of a stellar performance by Weldon Henley, who two-hit the Tigers, winning 4 to 0. Eddie followed with his own 2-0 shutout on the 29th. In the fifth and final game of the series, Waddell beat them 4 to 1, the A's taking four of five to end the month of July.

The A's were now 46-38, having gone 15-12 for the month. Unfortunately, the teams ahead of them were playing better ball, and they slipped to 5th place, still only 5 1/2 games out. Given the four teams ahead of them, the A's would have to play their best the rest of the way and hope that none of the four teams would get hotter. Eddie was 13-12 on the season and had several tough-luck losses.

The month of August began with news that the two major leagues could not agree to hold a World Series at the end of the season. Ban Johnson, the American League president was livid, per the *Philadelphia Inquirer*: "... No thoughtful patron of baseball can weigh seriously the wild vaporings of this discredited player (McGraw), who was 'canned' out of the American League by its Board of Directors on the first of July, 1902. The true caliber of the National Club owner is disclosed when he attempts to take refuge behind such an irresponsible character such as McGraw. It is indeed a loathsome bird that befouls its own nest. The incidents of the last fortnight prove, beyond the fear of contradiction, that there are two or three of that species in the National League."

McGraw's New York Giants were leading the National League handily, at 62-24, 9 1/2 games ahead.

Meanwhile, the Athletics were in St. Louis to face the Browns. Chief pitched a four-hit shutout, topping the Browns 4 to 0. The offense erupted for Waddell in the second game, the A's winning handily 14 to 3. The A's continued to hit well in the third game, winning 10 to 4 behind Henley. The final game of the series was rained out on the 4th.

Next up was Chicago on June 5th. Eddie took the mound and trailed 3 to 1 into the top of the 9th. The A's rallied for three thanks to some sloppy play by the Sox, who fell out of first place.

The next day, behind Nick Altrock, the Sox got their revenge, beating Bender 8 to 0. Waddell had the A's back on the winning side, 5 to 2, on Sunday the 7th. After play, the A's were only 4 1/2 back of three teams tied for first: Boston, New York, and Chicago.

Eddie picked up the sphere the next day, pitching to a 6 to 1 lead into the 9th when the Sox came to life. The rally was staunched at 4, the A's winning 6 to 5. Philadelphia had inched another game closer to the three leaders.

After an offday on the 9th and a rainout on the 10th, the A's were four games back in 4th place. On the 11th, they narrowly edged Cleveland 2 to 1 in thirteen innings, Waddell going the distance and striking out 14. The next day, Henley threw a brilliant three-hit shutout, the A's winning 5 to 0. They notched up a game, now only three back. Eddie was not at his best for the next game, being pulled after three innings, trailing 3 to 0. Bender came on, but the A's fell 7 to 2. By the offday on Sunday, the 14th, the A's were still three games back in 4th place.

To open the Detroit series, Waddell threw an eight-hit shutout, winning 2 to 0. Henley won the next game in Detroit 6 to 3, but the A's were still holding at three games back. Eddie was next up, battling for thirteen innings with the Tigers before the game was called because of darkness, tied at three. The A's inched a half-game closer by not losing. The team spent the next day traveling back to Philadelphia.

In a heart-breaker at Columbia Park on the 19th of August, the A's fell 2 to 1 in eleven innings. Rube had struck-out 14 and scattered eight hits. The winning run scored for the Naps on an errant throw by Monte Cross. The next day, once again, Henley was brilliant, shutting out the opposition 2 to 0.

On the offday on Sunday the 21st, the A's were still 2 1/2 games out, in 4th place. When play resumed on Monday the 22nd, Plank was on the mound, and pitched masterfully, winning 3 to 1. The A's were now only two games back. If only they had had a little better luck earlier in the season, they would easily be atop the league.

Waddell was next up. He struck-out 10 Naps but was trailing 2 to 0 in the bottom of the 9th. The A's rallied for two runs to take the game into extra innings, but Rube yielded two runs in the top of the 10th. The A's got only one back, falling 4 to 3.

The Tigers came to town on August 24th and promptly won 7 to 5, beating Henley. They followed this with a 7-to-2 trouncing of

Waddell. Bender ended the losing streak the next day, winning 7 to 4. Eddie battled for the split the following day, winning 4 to 3 in ten innings.

After the offday on Sunday, Chicago was in town. Rube was on the mound, and he struck out 11 Sox, winning 4 to 1. But, Henley lost the next one 3 to 0.

On the final day of August, Plank and Owen battled through eight innings, tied at zero. In the bottom of the 8th, the A's finally scored, Pickering singling in Powers. Eddie won 1 to 0, a five-hit shutout on his 29th birthday.

As the month of August ended, the A's were 62-45, in 3rd place, 4 1/2 games back. Their 17-7 month only netted them one game and two positions in the standings. Eddie had improved to 18-13, going 5-1 for the month.

The A's faced the Browns at home on September 1st. Waddell lost to Glade, 2 to 0. The next day, the grounds were too wet to play. The teams then split a doubleheader on the 3rd. Henley lost the first game 4 to 2. Plank won the second game 5 to 2.

After the offday on Sunday the 4th, the team was in New York for a Labor Day doubleheader against the Highlanders. In the first game, Chesbro beat Coakley 2 to 1. In the next game, Waddell started but only faced five batters before he was replaced by Bender. Said the *Philadelphia Inquirer*: "The sun was shining very bright for Waddell until the first five men in the batting order secured their safeties, a base on balls and a sacrifice which were turned into two runs. It equaled the elephant's lead and quite disturbed Captain Cross. 'That'll be all for you,' he said, and then beckoned Bender to come out. The Indian did so amid war whoops from the stands. That's old music for him and just fixed him for his work." Bender did not allow a run in nine innings of relief, and the A's won 7 to 2.

The teams played another doubleheader on Tuesday the 6th, New York winning both. Waddell struck out 14, but lost 5 to 2, followed by Henley's 2 to 1 loss to Griffith. Eddie salvaged a win the next day, shutting out New York on six hits, 3 to 0.

The teams then switched to Philadelphia for a doubleheader on the 8th. New York again swept the A's, Waddell losing 3 to 2 and Bender 5 to 1. The A's turned the tables the next day, sweeping a doubleheader. Henley took the first game 3 to 2, while Waddell finished up 5 to 1.

Boston was next in town on September 10th. The Athletics were eight games behind in 4th place. It was one of their last chances to make a move against the top team in the league. It was a pitchers' duel for the ages. Eddie Plank and Cy Young held both teams scoreless through twelve innings, yielding only six hits each. In the top of the 13th inning, Eddie held the Americans scoreless again. In the bottom of the 13th, Danny Murphy singled. Monte Cross then singled him to second. After an infield hit by Powers, Plank came to the plate with men on the corners. He ripped a ball down the right-field line that scored Murphy, winning the game.

After an offday on Sunday the 11th, the teams were back at it on Monday, splitting a doubleheader. Waddell again gave up early runs and was pulled for Bender, but the A's fell 6 to 4. Coakley saved the second game 6 to 2, helped by clutch hitting from Lave Cross.

The teams played to a scoreless tie after seven innings on Tuesday, the game called because of the weather. The next day's game against Washington was also postponed.

There was no better tonic for the A's than a doubleheader against the last-place Washington Senators. The teams faced off for two on the 15th, Plank taking the first one in workman-like fashion, 8 to 4, Bender winning the second in relief of Waddell, 4 to 3. The A's had crept back to six games behind, in 4th place. Henley dropped the final game of the series 5 to 3.

The A's were off to Boston for a series starting on September 17th. Coakley won the game 4 to 3, knocking Boston out of first place, putting New York in the lead.

After a Sunday off, Plank mowed down the Americans, winning a three-hitter, 3 to 1. Unfortunately, the A's were now chasing the Highlanders and not the Americans. On the 20th, Cy Young and the boys ripped Bender 11 to 1. This was followed by a doubleheader sweep by Boston the next day, Henley losing 5 to 1, and Coakley 4 to 3. The A's were then off for two days.

On September 24th, the A's were in Chicago. Henley lost to Patterson, 4 to 0. Coakley lost by the same score the next day, the A's having trouble hitting. Eddie salvaged the final game 2 to 1.

The A's moved on to St. Louis for a doubleheader against the Browns on the 27th. Henley lost the first game 4 to 2, and then

Bender and Willie Sudhoff exchanged ten scoreless innings before the game was called. A doubleheader on the 28th was swept by the Browns. Coakley lost 5 to 1, and Fairbank 5 to 0. The following day, the teams split another doubleheader. Waddell threw a two-hit shutout in the first game, winning 1 to 0. Henley dropped the second game 6 to 1.

To close out September, the Athletics were in Detroit for a doubleheader. Eddie won the first game 9 to 4. Applegate lost a seven-inning game 5 to 4. The A's finished the month 76-64, nine games out, in 5th place. The team had gone 14-19 at a critical point in the pennant race. Eddie's record was 24-13. He had won six games in September.

October began on a bad note with the A's losing two to the Tigers in Detroit, Waddell losing 3 to 2, and Bender 2 to 1.

After an offday on Sunday the 2nd, the team was off to Cleveland for two against the Naps. Coakley took the first game, 2 to 0, but Applegate lost the second, shortened to seven innings, 7 to 2. On Tuesday, the 4th, Weldon Henley threw an excellent game, winning 4 to 0. The teams were rained out the next day.

The A's traveled to Washington for a series on the 7th of October. The teams split a doubleheader, Waddell winning the first 3 to 2, while Bender dropped the second by the same score. The teams split another doubleheader the next day. Plank dropped the first, 12 to 5. Coakley won a six-inning game 2 to 0. After an offday, the teams played two more on the last day of the regular season, October 10th. Applegate won 7 to 6, and Waddell lost 4 to 3.

The A's finished 1904 in 5th place, 12 1/2 games back of the champion Boston Americans. The A's record was 81-70. The Americans edged the Highlanders by one-and-a-half games.

Eddie finished the season 26-17 with a 2.17 ERA. It was the highest win total of his career, to be matched once more. Waddell was 25-19 with a 1.62 ERA. Weldon Henley finished 15-17, and Chief Bender 10-11. Jack Chesbro led the league with 41 wins.

Harry Davis led the team with a .309 average, well behind Lajoie's .378, and a league-leading 10 home runs. Topsy Hartsel led the team with 79 runs scored. Danny Murphy hit .287 and led the team in RBI with 77 and stolen bases with 22. Lave Cross hit .290 and led the team with 31 doubles. As a batter, Eddie Plank was the best pitcher, hitting .240 with 31 hits and 11 RBI.

In the end, the A's offense was not up to the caliber of their pitching, leading to too many low-scoring losses. The team had come close, pulling to within two games in late August, but could not sustain the pace against tougher competition.

On October 15th, some of the Athletics played an exhibition game against the Trenton Y.M.C.A. The game was a scoreless tie, Waddell and Plank pitching. Eddie provided five innings of hitless ball, striking out 9.

On Friday, October 21st, Eddie organized a game between the Gettysburg town team and the college. Eddie pitched and Lave Cross also played. Robbin Wolf caught Plank, Al Holtzworth, Charles Stock, John Wisotzkey, Albert Minnigh, and Edgar Crouse made up the town team. Ira Plank (now in the Connecticut League) pitched for the college team. Per the *Gettysburg Compiler*, "He (Eddie Plank) simply toyed with the college team, let a player hit an easy ball and the next time the same man would fan the air with the bat and never touch the ball. He made the game appear as easy as he could for the college team. The score was 14 to 1." The game benefitted charity.

October 27, the first underground line of the New York City Subway opened.

November 8, Theodore Roosevelt was reelected President of the United States, defeating Democrat Alton B. Parker.

When the official American League batting statistics were published on Tuesday, December 6th, Nap Lajoie had run away with the batting title at .381. Willie Keeler was his closest competition at .343. Davis was 3rd at .308.

The official American League fielding statistics followed on Sunday, December 18th, Eddie Plank was the top fielding pitcher on the team, in 8th place overall. He was also tied for 3rd in wins with Cy Young, behind Chesbro, 41, and Bernhard, 29. Waddell was 5th with 25.

December 31, the first New Year's Eve celebration was held in New York's Times Square.

Few scenes gathered at the Baltimore and Ohio Station Saturday afternoon when Connie Mack and the team of ball players of this burg left for the balmy South.

Caricatures of Bender and Waddell at spring training in 1904.

BOSTON.

	ab.	r.	bh.	tb.	sh.	sb.	po.	a.	e.
Dougherty, lf	4	0	1	1	0	0	1	0	0
Collins, 3b	4	0	2	3	0	0	2	0	0
Stahl, cf	4	1	1	3	0	0	3	0	0
Freeman, rf	4	0	1	3	0	0	2	0	0
Parent, ss	4	0	2	2	0	0	1	4	0
LaChance, 1b	3	0	1	1	1	0	9	0	0
Ferris, 2b	3	1	1	3	0	0	0	3	0
Criger, c	3	1	1	2	0	0	0	0	0
Young, p	3	0	0	0	0	0	0	2	0
Totals	32	3	10	18	1	0	27	9	0

PHILADELPHIA.

	ab.	r.	bh.	tb.	sh.	sb.	po.	a.	e.
Hartsel, lf	1	0	0	0	0	0	0	0	0
Hoffman, lf	2	0	0	0	0	0	2	1	0
Pickering, cf	3	0	0	0	0	0	1	0	0
Davis, 1b	3	0	0	0	0	0	5	0	1
L. Cross, 3b	3	0	0	0	0	0	4	1	0
Seybold, rf	3	0	0	0	0	0	2	0	0
Murphy, 2b	3	0	0	0	0	0	1	2	0
M. Cross, ss	3	0	0	0	0	0	2	3	0
Schreck, c	3	0	0	0	0	0	7	0	0
Waddell, p	3	0	0	0	0	0	0	1	0
Totals	27	0	0	0	0	0	24	8	1

Boston ....0 0 0 0 0 1 2 0 x—3
Philadelphia ......0 0 0 0 0 0 0 0 0—0

Earned runs—Boston, 2. Two-base hits—Collins, Criger. Three-base hits—Stahl, Freeman, Ferris. Sacrifice hit—LaChance. Double plays—Hoffman and Schreck; L. Cross and Davis. Struck out—By Young, 8; by Waddell, 6. Time—1h. 25m. Umpire—Dwyer. Attendance—10,267.

Box score of Cy Young's perfect game against the A's on May 5, 1904.

ATHLETICS SALUTING THE FLAG.

Opening Day in 1904.

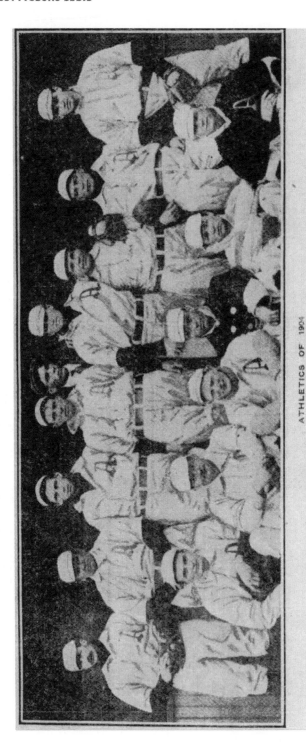

ATHLETICS OF 1904

Top Row, Reading From Left to Right—M. Cross, Seybold, Hoffman, Pickering, Bender, Barthold, Plannace, Schreckengost, Henley, Lower Row—Waddell, Lave Cross, Hartsell, Powers, Davis and Murphy.

The 1904 Philadelphia Athletics.

"CY" YOUNG WHO LET THE ATHLETICS DOWN WITHOUT A HIT
YESTERDAY

Cy Young in 1904 with Boston.

Cartoon of Plank winding-up.

Another Plank cartoon.

Plank with laurels.

Caricatures of Bender and Plank meeting as "old college chums."

Connie riding the elephant.

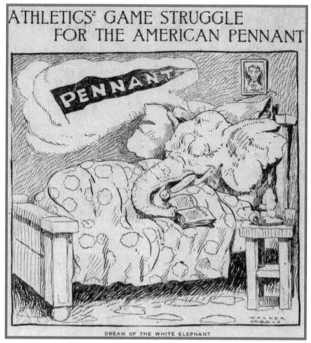

The elephant dreams of another pennant.

Captain Lave Cross, fielding a ball.

Portrait of Rube Waddell.

First baseman Harry Davis.

Shortstop Monte Cross.

Right fielder Socks Seybold.

"Schreck" the catcher.

Ollie Pickering, center fielder.

1905:
STRAW HATS

I T WAS SOMETIME this year that Eddie likely met Anna Cora Myers of New Oxford. During many of his visits home during his baseball career, Eddie would walk (and later drive) the short distance of a few miles from the Plank farm to the Myers' home. Anna was also left-handed and worked as a seamstress for a local tailor who was specifically looking for such handedness. Young Anna was over six years younger than Eddie, born on March 5th, 1882, the daughter of Washington Brugh Myers (1842–1911) and Sarah Ellen Dick (1842–1922).

On Sunday, February 4th, the *Philadelphia Inquirer* reported that both Connie Mack and his son were laid up due to severe colds, but contract work had been proceeding. Already signed for 1905 were: Barton and Noonan, catchers; Henley, Waddell, Bender, and Coakley, pitchers; Davis, Murphy, M. Cross, L. Cross, and Knight, infielders; Seybold, Hoffman, and Lord, outfielders. Others expected to sign soon were: Plank and Applegate, pitchers; "Schreck" and Powers, catchers; O'Brien and Soffell, infielders; and Hartsel and Bruce, outfielders.

On March 1st, the Athletics headed south for spring training in New Orleans and Shreveport, Louisiana. Chief Bender missed the train and had to catch up. Several games were planned for New Orleans before training most of the month in Shreveport. The train went initially to New York, and then to Washington. After some delays, the train arrived in New Orleans on the 3rd. There had been a shortage of food, and the boys were hungry. They stepped out onto the streets of New Orleans to behold Mardi Gras celebrations were underway.

On March 4th, 1905, Theodore Roosevelt begin his first full term as President of the United States following his inauguration.

On March 25th, the A's played in Vicksburg, Mississippi. Next, on March 27th, the A's were in Shreveport, Louisiana, playing a local team. Two days later, the A's beat Birmingham 10 to 6 in Birmingham, Alabama. Four pitchers took turns including Eddie Plank. The team stopped at Atlanta on the 30th, winning 11 to 4.

On April 1st, the Athletics and Phillies began an exhibition series at Columbia Park. The A's won the first two games as the teams played home and home. In the 3rd game, Eddie narrowly lost to the Phillies, 4 to 3. The A's took three of the first five games. On Sunday, the 9th, the A's played an exhibition in Newark, and narrowly won 3 to 2. The Phillies and A's were back at it on the 10th, Plank winning 5 to 1, the A's taking the series four games to two.

On the 12th of April, in preparation for the start of the season, Connie Mack released pitcher Applegate and infielders Soffell and O'Brien to Toronto of the Eastern League.

For Opening Day, Friday, April 14th, 1905, the American League champion Boston Americans were in Philadelphia. The team had arrived the prior day and were staying at the Bingham Hotel. League President Ban Johnson and Boston President Taylor attended the game, scheduled for 3:30. A music selection opened the festivities provided by Kendle's First Regiment Band. Mayor John Weaver threw out the first pitch.

The game got underway as planned, Chief Bender facing Cy Young. The *Philadelphia Inquirer* noted the voice of umpire Silk O'Loughlin in its story, "Silk O'Loughlin, the colorful voice umpire, early in the game rose to the limelight as a popular favorite. Silk has a way of pronouncing the word 'two' that is all his own. It is slightly reminiscent of Hopper's 'Casey at the Bat,' yet different. The crowd quickly caught on. Every time the second strike or ball called for official declaration there was breathless silence while Silk unfolded his new pronunciation. It was alone worth the price of admission."

Chief held the champs scoreless for eight innings while the A's built a three-run lead. The Americans rallied for two in the 9th, but it was not enough. The home team won 3 to 2, much to the pleasure of the full house at Columbia Park.

In the second game, the next day, Andy Coakley fell behind 5 to 0 by the 3rd. Team captain Lave Cross pulled him in favor of

Rube Waddell, who shut down the champs the rest of the way. The A's rallied offensively, Topsy Hartsel, Lave Cross, and Ossee Schrecongost knocking two hits each, including Lave's game-winning walk-off RBI in the bottom of the 9th. After two games, the Boston Americans didn't look so invincible. There was an optimistic vibe throughout Columbia Park.

After the Sunday day off, the teams were to play again on Monday the 17th. However, because of frigid temperatures, the game was postponed.

The Highlanders were in town for the game on the 18th, but it was again too cold and wet. The A's continued to sit on their 2-0 start against the best team in the league.

Eddie Plank finally took his turn on the mound, facing Jack Chesbro on the 19th. Staked to an early 2 to 0 lead, the teams exchanged the lead several times, arriving at a 6-to-6 tie after seven innings. In the bottom of the 9th, Lave Cross singled, followed by Seybold, who was hit by a pitch. Danny Murphy then sacrificed the runners into scoring position. Nineteen-year-old rookie shortstop John Knight, a Philadelphia native, stepped into the box and ripped a drive over the pulled-in centerfielder to win the game in walk-off fashion. It was another dramatic win for the White Elephants, and the first win of the season for Plank.

The next day, Bender took the mound and had an easier time of it. Leading 2 to 1 through the top half of the 7th, the A's pulled away with six runs late in the game, winning easily, 8 to 1.

The team was in high spirits on the train to Boston. On the 21st, Waddell pitched well early but seemed to tire into the 6th and 7th as the Americans tallied four runs. In the top of the 8th, the A's bats finally came to life, putting up five. They held on for a 5-to-4 win.

The next day, they ran into George Winter, who hurled a six-hit shutout, Henley taking the loss, 3 to 0.

Following the offday on the 23rd, Plank took the mound on the 24th against Tannehill. Eddie was wild, hitting three batters and throwing a wild pitch. He lost 3 to 1.

In the series finale, the A's found their bats and won easily, 10 to 6, Bender benefiting.

The A's traveled south to New York City to face the Highlanders. Coakley lost a close one, 4 to 3, New York winning it in the bottom of the 9th.

Eddie was on the mound for the next game, and despite hitting three batters, he held the opposition scoreless through eight, tied 0 to 0. The A's failed to score against Clark Griffith in the 9th, and the Highlanders manufactured a run to win 1 to 0, a very tough loss for Plank.

On the 28th, the A's won 7 to 5 behind Chief Bender, scoring four in the 9th. Chief contributed a single to the cause.

This was the last game in April for the Athletics, who finished the month 7-4, tied with the Highlanders for 1st place. Eddie was a tough 1-2.

The Washington Senators were in town on May 1. Coakley dropped a close one, 5 to 4. Eddie lost a forgettable game 9 to 5 on the 2nd. Trailing 4 to 0 into the bottom of the 9th of the third game, things finally began to look up when the A's rallied to tie. But, Bender coughed up a run in the 11th, and the A's had lost three to Washington, who were now alone in 1st place in the American League. Rube Waddell avoided a sweep by throwing a two-hit shutout on the 4th, the A's winning 6 to 0.

The teams then shifted to Washington where the home team tripped up Henley 4 to 2. "Gettysburg" Eddie was on the hill in the capital the next day, beating "Long" Tom Hughes 2 to 1. The next game did not start well with captain Lave Cross being hit in the nose by a sharply-hit ball. Said the *Philadelphia Inquirer*: "Some slight obstruction in the playing field caused a terrific smash from Huelsman's bat to take a nasty bound off the ball's regular course and Cross was unable to stop the drive from hitting him at the top of the nose and smashing the bone where it bridges to the forehead. A pebble that was dug up by the ball was forced into the side of Lave's nose and evidently disrupted a blood vessel, as it was more than an hour before a doctor could stop the bleeding after Captain Cross had retired to the hotel." Rube won a grueling game, striking out a dozen while winning 3 to 2. Bender lost another, 3 to 1, on the 9th. The A's gladly headed out of town on the 10th, having lost five of eight to the Senators.

The A's returned to Philadelphia and were scheduled to take a train to St. Louis on the 11th. Fortunately, at the last minute, Connie scheduled them to play a charity game in Reading, and the train ride west was postponed. That train, the *Cleveland and Cincinnati Express* of the Pennsylvania Railroad crashed near

Harrisburg leaving several dead or missing and dozens injured. Athletics' fans were relieved the team avoided fate.

This same day, Albert Einstein submitted his doctoral dissertation "On the Motion of Small Particles," describing the concept of Brownian motion. Over the rest of the year, Einstein published four papers, formulated the theory of special relativity and explained the photoelectric effect by quantization. It was his most prolific year.

Henley lost the first game to the Browns on the 12th. Rain prevented a game the next day. On the 14th, Plank allowed "only four measly hits" en route to an easy 10-to-2 victory. Eddie was hot at the plate with two hits and two runs scored. The headline the next day was "Big Chief Bender with His War Paint on Just Whitewashed the Browns." Chief threw a two-hit shutout, winning 4 to 0. Rain again interfered with the series on Tuesday the 16th.

The first game in Chicago, scheduled for the 17th, was rained out. The A's finally took the field on the 18th, Rube defeating Chicago 3 to 0. Nick Altrock beat Eddie the next day, 2 to 1, ending the shortened series.

In Cleveland on the 20th, Bender lost the opener 4 to 1 to Addie Joss. Waddell returned the favor on Monday the 22nd, winning 6 to 1. Eddie then continued the series with a 7 to 4 victory. Once again, he helped himself at the plate with a double and a run scored. The Naps earned a split the next day, Henley losing 6 to 5 in thirteen innings.

The first game in Detroit was a wild one won by the A's 9 to 7. Waddell got the win with help from Bender. Davis, Seybold, and Murphy each had two hits. Chief tamed the Tigers the next day, 5 to 2. The following game, on Saturday the 27th, was lost by Eddie 3 to 2.

The A's traveled home for a series starting Monday, May 29th against the Highlanders. Rube Waddell won a close one, 2 to 1. Coakley won the next one 6 to 5 thanks to three hits from Topsy Hartsel. Chief lost the game on the 31st 8 to 3.

The A's closed out May at 19-15, 2 1/2 games back of Cleveland, in 3rd place. Eddie was a mediocre 4-5 so far.

On June 1st, Plank was on the mound back home at Columbia Park to face the Senators. At the plate, he knocked out three hits.

On the mound, he was hurling a shutout until the 9th, when he yielded five runs and needed help from Chief Bender. The A's won 6 to 5. Waddell won the next one 3 to 1, followed by an easy 8 to 1 victory for Coakley. The game included a steal of home by Topsy Hartsel. After a Sunday off, the Senators won the final game 6 to 4, beating Bender.

The first game against Chicago on the 6th went to Waddell and the A's 4 to 1. This was followed by Altrock shutting out Bender 8 to 0. Eddie was on the mound for the next game, winning 6 to 3, yielding only 3 hits and striking out 9. Rube then lost his first game of the season, 3 to 2, resulting in a split of the series.

On the 10th, the Tigers were in town, and the A's had some fun, winning 15 to 8. Bender won the game in relief of Coakley. Most of the lineup had multiple hits, 20 in all.

After an offday on the 11th, rain prevented play on the 12th. Finally, on the 13th, the A's bats were all wet, losing 1 to 0, Waddell taking another tough loss. Eddie turned it around and was on top of his game the next day, winning 4 to 1.

The Browns rudely entered town on the 15th, shutting out their hosts 5 to 0, Harry Howell three-hitting the A's, Bender taking the loss. Rube and the A's came roaring back, winning the next one 10 to 1. Eddie notched another the following day, on the 17th, winning a tight one 2 to 1.

After the Sunday offday, the A's won an exciting game on the 19th, 5 to 4, made more so by Danny Murphy's amazing one-handed catch in the 9th to preserve the win for Henley.

The 1st place Naps were next in town on the 20th of June. Rube Waddell struck out 11 but lost 3 to 2. Plank was in "fine form" the following day, easily beating the Naps 7 to 3. The next games were delayed and then shortened by rain to only six innings. Coakley won 2 to 0, giving up only one hit. Waddell then took the last game of the series, 3 to 0, making it three straight against Lajoie's Clevelanders.

Rain prevented play on the 24th in Washington, followed by the Sunday offday. Weather also prevented play on the 26th. Finally, on the 27th, Plank pitched a "splendid game" to beat the Senators 1 to 0. Rube had them in the next game 3 to 0 until the 8th, when they erupted for six runs, downing the A's 6 to 3. After all the weather and waiting in Washington, the series was split 1-1.

On to New York on the 29th, the hot Highlanders beat Chief 13 to 4. "Uncle Rube" came to the rescue of "Professor" Plank the next day, Eddie holding a 7 to 4 lead in the 9th. Waddell shut the door, preserving the win. Eddie helped his cause with three hits of his own.

Over in the National League, Archibald "Moonlight" Graham came in as a defensive substitute late in a game for the Giants against Brooklyn at Washington Park. Graham did not get to bat. It was his only appearance in the major leagues, memorialized in the book *Shoeless Joe* by Ray Kinsella and the subsequent movie, in 1989, *Field of Dreams*.

The A's closed June at 34-23, in 3rd place, only two games back of Cleveland. Eddie was now 10-5, having won all six of his starts.

On Saturday, July 1st, the A's took two from the Highlanders. Waddell won the first one 3 to 2. Coakley was brilliant in the afternoon, throwing a four-hitter, winning 1 to 0. Henley followed on Monday with a three-hitter of his own, 3 to 0. The A's had taken four of five.

Over at Detroit, Cleveland star second baseman Napolean Lajoie was spiked and sustained a minor injury.

On July 4th, the A's were in Boston for a doubleheader. Said the *Philadelphia Inquirer* of the second game, "In the longest and, in many respects, the most remarkable game ever played in the American League, the Athletics defeated the Bostons this afternoon 4 to 2." Cy Young and Rube Waddell toiled for nineteen innings until the A's scored twice in the 20th. The A's had also won the morning game behind Coakley 5 to 2.

In Detroit, it was announced that Cleveland manager and star player Napolean Lajoie was ill from an attack of blood poisoning, believed to have been caused by dye from his stocking leeching into his wound.

Henley dropped the game on the 5th, 4 to 3 in ten innings. Coakley won the next one 7 to 4. Waddell faced Young again in the finale, the game tied 1 to 1 into extra innings. The A's won, Bender getting the victory in relief.

The teams then moved to Philadelphia and split a doubleheader on the 8th. Before a packed house, Henley beat Winter 11 to 4 in the morning. Eddie was knocked out of the 2nd game, losing 11 to 8.

The A's headed west to Cleveland for a series on the 10th of July. Lajoie was still not in the lineup, battling blood poisoning. Quietly, it was feared he might lose his leg. Meanwhile, Coakley won the first game 6 to 3. At this point, the teams were now tied, each a half-game behind Chicago. Eddie was hit around again and was pulled early in the game, the A's losing 7 to 0. After rain on the 12th, Waddell dropped the game on the 13th, 9 to 3.

After a rainout, the A's were in Detroit on the 15th. Eddie lost the first game 5 to 2. Waddell lost on his turn, 4 to 3. Plank was back on the mound for the finale, winning 6 to 3.

Rube Waddell won the first game in St. Louis on the 19th, 7 to 3. After a rainout, Coakley lost the next day in thirteen innings, 3 to 0. The teams then split a doubleheader on the 22nd. Weldon Henley threw a no-hitter in the first game, winning 6 to 0. Henley issued 3 walks. In the afternoon game, Waddell lost narrowly, 3 to 2.

The A's were in Chicago on the 23rd. Eddie Plank twirled a beautiful two-hit shutout, winning 1 to 0. The Sox returned the favor the next day, Altrock beating Bender 2 to 1. Waddell had it much easier in the following game, 8 to 2. Unfortunately, Henley dropped the next one, 5 to 2. In the rubber game, the teams played to a 4-to-4 draw in ten innings, Plank on the mound.

As the team arrived home from their road trip, Connie was in high spirits. He said, "Bar accidents, the Athletics should go right down the line from now on, and by Saturday night next they should be in the lead in the race for the American League pennant. No team in the league is playing steadier or better ball than our bunch. Our pitchers are doing finely. As you have doubtless noted by the scores of the games in which he has pitched, Henley has rounded into shape." Connie continued, talking up the rest of the team and the unfortunate loss of Lajoie to the Naps.

The White Sox probably did not appreciate Connie's remarks in the paper the next morning. They beat Rube Waddell 5 to 2.

Following the game, White Sox Business Manager Fredericks said, "It will be the Chicagos first and the rest scattered. We've walloped Waddell, and all we have to do to clean up here is to get away with Plank ..."

The next game, on the 31st, Eddie went out and shut down the White Sox, winning 4 to 1.

The A's ended the month of July 49-35, two games back of Cleveland, in 3rd place. The White Sox were in 2nd place, half-of-a-game out. Eddie was now 12-8.

August opened with the headline "After a Hilarious Time, Athletics Again Down Sox." A dispute by the White Sox that rookie John Knight had left third too early when tagging up to score led to arguments and ejections, and spilled over after the game. The A's won the game 5 to 4, Bender picking up the win in relief of Henley. After the game, the *Philadelphia Inquirer* picked up the story, "While going through the field gate after the game was over, (umpire Jack) McCarthy, on passing (White Sox first baseman Jiggs) Donahue, was grossly insulted by the latter. McCarthy replied that Donahue had no business to talk in the way that he did, and before he could get in position to defend himself, he was knocked down by the burly Chicago first baseman. Regaining his feet, the latter set sail, but before further damage could be done, officers and players interfered, and the offending player was hustled to his bus. The attack was as cowardly as it was unwarranted." Donahue was subsequently suspended indefinitely.

The next day, Connie's prognostication came true, as reported by the papers. The A's won again, beating Chicago 4 to 3 behind Rube Waddell. Philadelphia was now tied with Cleveland atop the American League and Chicago was a half-game back in 3rd place.

Detroit was in town on August 3rd. Coakley won a close one, 3 to 2. The next day, the teams split a doubleheader. Eddie won the first game 8 to 0, scattering nine hits. Henley lost the afternoon contest 3 to 2. Waddell took the following game 5 to 3. After the Sunday offday, Bender lost badly on Monday the 7th, 9 to 3.

Next up was Cleveland, stopping by Columbia Park on the 8th. Despite still missing Lajoie, the Naps edged Plank 5 to 4. Rain interfered with the next two contests, but the A's held their lead over Cleveland and Chicago. The teams finally played on Friday the 11th. Waddell won 7 to 6, the A's scoring four times in the bottom of the 8th.

On the 12th, last-place St. Louis came to town. Eddie won the game 6 to 4. After the Sunday offday, Bender won a tight one, 2 to 1. Waddell took the hill the next day and won a rain-shortened game 2 to 0. Rube gave up only one hit in the five-inning affair. He struck out 9. Coakley won the next one 6 to 4, Lave Cross providing four hits. The A's ended the long homestand with a three-game lead over the Naps.

In Detroit on the 17th, Plank marched to victory, 6 to 2, scattering ten hits. This was a brief stop on the way to St. Louis.

Facing the Browns at Sportsman's Park, the A's battled to a 3-to-3 tie before the game was called because of darkness after sixteen innings. Coakley and Waddell split the duties. The next day, the 19th, the A's lost 1 to 0, Coakley losing a tough one to Harry Howell. The Browns then swept two, Plank losing 3 to 2 and Henley 6 to 4. Coakley got one back the final game, 4 to 2.

Heading to Chicago, the A's now had a 3 1/2 game lead over both the White Sox and Naps. The teams split a doubleheader on the 22nd. Waddell won the first game 4 to 0, giving up six hits. Henley lost the second game 2 to 1 in thirteen innings. Not resolving much, they split two more games the next day. Eddie dropped the first game 3 to 1. Coakley, with help from Waddell, won the afternoon game 4 to 2.

During the offday on the 24th, the Tigers signed an eighteen-year-old outfielder named Ty Cobb. Two weeks earlier, Cobb's mother had shot his father, fearing he was a burglar.

The A's were in Detroit behind Coakley, who won 6 to 4 the next day. The Tigers returned the favor against Henley the following day, 5 to 4. After the Sunday offday, the teams played again on Monday the 28th. Eddie held off the Tigers 5 to 4, Waddell pitching in a save. Cobb did not play during the series.

The Cleveland Naps, with Lajoie back in the lineup, were up next for a doubleheader on the 29th. Waddell threw a three-hitter in the first game, winning 6 to 0. Coakley won the second game 4 to 2. The next day, the A's won again, 6 to 2. Socks Seybold hit one out in support of Plank. Waddell completed the sweep with a brilliant four-hit shutout on the 31st.

The A's ended August in great shape, as Connie predicted, 69-44, in 1st place. The White Sox trailed by 2 1/2 games. The Naps were now fading, 8 1/2 games back in 3rd place. The Athletics had gone 20-9 for the month. Eddie was 17-11 and turned thirty years of age.

After a travel day on the 1st, the game with Washington was rained out on the 2nd. The Sunday offday followed on the 3rd.

On Monday, the 4th, Labor Day, the A's were happy to finally play the Senators at Columbia Park. They swept both games, 5 to 0 behind a two-hitter from Bender and 5 to 4 behind Coakley, saved by Waddell.

Now 4 1/2 games up on Chicago, the A's headed to Boston to play the Americans on the 5th of September. Waddell was amazing, striking-out 17 Americans, but lost 3 to 2 in thirteen innings. The Athletics, behind Plank, trailed the next game 1 to 0 in the 7th. The A's scored a run each in the 8th and 9th to pull out a 2-to-1 victory. It took Coakley thirteen innings to defeat Boston the next day, also 3 to 2. Waddell was back for the fourth game but fell behind early. Rookie Jimmy Dygert relieved and picked up his first major-league win, beating Cy Young 5 to 3. The A's had taken three of four from last year's American League champions.

The boys were in high spirits. It being after Labor Day, it was a tradition for men to toss their straw hats, fashionable in the summer but not the fall, onto the field this time of year, or otherwise have them destroyed. Waddell and the boys took it upon themselves to enforce this fashion tradition as they traveled back to Philadelphia, smashing hats wherever they could. On the Providence platform, or in the train while at Providence station, Waddell noticed that teammate Andy Coakley was still wearing his straw hat. A tussle ensued as Waddell sought to destroy the hat. At one point, he slammed his left shoulder against a seat. Connie heard the ruckus and asked the boys to settle down. Rube went to his corner, removed his shirt and fell asleep next to an open window. The next morning, he could not lift his precious left arm above his head. He would be lost to the team for the rest of the season.

After this impactful trip to Boston, the A's returned to Columbia Park to play the Highlanders twice on the 9th of September. Eddie won the first game easily, 6 to 2. The second game was called because of darkness, tied at 7 after nine innings, Henley on the mound.

After the Sunday off, the doubleheader scheduled for Monday the 11th was postponed due to rain. The teams played two on the 12th, Coakley winning the first 4 to 3 and Dygert losing the afternoon game 7 to 4.

The Boston Americans were in town on the 13th. Eddie was masterful, giving up only two hits while shutting them out. Danny Murphy hit a home run in the 7th, the game's only run. Plank and the A's won 1 to 0. The next day, Bender was wild, walking 8 Bostonians en route to a 4 to 3 loss. On the 15th, the teams split a doubleheader. Coakley beat Winter in the first game, 4 to 3. Dygert lost the afternoon game 3 to 2. The A's closed out the series with a 6 to 2 win on Saturday, the headline reading "Boston Could Not Hit Eddie Plank's Twisters." Eddie scatted five hits.

The banter about town on Sunday the 17th was all about the pennant. It was assumed the team would hold on and win, though Chicago was holding steady, if not gaining ground.

The Athletics rode the train to New York, only to be rained out. Meanwhile, the Sox moved to four games back. The next day, the A's and Highlanders each won a game, the Sox moving to 3 1/2 back. Coakley dropped the first game 5 to 0, Ambrose Puttman throwing a two-hitter. Bender beat Griffith 3 to 0 in the afternoon game. Bill Hogg followed up with a three-hitter, beating Henley 1 to 0. The Sox crept to 2 1/2 back.

On the 21st, the Naps were in town. Lajoie was not in the line-up against Plank. Napolean was continuing to recover from his blood poisoning, having tried to make a go of it while Cleveland was still in the race. Eddie beat the Nap-less Naps and Addie Joss 2 to 1. However, the Sox swept two from the Highlanders in New York and inched to only two games behind.

The next day, the A's and Naps split a doubleheader, Bender losing 8 to 4 and Coakley winning 4 to 1. In New York, Chicago lost, slipping to 2 1/2 back. The Sox swept the Highlanders in a doubleheader on the 23rd, but the A's did the same to the Naps, Henley winning 5 to 2 and Plank winning 3 to 2. The standings stayed the same through the offday on Sunday the 24th of September.

Chicago was off to Boston on the 25th and swept two from the Americans. The Mack Men hosted the Tigers, who had Cobb batting 5th and won 3 to 2 behind Bender. Chicago was back to two games behind.

On Tuesday, the 26th, the Sox again swept two from the Americans. This time Detroit got the better of the A's, 6 to 4, Coakley and Dygert unable to hold them off. The difference in the standings was now a measly half-game, and the loss of Waddell was starting to show.

On Wednesday, the 27th, the Sox and Americans split a doubleheader. In Philadelphia, Henley and the A's led 1 to 0 into the 6th, when the Tigers tied them up. The A's notched up a run, taking a 2 to 1 lead into the 7th. After three in the 7th and three in the 8th, the Tigers led 7 to 1 and all hope seemed lost. The A's rallied for three in the 8th, pulling to 7 to 5. The Tigers added one in the 9th and led 8 to 5 into the bottom of the 9th. Once again the A's rallied, but could only muster two, losing 8 to 7. The Sox and A's were now tied for 1st in the American League, though Chicago had two more losses.

And guess who was coming to town? The Chicago White Sox. Thursday, September 28th over 20,000 fans crowded Columbia Park to watch the two tied teams battle for the pennant. The headline in the sports section the next day read "Eddie Plank Pitches Athletics to Victory." It was Philadelphia 3, Chicago 2. Eddie did his best Rube Waddell impression, striking out a dozen. The A's now had a one-game edge.

The next day, the A's drove an 11 to 1 wedge into the Sox, Bender winning easily, the lead now at two games. Chicago would not go quietly, though, taking the next game 4 to 3, Eddie Plank losing a close one.

The A's finished September at 87-54. The White Sox were 88-57, one game back. Detroit was the next closest team, 14 1/2 behind. Eddie was now 24-12. He had gone 7-1 in September during a very tense pennant race.

The Athletics rested on Sunday, October 1st, the one-game lead intact. On the 2nd, the last-place Browns were in town and couldn't have arrived at a better time. Coakley four-hit them, shutting them out 4 to 0. With the Chicago loss in Washington, the A's now led by two games.

Both teams won on the 3rd, the A's winning 5 to 2 behind Henley and Bender. Meanwhile, the National Baseball Commission announced and the *Philadelphia Inquirer* was happy to report the World Series with the New York Giants would begin at Columbia Park on Monday, October 9th. Sheridan and O'Day were to umpire the series. Of course, the pennant had not yet been clinched, though it was looking increasingly to be in Philadelphia's favor.

Both teams won again on the 4th, the A's winning 4 to 1 behind Plank, who scattered five hits and had two himself. Meanwhile, the *Philadelphia Inquirer* boldly advertised they would pay the Athletics $1000 in gold should they win the World Series.

On October 5th, the White Sox did not play and the A's swept two from the lowly Washington Senators in D.C. Bender won the first game 8 to 0 and relieved Coakley to win the afternoon game 9 to 7. The A's were now three games ahead and only needed one more win or Chicago loss to clinch the pennant.

The next day, the A's did not do their part, losing 10 to 4 behind Coakley, who was relieved by Waddell. But, Chicago lost in St. Louis and the A's clinched.

The A's closed the season with a doubleheader on the 7th, Waddell pitching only one inning in the first game. Per accounts, he "did not look right" and was pulled after giving up a couple runs. Dygert finished, but the A's lost 5 to 4. The second game ended in a 3-to-3 tie, called after five innings as agreed so the Athletics could make their 6:50 train back to Philadelphia. Wilmington, Delaware, native Joseph Myers, a twenty-three-year-old rookie pitched for the A's. It would be the only five innings of his major-league career. Myers would go on to toil in the minors, winning 19 for the Harrisburg Senators in 1911.

The regular season ended with the A's at 92-56 and the Sox at 91-59, two games behind. Eddie was 24-12 with a 2.26 ERA. Rube was 27-10 with a 1.48 ERA and 287 strikeouts, all league-leading figures. Coakley and Bender each contributed 18 wins. Clearly, the A's had a formidable pitching staff, though the status of Waddell for the series was worrisome.

At the plate, no Athletic hit better than Harry Davis's .285, which trailed Elmer Flick's .308. Davis also led the team with 8 home runs and 83 RBI, both league-leading numbers. Danny Hoffman led the team with 10 triples and 46 stolen bases.

The *Philadelphia Inquirer* described the arrival of the Athletics in Philadelphia on the 7th: "No better evidence of the fact that this good old town is baseball dippy could be had than the reception which was tendered the Athletics last night on their arrival at the Broad Street Station. The train was due in at 10:05, but owing to a late start from Washington, and the fact that two extra parlor cars had been put on to accommodate the Athletic players and a bunch of rooters, the train pulled in about twenty minutes late. But that made no difference to the fans, who had started to assemble in the station as early as 9 o'clock. They were there to stick, even if the train had been delayed an hour or two. Long before 10 o'clock the space between the train gates and the waiting room was packed by a solid mass of good-natured humanity, while hundreds of others resorting to neat little schemes, got through the gates to be the first to welcome the champions on their return. When the train did pull in and the players got off it was almost impossible for them to work their way through the crowd. President Shibe, with a smile that would not come off, was the first to greet Manager Mack on the platform, and the champions followed their chief in the walk toward the gates ...”

Meanwhile, there was great anticipation for the series, the odds-makers giving the edge to John McGraw's New York Giants.

The Athletics laid low on Sunday the 8th. Connie even stayed away from Ban Johnson and the other baseball officials who arrived in town. Instead, he stayed in his office and received a congratulatory telegram from Charles Comiskey, the owner of the White Sox. The players also rested.

Early on the 9th, McGraw and his Giants arrived in town with much fanfare, many rooters joining them including the actor Jim Corbett, the comedian Louis Mann, and other Broadway stars. The Giants first dropped by the Continental Hotel and partook in a luncheon. Ticket sales began at Columbia Park at 11, the game scheduled to commence at 3:30. Meanwhile, the *Philadelphia Inquirer* included an item about Harry Davis's glove being stolen when the team had arrived on the train on Saturday night. Davis appealed for the return of the glove he had used all season and feared "with a new or strange glove he would be handicapped in covering the bag."

Over 20,000 made it into Columbia Park as thousands were turned away. Those multitudes sought every possible vantage point to watch the game including the tops of wagons, rooftops, and even telegraph poles. The weather was pleasant with a light breeze. The Giants arrived by "barouches, tallyhos, and automobiles" to Columbia Park, rooters carrying many of the players into the stadium on their shoulders. The Giants were dressed in black with white NYs on their jerseys.

The crowd roared when the A's appeared and began to loosen. Eddie Plank was to take the ball, facing Christy Mathewson.

When John McGraw and Lave Cross met at home plate to exchange lineups, Captain Cross brought with him a package for the Giant manager. Described the *Philadelphia Inquirer*: "McGraw ripped the package and revealed to the thousands of eyes that were fixed upon the group an effigy of a white elephant in miniature. There was a tremendous roar of laughter and approval, which was rather pertinent in view of the fact that it was McGraw who gave the Athletics their symbol when he remarked that in the club the American League had a 'white elephant on its hands.' Connie Mack proved the absurdity of McGraw's statement by carrying off the pennant in 1902 and again this year, and he must have felt that he had had sweet revenge as he sat on his players' bench and watched the manager of the Giants uncover the symbol his statement had given to the White Elephants. McGraw, however, took the incident good-naturedly and, laughingly, placed the effigy on his head."

Harry Davis was "happy as a lark" when a loyal fan returned his glove in time for the game.

The game did not start well when Eddie Plank plunked lead-off hitter Roger Bresnahan in the leg, giving him first base. It was for naught though as Plank and Christy Mathewson exchanged zeros for the first four innings. In the top of the 5th, New York scored twice, and it was all she wrote. Mathewson held the A's scoreless, touched by only four hits. Davis, Murphy, and Schrecongost all hit doubles but were stranded. While Plank pitched well, no one was going to beat Mathewson this day, who had gone 31-9 with a stingy 1.28 ERA during the regular season. The Giants took a one-game lead.

The series moved to the Polo Grounds in New York for Game Two. Chief Bender took the mound against Joe McGinnity, and would not disappoint, as the *Philadelphia Inquirer* described: "Superb is the only word that fitly characterizes the work the big copper-skinned athlete did on the slab for his team. He had the speed of an arrow shot from the bow of a Chippewa marksman, he was cool as an Esquimuax in a snow hut, and his aim was as good as that of Davy Crockett when that hunter was wont to hit a squirrel in the eye." Bender won the game 3 to 0, scattering four hits.

The Giants took an early train to Philadelphia and planned to rest. The A's took in a Broadway show then headed home. McGraw announced Mathewson would be back on the mound for Game Three. Rain prevented play on the 11th, the game moved to the 12th. Mathewson again dampened the A's' spirits, repeating his four-hit shutout performance. This time, the Giants rallied for nine runs off Coakley. The A's now trailed two games to one.

On the 13th, at the Polo Grounds, Eddie faced Joe McGinnity in a game in which neither pitcher yielded an earned run. Both teams managed only five hits. Plank struck-out 6 to the "Iron Man's" 4. Unfortunately, it was the A's who fumbled, making a key error in the 4th inning that led to the only run of the game. The Giants won 1 to 0 and now led three games to one.

Christy Mathewson got the call again to face Bender for the fifth game, also to be played at the Polo Grounds. Should the series continue, it would shift back to Columbia Park for the final games. However, it was not to be. Once again, the A's could not score on Mathewson, who threw a six-hit shutout. Bender was also superb but lost 2 to 0. The Giants were World Series champions.

The inevitable postmortems followed in the Philadelphia papers. Some wondered what would have happened had Mathewson been laid up for over a month like Rube Waddell. Some argued the A's were tired from their tough fight with the White Sox, made harder by the loss of Waddell, while the Giants had been rested from their easy cruise to the finish. Waddell was blamed for the team losing a lot of money when he was in Providence Station the night after the last game in Boston. "In skylarking, he tripped over a grip, and in falling he injured his left arm," recounted the *Philadelphia Inquirer*. In summary, Rube and weakened their chances when he was goofing off and was injured.

In the end, none of this mattered. Christy Mathewson had just thrown three shutouts in the World Series. The absolute best Waddell could have done was to tie him.

On the 19th, the A's were in Pottsville for an exhibition against a local team. Eddie played a bit of right field while the team won 8 to 3.

On the evening of Monday, October 23rd, 1905, the town came out for a parade to honor the American League champions. Even McGraw's Giants came from New York in a show of respect.

This was followed by a dinner held by the Athletics at the Bingham House. Said the *Inquirer*, "It was a glorious dinner, from oysters to cigarettes." Ban Johnson spoke and mentioned how special the parade was. "In no other city could such a parade be given. It was wonderful and inspiring." He then proceeded to congratulate the Athletics and perpetuated the idea they must have been worn out from the tough fight with the Sox. He also mentioned he had never had to discipline any of the Athletics' players, having played "clean and sportsmanlike baseball."

On Wednesday, November 1st, it was announced in the *Gettysburg Compiler* that Eddie Plank had arrived home and was "the same Eddie as well as being at the top notch of his career."

A banquet was given in honor of "Our Eddie" at Hotel Gettysburg that evening.

On November 27th, Connie drafted thirteen players to compete for positions next spring. One of them was Rube Oldring.

On December 23rd, the Washington Senators announced the signing of former A's team captain and third baseman Lave Cross to a contract. Mack had promised Lave his release when signing his contract the prior spring. Cross was considering retirement, but several clubs showed interest. The A's received no cash or players, but only future considerations. Harry Davis was signed to a contract to be the team captain for 1906.

Meanwhile, Rube Waddell was in the care of a doctor who was looking after his sore arm.

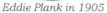

Eddie Plank in 1905   Anna Cora Myers circa 1902.

THE ATHLETICS' SIX NEW PLAYERS WHO LEFT YESTERDAY WITH THE OLD GUARD FOR NEW ORLEANS AND SHREVEPORT, WHERE THE TEAM WILL TAKE ITS PRELIMINARY TRAINING

The Athletics waiting for the train to spring training in 1905.

Cartoon of the Athletics arriving in New Orleans during Mardis Gras.

THE ATHLETIC BUNCH, OF WHOM MANAGER MACK EXPECTS GREAT THINGS THIS SEASON
Reading from left to right on the top row are Noonan, Soffic, O'Brien, Knight, Plank, Davis, Seybold, Monte Cross; Second row—Powers, Waddell, Hartsel, Barton, Metzner. Third row—Loftman, Lave Cross, Lord and Bruce.

The 1905 Philadelphia Athletics.

MAYOR WEAVER THROWING THE BALL ONTO THE FIELD AND A VIEW OF THE CROWD IN THE
LEFT FIELD BLEACHERS

Philadelphia Mayor Weaver throws out the first pitch at Columbia Park in 1905.

Eddie Plank following through in 1905.

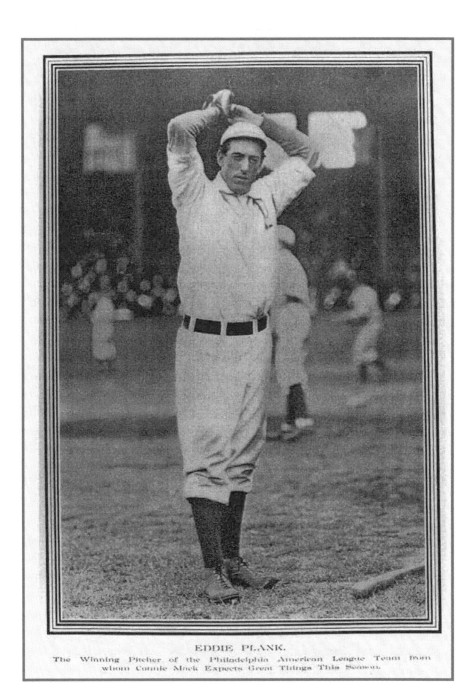

EDDIE PLANK.
The Winning Pitcher of the Philadelphia American League Team from whom Connie Mack Expects Great Things This Season.

Eddie Plank winding-up circa 1905.

Caricature of Eddie Plank in 1905.

Caricature of Rube Waddell in 1905.

Caricature of an upset fan after three straight losses to lowly Washington.

Connie riding the elephant to the pennant in 1905.

Cartoon of Plank winding-up to pitch – but wrong-handed.

Crowd for Boston at Philadelphia at Columbia Park, July 8, 1905.

Socks Seybold hits a home run on September 3, 1905.

Pitcher Andy Coakley at the plate on September 4, 1905.

Chief Bender and the crowd on September 29, 1905.

Cartoon of Chief Bender and photo of Topsy Hartsel prior to Game One
of the 1905 World Series.

The 1905 American League champion Philadelphia Athletics.

Chief Bender during the World Series.

Cartoon of Plank in the World Series.

Caricature of Chief Bender during the World Series.

1906:
FADED TO WHISPER

THE NEW YEAR'S Day edition of the *Philadelphia Inquirer* included an optimistic outlook from Connie Mack regarding the upcoming baseball season. Connie expected Waddell to be healthy and mentioned he looked forward to Harry Davis taking over as team captain.

In late February, the team members began collecting in Montgomery, Alabama, for spring training. Connie Mack had traveled ahead to prepare. The Philadelphia train left the Baltimore and Ohio Station at 2:14 on Tuesday the 27th. New captain Harry Davis and many of the veterans were on this train, including Rube Waddell, Monte Cross, Topsy Hartsel, Chief Bender, Danny Murphy, and Socks Seybold. Per the *Philadelphia Inquirer*, the team left "amid the shaking of dainty handkerchiefs and the waving of hats." The plan was to pick up Plank in Baltimore. The ride south was wrought with delays, taking an additional six hours to complete, thirty-three in total. The team put up at the Glenmore Hotel in Montgomery.

On the afternoon of March 1st, the players rode trolleys to Athletic Park in Montgomery where practice began. Harry Davis led the drills and it was noted that Waddell, Schrecongost, and Seybold appeared a bit overweight. Rube, however, showed no signs of the recent arm soreness.

In Eddie's first exhibition action on March 6th, he was a bit rusty, giving up three runs in the 1st inning against a local Montgomery team. The squad then split up, some going to New Orleans for exhibitions, while Eddie and many veterans stayed in Montgomery.

On the 13th, the club was back together in Montgomery, staying at the Glenmore. Waddell was a no-show at practice this day, apparently involved in a wild night out that involved some highwaymen and the police—at least that was the story that was circulating. Meanwhile, Bender and Plank were deemed "ready for championship ball."

Unseasonably cold wet weather interfered with much of the next week. Things were so slow, the *Philadelphia Inquirer* published goofy photos of some of the players and included a report of Waddell responding to a local fire in Montgomery which he helped put out.

On the 23rd, the veterans were off to Memphis to play the Southern League team, winning easily, 8 to 1. "Waddell, Bender, and Plank had the Memphis men pulling away from the plate," reported the *Philadelphia Inquirer*. However, the game at Nashville on the 26th was tougher, ending tied at two after eleven innings. Eddie and Chief threw shutout ball, Rube yielding two unearned.

Back in Philadelphia on March 31, the team began an intercity series with the Phillies. The first game was delayed by weather until April 2nd, the A's winning 7 to 1 behind Jimmy Dygert. The next day, Eddie helped himself with two hits en route to a 3 to 0 six-hit shutout. Chief followed with his own six-hitter the next day, winning 1 to 0, the A's up three games to none. The Phillies got one back, 4 to 1, topping Coakley on April 5th, but the A's won the rain-shortened series four games to one.

A farewell banquet was held to honor former team captain Lave Cross on April 10th, Lave coming from Washington, D.C., to attend. Many American League players and dignitaries were present. Eddie was likely not present, suffering from a case of "the grip."

For Opening Day, April 14th, the A's were in Washington, the A's winning 4 to 3 behind Chief Bender. Following the Sunday offday, the A's won again, 5 to 3, on Monday, Waddell winning in relief of Dygert. Dygert and Coakley lost the following day, 5 to 2.

On April 18th, an earthquake in San Francisco, California, destroyed much of the city, killing over 3,000 and leaving up to 300,000 homeless.

Meanwhile, on the east coast, the teams switched to Columbia Park for the home opener on the 18th. Bender was masterful again, winning 4 to 2. Eddie finally could go on the 19th and was leading after five innings, 9 to 2, but weakened, the Senators hitting him hard for five runs. Dygert ended up losing the game in relief.

The New York Highlanders were next in town on the 20th. Coakley took the first game 11 to 3, Rube taking game two the next day 3 to 1.

On Saturday, the 22nd, the A's played an exhibition against the Eastern League champion Providence Grays, winning 1 to 0 behind Coakley.

Following the offday, the Highlanders won on the 24th, 7 to 4, defeating Chief.

Boston visited on the 25th, pitting Cy Young against Rube Waddell. The A's won 5 to 0, but the Americans got their revenge, 12 to 0, the following day. "Plank Twisted the Beaneaters" read the headline for game three on the 27th, Eddie beating Cy Young 3 to 0, tossing a three-hitter. Waddell lost a close one, 7 to 6, the next day.

The Senators were in town to close out April, the Chief winning 6 to 3. For April, the A's were 8-5 and occupied 1st place in the American League, one game up on Cleveland. Eddie started the month with the flu, and was only 1-0, albeit a shutout of Cy Young.

The first game in May, on the 1st, was a 16 to 2 laugher over the Senators, Plank benefiting. Eddie scattered seven hits.

The A's traveled to New York on the 2nd for a game against the Highlanders but it was rained out. On the 3rd, Dygert lost 6 to 5. The next day, a 6-to-2 loss, Bender, Waddell, and Plank all pitched, Bender taking the loss. Chief won easily on the 5th, 9 to 3, and swatted a three-run home run.

The A's were next off to Boston for a series that opened on Monday the 7th. Waddell won the first game 4 to 0, beating Winter. The next day, Chief Bender, Mack's emergency substitution in right field for Topsy Hartsel, hit two inside-the-park home runs in three at-bats late in the game as the A's rallied to win 11 to 4 with seven runs in the 9th. Coakley was the winning pitcher.

Eddie and Cy Young faced off on the 9th. Tied at one into the top of the 5th, the A's scored four to go up 5 to 1. Eddie cruised to a 9 to 6 victory. Cy was signaling it was to be a down year for Boston. Chief finished the four-game sweep, 5 to 1.

A highly anticipated series with the White Sox in Philadelphia was interrupted by rain on the 11th. In the first game, the A's won 4 to 0 behind Waddell. Following the offday on Sunday, however, the teams were rained out again on Monday. "Plank and Altrock Exceptionally Effective" read the headline as Eddie and the A's edged the Sox 1 to 0 on the 15th.

On May 16th, Detroit was at Columbia Park and Ty Cobb was leading off. Chief Bender won easily 9 to 2. The next day, Rube Waddell one-hit the Tigers, winning 5 to 0. The only hit was a lead-off bunt single by Ty Cobb in the 1st inning. The next day, May 18th, Eddie Plank faced Ty Cobb for the first time, yielding a double in four at-bats. Eddie and the A's won 4 to 3. Coakley made it eleven straight wins, topping Donovan and the Tigers 2 to 1 the next day.

Eddie made a quick trip home to visit his parents on Sunday the 20th. He stayed a couple days.

The 2nd place Naps were in town on the 21st of May. The A's dropped the game 2 to 1 in thirteen innings, Bender taking the loss in relief of Waddell. Bender lost the next one 8 to 5, Lajoie knocking three hits. Eddie ended the brief losing streak with a 4 to 3 win in ten innings thanks to Harry Davis's walk-off home run. But, the Naps took three of four, besting Coakley 9 to 7 on the 24th.

St. Louis lost to Dygert at Columbia Park, 6 to 2, on the 25th. Chief won the next one 3 to 2. After the offday on the 27th, the Browns and A's were rained out on the 28th.

At Boston on the 29th, the A's faced the struggling "Beaneaters." Eddie won 2 to 1. Boston then took a doubleheader on the 30th, 5 to 1 over Coakley and 5 to 3 over Bender, Winter winning the second game.

May ended with the A's in New York to face the Highlanders. Dygert lost to Clark Griffith 7 to 3.

The A's finished the month 24-13, half of a game ahead of New York, in 1st place. Eddie was 7-0 on the season.

The next day, June 1st, the Highlanders walked into 1st place after a 10-to-2 drubbing of Coakley. On the 2nd, the teams split a doubleheader, Plank and Dygert losing the first game 14 to 4, Chief Bender winning the second 7 to 1.

After an offday on the 3rd, the A's were off to Chicago to face the White Sox. Eddie lost a close one, 3 to 2. This was followed by a 7-to-1 loss by Waddell and a 4-to-3 loss by Bender. Rain on the 7th prevented a four-game sweep.

The team was then off to St. Louis on the 8th to begin a series on June 9th. The headline read "Plank Pitched in Splendid Form and Had Losers Faded to Whisper." Eddie gave-up only five hits in winning 2 to 0. Coakley also won the next day, 5 to 2. Dygert made it three straight with a 5-to-1 win on the 11th.

The next stop on the western swing was Detroit on the 12th. Bender lost the first game 8 to 7. Eddie won the next game 5 to 4, Cobb going 0 for 5. Coakley lost by the same score on the 14th. Dygert threw a three-hit shutout on the 15th, winning 4 to 0. Cobb had two of the hits.

In Cleveland on the 16th, the A's lost 9 to 4 behind Bender. After the Sunday offday, Eddie won on the 18th, 3 to 2. The next day, Rube Waddell, back from a sprained thumb, beat Addie Joss 2 to 0. This put the A's back into 1st place by a half-game. Dygert dropped the next one, however, 7 to 3, and the teams switched positions.

On to Washington on the 21st, rain, wind, and hail shortened the game to seven innings. Bender ended up tied 1 to 1.

Back in Philadelphia on the 22nd, the Boston Americans were in town. George Winter beat Coakley, Waddell, and Dygert 6 to 4 in twelve innings. Eddie followed this with a five-hit shutout on the 23rd.

The next day, Waddell and Dinneen exchanged zeros until Bris Lord tripled and Danny Murphy singled him home in the 9th for the walk-off win. On the 26th, Bender beat Young 3 to 1.

That day, in Le Mans, France, the first Grand Prix was held.

The A's took the train to Washington on the 27th. Eddie won the game easily, 5 to 0. Rube dropped the next one, 4 to 2. The teams split a doubleheader on the 29th. Coakley won the first game 9 to 5 and Dygert lost the afternoon game 6 to 5, former captain Lave Cross tallying three hits for the Nats. The A's won on the last day of the month, 6 to 5, Bender saving it for Waddell. The A's ended the month 38-25, tied for 1st with New York, with Cleveland a game behind. Eddie was 12-2 on the season.

On July 1, a Sunday, Eddie was home to visit his parents. The following day, on the 2nd, New York was in town in a battle of first-place teams. They played two and split. Eddie won the morning game 5 to 4, but Coakley dropped the afternoon game 5 to 1. When play ended, the A's, Highlanders, and Naps were all tied for 1st place.

The game on the 3rd was called because of rain after two innings, tied at one apiece.

On Independence Day, July 4th, the A's and Highlanders again split a doubleheader. Waddell won 3 to 1, but Bender lost 2 to 1. The Naps swept their doubleheader and now led both teams by a game-and-a-half.

The Senators were in town on July 5th. A rookie named Jack Coombs hurled a six-hit shutout in his debut, winning 3 to 0. Veteran Plank won the next one on the 6th, 2 to 1.

The Naps were at Columbia Park on July 7th. Rube won the game in ten innings, 3 to 2, putting the A's back in 1st place. After the Sunday off on the 8th, Coakley lost on the 9th, 6 to 0. Rain canceled the game on the 10th, but Waddell beat them 5 to 1 on the 11th.

On July 12th, Ty Cobb and the Detroit Tigers were in town. Eddie yielded only two hits, winning 2 to 1. Cobb did not play in the first game. However, the next day, Cobb pinch hit and scored the winning run in the 9th in Coomb's 4 to 3 loss. Rube won the next one, 5 to 4. All runs were scored in the 3rd inning.

After an offday, Dygert won 2 to 1 on the 16th.

Rain prevented the start of the Browns series on the 17th. The teams split a doubleheader on the 18th. Eddie lost the first game 4 to 2, but Coombs won the afternoon game 10 to 5. In the next game, Waddell was replaced after yielding two runs in the 1st, the team losing 4 to 0. On the 20th, Bender won 5 to 2.

Saturday the 21st, Chicago came to town. Eddie fell behind 2 to 0 in the 1st but held on to win 3 to 2. He helped himself with two hits, including a triple. After the offday, the teams played a doubleheader on Monday the 23rd. Combs dropped the first game 4 to 0, but Dygert led the way 5 to 0 in the afternoon game. Bender followed with a 7-to-1 win the next day. The A's then swept a doubleheader on Wednesday the 25th. Eddie won the first game easily, 5 to1, while Coombs won 4 to 2.

During the offday on the 26th, as they left town on a westward trip, Connie arranged for a charity game in Reading, Pennsylvania, to benefit St. Peter's Roman Catholic Church. The A's won 7 to 2, Plank pitching a couple innings.

The team arrived in Detroit on the 27th along with some rain that canceled the game. Waddell stayed behind and would miss at least ten days due to his "split thumb." On the 28th, the A's won 8 to 2 behind Chief Bender. After the Sunday offday, the headline from the Monday game read "Plank Pitches All Around

Tigers." Eddie won 6 to 3 and Cobb was again on the pine. Dygert
lost the next one 5 to 3.

The A's closed the month 56-33, a game-and-a-half ahead of
New York and five ahead of Cleveland, in 1st place. Eddie was
18-3 on the season and now thirty-one years old.

Bender lost the first game in Cleveland on August 1st, 8 to 3.
Coombs won the next one 3 to 2 in ten innings. Eddie won the
game on the 3rd, 10 to 7, benefiting from five 9th inning runs. It
was his 19th and last win of the season. Dygert and the A's won
easily, 8 to 1, the next day. The A's were 2 1/2 games up on New
York and seven up on Cleveland. It would be their high-water
mark.

In Chicago on the 5th, the A's lost 10 to 2, Chief losing 10 to 2.
Coombs lost the next one 7 to 2. Ed Walsh beat Rube Waddell 4 to
0 on the 7th. Eddie threw a brilliant two-hitter, losing 1 to 0 in ten
innings and Dygert lost the next day in ten innings 3 to 2, completing the five-game sweep by the White Sox. The A's were now
only a half-game ahead of New York and 2 1/2 ahead of Chicago.

On the 10th in St. Louis, Bender lost a heart-breaker, 1 to 0.
Coakley lost another close one, 5 to 4, the next day. The White
Sox and Highlanders were both a half-game back.

Chief continued the losing streak, falling 7 to 4 on the 12th.
Chicago moved into the lead. The teams split a doubleheader
header on the 13th, Waddell winning the first 8 to 0, but dropping
the second game 5 to 1 with help from Coombs.

The team hurried home on the 14th to open a series at
Columbia Park against the Naps on the 15th. The teams played
to a 3-to-3 tie after twelve innings. The teams then split a doubleheader on the 16th. Waddell lost the first game 4 to 1. Bender
won the second 2 to 1. They again split a doubleheader on the
17th. Cleveland beat Coombs 6 to 4, followed by Coakley's 4-to-2
victory. In was announced in the *Philadelphia Inquirer* that "Eddie
Plank would not be called upon to pitch until his arm has become
perfectly well." The team had slipped two games behind the White
Sox at 62-45. They finished August 65-50, in 3rd place, 4 1/2
games back.

On August 16th, activity around the "Ring of Fire" continued
with devastating results in Valparaiso, Chile where a magnitude
8.2 earthquake left approximately 20,000 dead.

The A's and Boston faced off in a twenty-four-inning affair on September 1st, the A's winning 4 to 1. Jack Coombs and Joe Harris both went the distance, a record which still stands.

On September 13th, Eddie attempted a comeback and was a bit rusty. He went five innings in a 4-to-3 loss to Boston. It was his last appearance.

On September 18th, a typhoon and tsunami killed an estimated 10,000 in Hong Kong.

Unfortunately, without Eddie down the stretch, the team went 13-17, slipping to 4th place at 78-67. Waddell also missed significant time, and Bender was nursing a sore arm.

Eddie finished the season 19-6 with a 2.25 ERA. He led the league in winning percentage, though he made only 25 starts of his usual 40+. Rube Waddell finished 15-17 and Chief Bender 15-10. Dygert won 11 games and Coombs 10. Andy Coakley slipped to 7-8. Al Orth led the American League with 27 wins.

At the plate, Socks Seybold hit .316 to lead the team, trailing George Stone's .358. Danny Murphy batted .301. First baseman Harry Davis hit .292 with 12 home runs and 96 RBI, both league-leading figures. Topsy Hartsel led the team with 96 runs and 31 stolen bases.

Near the end of the season, nineteen-year-old rookie Eddie Collins got into 6 games and hit .200 in 15 at bats.

A season full of promise was curtailed by the sore arms of the team's top pitchers. The White Sox claimed the American League crown. They beat the cross-town Cubs in six games in the World Series.

On November 7th, the *Gettysburg Compiler* announced that Eddie was home for the winter, staying with his parents near town.

On November 9th, President Theodore President left to inspect the progress of the Panama Canal, becoming the first sitting president to leave the country.

Portrait of Eddie Plank, American League champion.

Cartoon of Schreck and Waddell.

PLANK'S PITCHING
FACE · · ·

Stretched Plank.

RUBE WADDELL

Snapped by The Inquirer's artist camera
style just after extinguishing the blaze at
Montgomery.

Warped Rube Waddell.

OSSE SCHRECK

Southern cooking has had a most peculiar effect upon him. He is hoping
to come home soon. This picture was snapped while the big catcher was looking at the Alabama River scroll up.

Stretched Schreck.

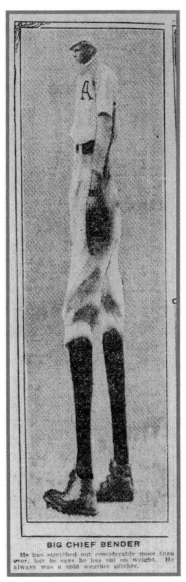

BIG CHIEF BENDER

He has stretched out considerable more than ever, but he says he has not put on weight. He always was a cold weather pitcher.

Goofy Chief Bender.

Cartoon of the Athletics returning from spring training.

Eddie during his first game in 1906.

The 1906 American League pennant race.

1907:
TIGER BY THE
TAIL

N ITEM IN the January 20th *Philadelphia Inquirer* mentioned Eddie's affinity for harness racing saying Eddie "loves the light harness flyer and leads the pitchers in his league, should also be among the leaders in the matinees."

Connie and many Athletics players headed out of Philadelphia at 4 PM on March 1, destined for Texas. Plank, Waddell, Dygert, and Coombs were the pitchers in the party. Seybold, Hartsel, Davis, Murphy, Schrecongost, and others represented the regular players.

After a seventy-two-hour train ride. the Athletics were training in Marlin, Texas, a small town south of Waco.

Over 6000 fans turned out to see Rube Waddell hurl in an exhibition in Dallas on the 10th. The A's beat the locals 4 to 2.

On March 24th, at Dallas, the A's won an exhibition 8 to 4 and had to hurry to catch the Texas and Houston train headed to New Orleans. In the game, Eddie pitched the first four innings and yielded two runs, but per the reporter, should not have yielded any because the umpire "being utterly unable to fathom the cross-fire delivery. Eddie had to split the plate to get a strike."

While Connie piloted the younger players in a split-squad through the Southern League, Harry Davis led the veterans into New Orleans to face the New York Giants on March 27th. New York beat Coombs 4 to 3 that day.

The next day, Eddie took the mound against McGraw's Giants. In the top of the 1st inning, after Plank retired the first two men, Devlin and Seymour each singled to the outfield and moved up a base on Oldring's throw to try to catch Devlin. Bowerman was next to bat. Eddie got ahead of him, one ball and two strikes. Before Eddie could throw the next pitch, the Giants were accusing him of a balk, which umpire Chief Zimmer disallowed. This set off a half-hour long argument by Giant players and McGraw. As play was finally about to resume, McGraw made a snide comment at Zimmer, who ejected him. This set off an angry face-to-face jawing between the two as the New York players gathered around. Zimmer maintained control and looked at his watch and at McGraw, who still refused to leave. Chief then declared the game forfeit, awarding the A's a 9 to 0 victory.

On the 29th, the Eddie was back on the mound against the Giants and won easily 7 to 0. McGraw refused to continue the series given the forfeit the day before.

Back in Philadelphia on April 3, the A's and Phillies held their traditional inner-city series during the first weeks of April. Meanwhile, on April 7th, Hershey Park opened in Hershey, Pennsylvania.

On April 11th, the Boston Americans were at Columbia Park to open the season. After the usual opening festivities, Jack Coombs battled Cy Young into extra innings, tied at four. Boston scored four in the 14th inning, giving Tannehill the win in relief. After rain and cold delayed the game on the 12th, Waddell beat Winter 4 to 2.

Following the Sunday offday, Plank took the mound on Monday the 15th, topping Boston 3 to 2, Murphy providing the key hit.

The A's were then off to New York to face the Highlanders. Dygert won the first game 9 to 6. On the 17th, Waddell was winning in the 9th, 4 to 2 when he allowed the first two batters to reach. Chief Bender was called in to relieve, and he lost the game, giving up three runs, the Highlanders winning 5 to 4. Coombs dropped the third game, 8 to 4.

Back in Philadelphia, the game on the 19th against Washington was rained out. The A's were back in the winning column the next day, beating the Senators 6 to 5, Bender getting the win.

After the Sunday off, the A's won on Monday, 8 to 7, behind Plank, who needed relief help from Dygert. Rain canceled Tuesday's game.

On Wednesday, the 24th, the A's were in Boston, Coombs beating Cy Young 6 to 1. Bender won the next day, 4 to 2. Dygert threw a one-hitter on the 26th, winning 1 to 0. Rube Vickers dropped the Saturday game 5 to 2.

On Monday, the 29th, the A's were in Washington to face the Senators. Jack Coombs won 2 to 1 with a two-hitter. The A's ended April with a 3-to-2 win behind Plank.

The A's finished the month 10-4, a half-game ahead of Chicago, in 1st place. Eddie started the season 3-0.

After a rainout, the A's lost 4 to 1 to the Senators on May 2nd, Bender taking the hit.

The New York Highlanders were in Philadelphia on the 3rd, beating Coombs 4 to 2 in ten innings. Al Orth won the next one easily for New York, 8 to 0.

After an offday and some rain days, the A's next played in Chicago on the 9th, Plank losing to Patterson, 6 to 0. After rain on the 10th, the A's lost again on the 11th, 7 to 2, behind Vickers. Ed Walsh topped Plank 10 to 3 on Sunday the 12th. The A's finally won, 9 to 1, behind Waddell on the 13th.

After a travel day, the A's were in St. Louis to face the Browns. Coombs fell behind early, 5 to 0, and was replaced by Vickers, and then Dygert. The A's roared back, tying the game at five in the 5th inning, and won with three in the 9th.

The Browns were less kind the next day, beating Plank 4 to 0. Waddell was roughed-up even worse on the 17th, losing 13 to 1.

The team transferred to Detroit for a game on Friday the 18th. Bender and Coombs were ripped, 15 to 8, Cobb tallying four hits. After a needed offday on Sunday, the A's won 1 to 0 on Monday behind Eddie Plank, who five-hit Detroit, two of the hits by Cobb. Waddell took his turn, also shutting out Detroit, 3 to 0, on Tuesday the 21st. Bender lost the next one 6 to 5.

In Cleveland on the 23rd, the A's dropped the first game 5 to 0 behind Coombs. Eddie lost the next one 3 to 0. Waddell lost the third game to Joss on Saturday, 5 to 2.

After a couple days off, the team was back in Philadelphia on the 28th to face Boston. Plank and Winter battled, Eddie prevailing 2 to 1 in eleven innings. The A's then took a doubleheader from the last-place Americans, 4 to 0 as Coombs topped Young, and 4 to 3 behind Waddell. The teams followed this with a double-header split on the 30th. Dygert won the first game 3 to 1, followed by Bender's 6-to-4 loss.

The A's ended the month with an 8-to-2 victory in Washington, Plank getting the win.

The A's completed May with a mediocre 19-18 record. They had slipped to 5th place, seven games back of the hot Chicago White Sox. Eddie's record was now 6-3.

After a rainout and an offday, the teams split a doubleheader on Monday, June 3rd. Coombs lost the first game 2 to 1, followed by Waddell's 8-to-4 win in ten innings.

This same day, Eddie took ownership of his parents' farm in Straban Township. At some point after this, he had a new house built on the property for his parents where they lived until David no longer wanted to farm. At that point, they moved to 1025 Old Harrisburg Road.

At Columbia Park on the 4th, Eddie lost 10 to 6 to the White Sox. After another rainout on the 5th, the A's won 3 to 0 on the 6th, Waddell beating Walsh. Plank got his revenge on the 7th, beating Chicago 5 to 4.

The Browns were next in town, falling 4 to 2 on June 8th, Dygert getting the win. After the Sunday off, the teams battled on Monday the 10th, Waddell winning 3 to 0. The Browns beat Eddie by the same score the next day, while Dygert flipped it the other way, 3 to 0, on the 12th.

From June 10th through August 10th, the Peking to Paris motor race was held. Prince Scipione Borghese, an Italian aristocrat, won the race driving a 7-liter 35/45 hp Itala.

Cleveland was in town on Thursday the 13th, Waddell losing 6 to 5. After a rainout on Friday, the A's won on Saturday, 8 to 6, Plank picking up the win. Following the offday on Sunday, the A's won 4 to 1 on Monday, Coombs shutting them down.

Detroit was next at Columbia Park on the 18th. Waddell lost 6 to 2, Cobb getting two hits including a triple. Dygert won the next one 4 to 1. Plank "did some clever work with the ball" to shut out the Tigers 4 to 0 on only four hits. Waddell was hit early in the next game and was replaced by Bender. The A's lost 5 to 2, Rube taking the loss.

On Saturday, June 22nd, the Washington Senators were in town. Coombs shut them out 4 to 0. The A's then swept a doubleheader on Monday the 24th, Plank 9 to 2 and Dygert 6 to 3 getting wins. Eddie hit a triple to help himself. Philadelphia nabbed two more on the 25th, 3 to 1 and 3 to 2, Coombs and Bender registering the wins. The last game was rained out.

After the offday, the A's dropped a game in Boston, 1 to 0 on the 27th. Coombs lost 1 to 0 and left after the 3rd inning with a sore arm, replaced by Dygert.

The next day, Eddie allowed only two hits through nine innings and had two hits himself, but the game was tied 3 to 3. Bender lost it 4 to 3 in twelve innings. The next game, Waddell shut out Boston 3 to 0.

The A's ended the month of June 35-26, in 3rd place, five games back of Chicago. Eddie was now 9-5 on the season.

The A's started off July with a 5-to-1 loss to Boston, Cy Young beating Dygert.

In New York on July 2nd, Waddell, Bender, and Dygert all participated in an 8-to-7 loss. The next day, "Plank's Home Run Did the Trick" as Eddie won 3 to 1, including a four-bagger of his own. The teams then split the doubleheader on the 4th, Bender winning 3 to 1 and Waddell losing 7 to 3.

The A's then headed west, arriving in Detroit for a game on the 5th. Dygert lost the game 5 to 0, Cobb getting three hits. The next day, they were in Chicago, tying the White Sox 1 to 1, Plank battling for all thirteen innings. He even had two hits at the plate. Ed Walsh shut out Dygert on the 7th, 6 to 0. Chief won the next one 5 to 2. Young Bill Bartley started on the 9th and lost 5 to 1. It would be his only big league decision.

"Sox Tied Up by Eddie Plank" was the headline the next day. Eddie beat Ed Walsh 2 to 1.

Off to St. Louis, the A's beat the Browns 6 to 5 on July 11th. Rube Waddell got the win with help from Chief. Bender then followed with an easy 9-to-1 win. Waddell took the next, 2 to 1.

After the Sunday off, the A's were rained out in Cleveland on the 15th. Well-rested, Eddie beat Addie Joss 3 to 2 on Tuesday the 16th. The hot A's won again the next day, 5 to 1, behind Waddell. Bender followed with a five-hit shutout.

Off to Detroit again on the 19th, the A's fell 6 to 1 behind Dygert. On Saturday, the 20th, the A's lost again, 4 to 3, nipping Waddell. After the Sunday off, Eddie took the mound on the 22nd and was leading 3 to 1 into the 8th when the Tigers scored five. They won 6 to 3. The A's traveled home on the 23rd.

On July 24th, in Philadelphia, the A's faced off against the champion White Sox who currently led the A's by six games. Waddell won the first game 3 to 1. The A's then took a double-header on the 25th, Bender two-hitting Ed Walsh 2 to 0 in the first game and Dygert winning the second 7 to 3. The A's were now three games back. Eddie made it two games back with a clutch 4-to-3 win on the 27th. The A's had won four in a row. Chicago got one back the next day, 7 to 2, Walsh beating Waddell.

After the Sunday off, St. Louis came to town, but the game on Monday the 29th was rained out. Bender won 2 to 1 on the 30th. Eddie "vultured" a win on the 31st, picking up for Dygert in extra innings after the Browns tied the game at seven. The A's won in the 11th inning, 8 to 7.

The A's finished July 51-36, 2 1/2 games back of the Chicago White Sox. Cleveland and Detroit were also ahead of them. Eddie's season record now stood at 14-6.

Eddie started August with a four-hit shutout of the Browns, winning 2 to 0.

On August 2nd, the A's easily beat the Naps, 9 to 1, Bender the beneficiary. Over in Washington, Walter Johnson of the Senators made his debut, losing 3 to 2 to Detroit. Ty Cobb was the first hit yielded on a bunt single. On the 3rd, the Naps got one back 5 to 3, Waddell falling.

After the Sunday off, the A's swept two from the Naps on Monday. Eddie won the first game 6 to 2. Waddell took the afternoon game 12 to 6. The A's were now in 3rd place, two games behind Detroit, Chicago a half-game out. The A's won again, 4 to 2, on the 6th, Dygert pulling them to within a game-and-a-half.

Bender's 4 to 2 win on the 7th against Detroit at home made it a mere half-game, the Tigers and White Sox now tied for 1st.

Eddie lost 5 to 3 on the 8th. Rain prevented the game on the 9th. Chief thwarted the Tigers from scoring on the 10th, winning 1 to 0. The A's were now only a half-game back of Detroit, in 2nd place. After the Sunday off, the A's moved into first place on the 12th, winning 7 to 3 behind Waddell. Eddie padded the lead, winning 3 to 0 on a three-hitter, but Detroit inched back a game with a 9 to 2 win on the 14th, Dygert taking the hit.

Back on the road, the A's were in Cleveland on the 15th. Bender won 3 to 2. The teams split a doubleheader on the 16th, Dygert losing in relief of Coombs, 8 to 7, and then winning 7 to 2.

The Naps beat Plank 6 to 0 in the next game, but the A's returned the favor 10 to 8 on Monday the 19th. Dygert picked up the win again.

Next, the A's were in Chicago and dropped the first game 4 to 1 behind Plank, all the runs scoring in the 1st inning. The Sox were now only a half-game back. Chief lost a heartbreaker the next day, 1 to 0, vaulting the Sox into 1st place. Waddell flipped it back, winning 2 to 0 and yielding only two hits on the 22nd.

Off to St. Louis, the A's won 1 to 0 on the 23rd of August. Plank scattered six hits for the win. On the 24th, the A's and Browns split a doubleheader, a 6-to-4 win for Coombs and a 6-to-4 loss for Bender. The Sox and A's were now tied for 1st place. The teams split another doubleheader on Sunday the 25th, Dygert losing 2 to 1 and Waddell winning 1 to 0. The idle Sox were now a half-game up.

After traveling home on the 26th the A's were off until the 29th when New York came to town. Eddie lost 5 to 2. Waddell won the next day 6 to 3. Chief won the last game of the month 3 to 0, a nice thirty-second birthday present for Eddie.

The A's ended August at 69-46, 1 1/2 games behind Detroit. Eddie was now 18-10 on the season.

Washington was in for a doubleheader on Labor Day, September 2nd. Coombs dropped the morning game, 3 to 1. Eddie beat Walter Johnson 3 to 2 in the afternoon. The A's were a game back of Detroit.

The bats then went wild in a doubleheader on the 3rd, the A's sweeping. Dygert won the first game 15 to 9, Waddell the second, 9 to 1. Detroit won their game, the A's pulling to within a half-game.

The Highlanders came to Philadelphia on the 4th. Detroit's loss coupled with Bender's 4 to 2 win put the A's back in 1st place by a half-game.

The A's played two on the 5th, Waddell losing the first game 6 to 3. Bill Bartley and Jack Chesbro battled to a 2-to-2 tie through eight innings in the second game, which was called because of darkness. Detroit lost in Cleveland, the standings remaining the same.

The next day, Philadelphia and New York were at it again for two more games, the A's sweeping. Eddie won the morning game

6 to 4, Dygert the afternoon, 6 to 2. Detroit won their game but was now a full game behind.

Chief was big the next day, winning 8 to 3 to keep pace, however, the Tigers won on Sunday the 8th while the A's rested, pulling to within a half-game again.

Off to Boston for a game on the 9th of September described as one of the quickest and most exciting of the season. Rube Waddell and Cy Young exchanged zeros for thirteen innings, the game ending in a scoreless tie. The Tigers, meanwhile, lost to the White Sox and slipped to a full game back. The A's and Americans split the doubleheader on the 10th, Winter and the Americans beating Coombs 5 to 0 in the first game after which Eddie shut out the Americans 3 to 0 in a game called after seven innings. Detroit did not play, so the standings did not move. Both teams lost on September 11th, Chief dropping the game with Boston 5 to 4.

The *Gettysburg Compiler* on September 11th contained an article by George W. Graham from the *North American* describing Eddie Plank as "... the team's other great southpaw. He thinks all the time. One of the cardinal rules is never to pitch a ball over the center of the plate, and he remarked to the writer once he did so it was an accident. 'Work the corners' would be his advice to young pitchers. Plank invented what is known as the cross-fire. It is his best ball being especially deadly when used against left-hand batsmen. Any of them will tell you they would sooner bat against Waddell than Plank. The cross-fire is delivered side-arm and cuts across the corner of the plate so close and sharply that the batter never gets a chance to meet it fairly."

Boston came to Philadelphia on the 12th of September. Dygert won 7 to 1 while Detroit won and tied. The standings remained one game to the A's' favor. The next day, while the Tigers split a doubleheader, the Americans and A's were tied at six after seven innings. Coombs and Winter were the starters. Eddie relieved and threw several scoreless innings, but the offense could not break through. The game ended 6 to 6 after thirteen frames. Finally, on September 14th, the A's got some breathing room. The Tigers dropped two in St. Louis while the A's swept the Americans at home. Bender beat Young in the first game 7 to 6. Dygert won the afternoon game 5 to 2. The Tigers fell to three games behind, in 3rd place, the White Sox now in 2nd place 2 1/2 back. While the A's rested on Sunday, the Sox lost their game, slipping into a 2nd place tie at three games back.

The Highlanders were next in, Plank against Chesbro on September 16th. Eddie allowed a couple runs in the 1st inning and was "out of form." The Highlanders held on to win 3 to 2. Meanwhile, the Tigers beat the White Sox, pulling a game closer. New York got to Coombs early in the second game and won easily 11 to 3. Detroit won again and was now only a game back. While rain delayed the third game with New York, the Sox and Tigers split a doubleheader. The weather was a factor again on the 19th, preventing all three contenders from playing.

Back in action on the 20th, the Browns came to town and downed the A's 4 to 1, Waddell taking the loss. Meanwhile, Detroit won their game and Chicago swept a doubleheader. The standings were now extremely tight with the Tigers and A's tied for 1st, the Sox only a game-and-a-half back.

Eddie was back in form the next day, winning 6 to 0 while Detroit split a doubleheader. The A's regained a half-game lead.

Following a Sunday offday and rain on Monday, the Chicago White Sox were in town on the 24th. Walsh beat Waddell 8 to 3, and the A's fell a half-game back of Detroit, who won. "Eddie Plank Keeps the Athletics on Top" read the headline the next day, the A's winning 5 to 0 on Plank's two-hitter. Detroit won their game, keeping their narrow half-game lead.

Jimmy Dygert won the final game 3 to 1 against Walsh on the 26th, pushing the White Sox further behind and keeping pace with the winning Tigers.

September 27th, Ty Cobb and the 1st place Detroit Tigers were in town to defend their minuscule half-game lead. Eddie Plank took the mound against Wild Bill Donovan before 17,000 fans at Columbia Park. The *Philadelphia Inquirer* described some of the ardent rooters: "... an aggregation of crazed Icemen, prototypes of the Great and Only Iceman, marching in a bunch with a weird collection of noisemakers including a worn bass drum, an ancient pair of cymbals, and a horn that had done service on a fish wagon. They bore aloft a wonderful canvas banner upon which had been painted 'We Are the Icemen Rooters Club, Patented.' And all through the performance their drum boomed and their cymbals clanged and their horn screeched and they dared anyone to say they weren't happy ... When Plank fanned Cobb, the stick wonder of the Tigers, in the seventh the band brayed 'Go Way Back and Sit Down' which didn't cheer up the sore slugger at all."

Unfortunately for Eddie and the A's, Ty's boys won this one 5 to 4 and were now ahead by a game-and-a-half.

Rain prevented play on Saturday the 28th and no game was scheduled on Sunday the 29th. The series resumed on Monday the 30th, a doubleheader on the slate. Over 24,000 fans crowded Columbia Park, many of them stationed in the outfield, behind a rope. Many thousands more watched from housetops and other vantage points. Jimmy Dygert was the starting pitcher for the A's, but got into trouble early, and was replaced by Rube Waddell. Meanwhile, the A's built a 7-to-1 lead through seven innings. After some sloppy play and some great hitting by the Tigers, the A's took an 8-to-6 lead into the 9th inning, Waddell still on the mound. Crawford singled in the top of the 9th, followed by Ty Cobb. The Georgia Peach promptly sent a ball over the right-field fence, tying the game. It had been said that Connie Mack was so stunned by the swat, he fell off the bench. Plank was then inserted into the game in place of Waddell. Each team scored a run in the 11th inning, and the A's should have won the game in the bottom of the 14th inning.

"... that they did not win out in the 14th was due to an outrageous and high-handed usurpation of umpirical authority on the part of Silk O'Laughlin. Harry Davis led off with a fly to deep left. All through the game when a ball was hit into the crowd the spectators broke ground for the fielders, and in this instance an officer, getting out of Crawford's way, ran across him. There was not the slightest evidence of interference, Crawford reached the ball while on a full run. It struck his mitt and dropped out again. The claim of interference was made and, to the surprise of everyone, it was allowed by O'Laughlin. Of course, a vigorous kick followed, in the course of which the players, being keyed up to high tension, became unusually demonstrative. Rossman became exceptionally offensive, and in the excitement, Donovan pushed Monte Cross. Waddell, thinking that Cross was in danger, got into it, and a few of the more hot-headed of the spectators rushed on the diamond. The police were quickly on the job, and what might have been a serious affair was averted. There was not the slightest justification for O'Laughlin's misinterpretation of the rules. Crawford was not interfered with. He reached the ball and muffed it. That was all there was to it. That decision cost the Athletics the game, for Murphy followed with a single on which

Davis could have easily scored from second. And it may cost them the championship."

Eddie toiled for three more innings until the game was called due to darkness, tied at nine. "The game and the crowd will make the day ever memorable in baseball history as the greatest ever," concluded the *Philadelphia Inquirer*.

The A's ended the month of September 83-55, a half-game behind the Tigers who were 87-56. Eddie was 23-12 on the season.

Cleveland was in town to start the month of October. Jimmy Dygert took the slab for the A's and impressed, allowing only four hits in a clutch 4-to-0 victory. Unfortunately for the A's, the Tigers beat Washington to maintain the game-and-a-half margin. The next day, Wednesday, October 2nd, the Tigers swept two from the Senators in Washington. Eddie was on the mound for the A's against the Naps. It did not go well, resulting in a tough 4-to-3 loss. The A's were now three games behind.

Detroit won again on the 3rd. Little Jimmy Dygert did it again for the A's, hurling a two-hit gem that kept pace, the A's winning 4 to 0.

On October 4th, the A's traveled to Washington to play a doubleheader. The teams split the two games, the Senators winning the first one 2 to 1 in ten innings, Walter Johnson defeating Eddie Plank. The second game was an easy 8-to-0 win for the A's behind Dygert, who pitched another shutout! Detroit did not play this day, keeping the deficit at three games.

The A's were almost out of chances. The next day, Washington and Philadelphia played two more, the A's sweeping them both. The A's won the first game 4 to 2 in 15 innings, Vickers winning in relief. The second game was a five-inning 4-to-0 win also for Vickers. Meanwhile, in St. Louis, Detroit won and clinched the pennant.

Detroit lost a doubleheader the next day, but it didn't matter. The A's finished the season 1 1/2 games out in second place at 88-57. Eddie had a very strong season at 24-16 with a 2.20 ERA. He led the team with 40 starts and 343.2 innings pitched. Jimmy Dygert was 21-8, 2.34. Rube Waddell was 19-13, 2.15, and led the team in strikeouts with 232. Chief Bender was 16-8 and Jack Coombs 6-9. Addie Joss and Doc White led the league with 27 wins.

At the plate, rookie shortstop Simon Nicholls led the team with a .302 batting average, trailing Ty Cobb's .350. Harry Davis led with 8 home runs, trailing Dave Brain's 13, but Socks Seybold led with 92 RBI. Topsy Hartsel topped the team with 93 runs scored and 106 walks.

On October 12th, the Chicago Cubs won the World Series over the Detroit Tigers.

October 22nd, there is a run on the banks in New York as the Panic of 1907 began. The stock market dropped 50% from its high. On the 24th, J. P. Morgan and other millionaires pooled their money and invested millions in plummeting shares, ending the crisis.

The *Gettysburg Compiler* announced on November 6th that Ira Plank had signed a contract to pitch for the New York Highlanders next season.

On November 16th, Oklahoma was admitted as the 46th state.

On December 16th, the U.S. "Great White Fleet" began its circumnavigation of the globe. The friendly mission was ordered by Theodore Roosevelt to illustrate American naval power around the world.

As the first electric ball was dropped on Times Square on New Year's Eve, it was apparent the A's were an aging team. Monte Cross, 37, had already lost his job to Nicholls. But, Jimmy Collins at third base was also 37, and Socks Seybold was 36. Topsy Hartsel and Harry Davis were both 33. The catchers, Ossee Schrecongost, 32, and Doc Powers, 36, were also aging. Even Danny Murphy was 30. Connie knew this 1907 pennant run was likely the last for this crew.

On the mound, Plank at 32, was the oldest on the staff, with only Waddell past 30 years of age. The rest of the pitchers were still in their 20s and would be the core of the upcoming rebuild.

Eddie following through.

Eddie warming up.

Former major leaguer Chief Zimmer who umpired in the spring of 1907.

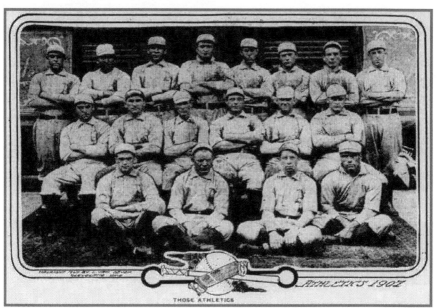

The 1907 Philadelphia Athletics.

Athletics in 1st place on August 12, 1907.

Topsy Hartsel at the plate on August 10, 1907.

A packed crowd at Columbia Park on August 10, 1907.

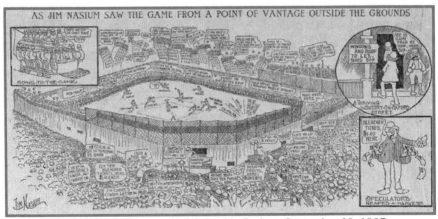

Cartoon depicting a packed Columbia Park on September 30, 1907.

Cartoon about confidence in winning the 1907 pennant.

Cartoon about the rain during the pennant race in late 1907.

Eddie Plank in the paper on September 30, 1907.

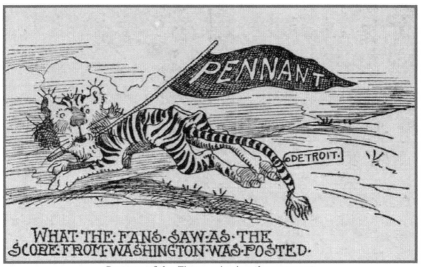

Cartoon of the Tigers winning the pennant.

1908:
GRAND UPHILL GAME

I N EARLY JANUARY, Connie Mack returned from a two-month trip to California. While he was primarily there for a vacation, he managed to sign a young pitcher, aged eighteen, named Harry Krause. Mack discussed several other young pitchers from the south he was keeping his eyes on. He also announced that, due to an early Mardi Gras, the A's would leave for New Orleans on or about February 26th, returning on April 1st. Given the near-miss the prior season, Mack was very optimistic about 1908 and wasn't planning any major changes to the lineup.

On January 13th, a fire at the Rhoads Opera House in Boyertown, Pennsylvania, killed 170. It was one of the worst tragedies in Pennsylvania's history and garnered thousands of dollars in donations from Philadelphians to assist the survivors.

In early February, Monte Cross announced his retirement and intention to manage the Kansas City team in the American Association. A large dinner was planned in his honor for February 24th, before the team headed off to spring training. Mack, who had just returned from a trip to the mid-west, was elated with the condition of third baseman Jimmy Collin's knee, which had been operated on during the off-season. "Last year Jim was hog fat and unable to play up to his best form because on account of his game leg he was unable to train."

Mack announced the spring training schedule which included stops in Mobile, Birmingham, Memphis, Nashville, Louisville, Indianapolis, Columbus, and Lancaster following training in New Orleans. The traditional inner-city series was scheduled for April 4th.

On February 8th, Connie announced the sale of Rube Waddell to the St. Louis Browns. The amount of money involved was not initially divulged. A lot of discussions followed for many weeks, recounting the good and bad of Waddell and his positive and negative effects on the team and pennant races.

On February 12th, the first around-the-world car race began, starting at Times Square in New York City, ultimately ending in Paris, France.

On February 24th, Connie Mack and Ben Shibe announced plans for a new ballpark, to be ready for next season, in North Philadelphia to be bounded by Lehigh and Somerset Streets, between 20th and 21st Streets. That evening, the dinner for Monte Cross at the Majestic Hotel was described by the *Philadelphia Inquirer* as "the greatest gathering of baseball people on record." Eddie did not attend, nor did most of the players.

On February 26th, the *Gettysburg Compiler* mentioned Eddie Plank would be helping to coach the college team for a few weeks at the beginning of the season to help assess the players and teach the pitchers. For months, Mack had tried to get Plank for the same salary he had received the last two years, $3500. The salary had stayed the same out of concern about Eddie's arm, which had been demonstrated as healthy. Each time Connie mailed a contract, Eddie tore it up. Eddie felt he deserved a raise and threatened to stay and coach the Gettysburg College team. Hearing this, with spring training approaching, Mack quickly sent along a contract for $4000 by registered mail. Eddie signed it and hurried off for spring training, passing through Hanover in the evening to catch the group in Philadelphia for the 8:55 PM departure. This same day, baseball announced the adoption of the sacrifice fly rule.

In the first game of the spring, on Monday, March 1st, in New Orleans, the A's upended the Pelicans 4 to 1. Eddie did not participate, but three of the younger pitchers did. The team took a break the next day for the Fat Tuesday celebration.

On March 4, a fire at the Collinwood School near Cleveland, Ohio, killed 174 students, teachers, and rescuers. It was another example of tragedy by fire that was all too common in the early 20th century.

The next day, the A's beat the Pelicans 3 to 2 behind three young pitchers. Socks Seybold scored the winning run in the 9th, but severely injured his knee sliding into home plate. He was seen using crutches later and would be lost to the team for some time.

Old teammate Lave Cross had started playing for New Orleans of the Southern League following his retirement from Washington the prior year. He had a part, as did Rube Vickers who was on loan from Connie, in beating the A's on March 8th, 5 to 3.

Eddie finally threw a few innings on the 9th in a game between the veterans and the "Yanigans," the pet name used for the younger players in camp in those days. The veterans won 12 to 7, but Chief Bender, playing second for the Yanigans, was robbed of a homer when a line drive hit a horse in the ass. The ball was ruled a double. The article in the *Philadelphia Inquirer* was not clear if the ball was retrieved and what condition it was in!

Eddie got some work against the Pelicans on the 11th, the team winning 6 to 2. Socks Seybold was now wearing a light cast and Rube Oldring was under the weather.

The A's won the game the next day, 3 to 2, Jack Coombs playing right field because of the shortage of outfielders. Said Connie of Coombs, "I am confident he'd make a first-class outfielder. He is a good sticker and being in the game every day he is bound to improve in that respect, and besides, he is one of the fastest men on the team."

On the 14th, Eddie played right field while Coombs pitched for a "patched-up" team that was weakened by the Yanigans playing in Gulfport. Lave Cross led the Pelicans with three hits as they beat the veterans 7 to 3.

On the 16th, the team began its homeward odyssey, stopping in Mobile for a 4-to-0 win. Coombs played right field, and Bender pitched most of the game.

Jimmy Collins had three hits and Coombs two as the A's topped Birmingham on the 19th, 7 to 1. Chief did most of the pitching.

In Memphis on the 21st, the team won 8 to 5 with Vickers and Dygert on the mound. After a rainout, the team was on to Nashville. Connie said the twenty-four players left with the team would likely stick with the club for the start of the season. Oldring and Seybold were still laid-up.

On the 23rd, the team stopped in Nashville in the rain and arranged to continue to Louisville. The train probably should have kept going as the Louisville team from the American Association routed the A's 9 to 4. However, the A's got their revenge the next day, 6 to 4. Jimmy Collins was the hitting star.

In Indianapolis on the 27th, the A's won 3 to 2. On the 29th, in Columbus, Ohio, the A's tuned-up with a 3-to-0 win.

The train stopped in Lancaster, Pennsylvania, for an exhibition against the Tri-State League team there. Eddie Plank pitched a few of the middle innings in an easy 7-to-0 win. Shortstop Simon Nicholls had four hits.

Back in Philadelphia, the A's scrimmaged the University of Pennsylvania at Columbia Park and won easily 9 to 3. The subsequent series against the Phillies was postponed due to rain and cold weather. They finally played the first game on April 6th, the A's winning behind Nick Carter, 5 to 0. The A's took the series, five days later, winning by the same score behind Bender. They were City Champions.

On April 14th, Opening Day, the Athletics were in New York to face the Highlanders. Carter started for the A's and Coombs was in right field. "Slow" Joe Doyle had the honors for New York. The two traded zeros for eleven innings before New York walked-off with a run in the 12th. It would be the only win for Doyle all season. Rain prevented a game on the 15th. The next day, the A's lost again, 2 to 1, Vickers taking the hit. On the 17th, the A's notched their first win, 8 to 2, behind rookie Biff Schlitzer.

In Boston on the 18th, Coombs, Collins, and Nicholls each had two hits in support of Jimmy Dygert as the A's beat the Red Sox 4 to 2. But, after the Sunday off, the Red Sox swept a doubleheader on Monday the 20th. Vickers lost to Cy Young 8 to 1 in the morning game. Carter lost the afternoon game 5 to 3. Vickers got one back the next day, 7 to 0.

On April 21st, American explorer Frederick Cook claimed to have reached the North Pole. The accuracy of his claim has been in dispute, though has gained more favor in recent times.

The Athletics' home opener was Wednesday, April 23rd, at Columbia Park against the New York Highlanders. Eddie Plank had the honor of starting and Jack Coombs was in right. This was a good thing this day. As described in the *Philadelphia Inquirer*, "... Jack Coombs delivered the goods in a way that started 18,210 fanatics on the road to padded cells ... for the faithful would have killed anyone insane enough to disagree with the dope that it was Jack's great stop of Conroy's drive to the crowd on the right field borderline in the seventh chapter, and his phenomenal throw to Murphy, thereby causing Camden's 'gentleman farmer' to die at second, that had much to do with the sorrow in the Highlander's camp."

During the opening festivities, while the "Star Spangled Banner" was played, the flag was raised to only half-staff in honor of the recent passing, on the 20th, of Henry Chadwick "The Father of Baseball." Chadwick, born an Englishman, was a writer and fan of baseball who devised the box score and many of the game's early statistics. He was the editor of the *Spalding Baseball Guide*, among others.

The mayor then appeared in Ben Shibe's box and threw the first ball out to umpire Sheridan to a great roar. Sheridan then tossed it to Plank, who delivered a first-pitch strike to Niles. The game was underway.

Coombs great play ended a potential Highlander rally in the 7th, helping Plank preserve a 2-to-2 tie. The A's added a run in the 8th, and Eddie notched his first win of the season, 3 to 2. He also hit a double in the game.

After Dygert lost 5 to 3 on the 23rd, Bender won a twelve-inning affair, 3 to 2 on the 24th. Meanwhile, a tornado ripped through Amite, Louisiana, and Purvis, Mississippi, killing 143 and injuring 770, just a few miles north of New Orleans where the A's had trained the prior month.

The next day, Dygert was ahead 4 to 0 in the 8th, when New York rallied for five runs. The A's answered with five in their own turn and won the game 9 to 5.

After the Sunday off, the Senators were in town on the 27th. Vickers won a close one, 2 to 1. Despite the triple-play pulled by Davis, Murphy, and Nicholls, the A's lost the game on the 28th, 6 to 4. Eddie took the loss, lasting only until falling behind 5 to 0 in the 5th. The A's won 3 to 2 behind Dygert the next day, but Carter dropped the last game of the month, 2 to 1.

The A's finished the month of April 8-7, one game back in 4th place. Eddie started the season 1-1.

May opened with a 5-to-4 extra-inning win at home against the Red Sox. Vickers picked up the win in relief. Dygert was brilliant on the 2nd, three-hitting Boston and defeating George Winter 2 to 0. After the Sunday off, the A's won again on the 4th, 3 to 2, Vickers beating Cy Young. This put the A's in a 1st place tie with New York. Schlitzer pitched the team into a 1st place lead with a 5-to-2 win on May 5th.

Rain interrupted the game on May 6th against Washington, allowing Mack to shift his pitching rotation. The *Philadelphia Inquirer* also revealed why Waddell was sold before the season: "It develops that Connie Mack was virtually forced to get rid of Rube Waddell by members of his team. The players put it up to Mack to dispose of the erratic southpaw or have discord in the ranks all season." Apparently, Waddell reneged on a gentleman's agreement concerning the money from the barnstorming tour some of the players participated in after the 1907 season. It caused a lot of hard feelings. The game was rained out again on the 7th. This was unfortunate, because Eddie's father, David Plank, was in town to see the game.

Chief Bender finally pitched in Washington on the 8th, losing 3 to 2. The A's slipped back to a 1st place tie with New York. The next day, they lost again, 6 to 2, and slipped to 2nd place. After the Sunday off, which was the first time Mother's Day was observed, the A's beat Washington 7 to 2 on Monday the 11th. Schlitzer picked up the win.

The A's were back home against the White Sox on May 12th. The A's' bats were lively, including a double by Plank, as Eddie won easily, 8 to 3. Chicago scored all their runs in the 1st inning before "Plank got his curveball working to perfection." The A's again tied for 1st place. On the 13th, Ed Walsh beat Dygert 2 to 1. The A's slipped back a game. Rube Vickers followed with a three-hit shutout, defeating the White Sox 1 to 0. The game on the 15th was rained out.

The St. Louis Browns dropped by on May 16th. A young utility infielder, playing right field, named Eddie Collins, now 21 in his third season, hit the game-winning single to lift Jimmy Dygert to a 1-to-0 victory. It would be the first of many contributions Eddie Collins would make to the A's over the years.

After the Sunday off, the A's beat the Browns 12 to 10 on Monday in what the *Philadelphia Inquirer* described as a "Grand Uphill Game." The A's used five pitchers, and Eddie Collins provided three base hits. The A's trailed 9 to 2 and 10 to 4 at different points before roaring back in the later innings. In the end, the A's found them tied, once again, with New York for 1st place.

However, it was short-lived thanks to former mate Rube Waddell, who beat Chief Bender 5 to 2 in his return to Philadelphia. The Browns also won on Wednesday the 20th, defeating Eddie Plank, 3 to 1.

On May 21st, the Cleveland Naps were in town. Rube Vickers won 1 to 0, but the A's lost by the same score the next day, Dygert losing in a six-inning affair. The Naps then beat Carter, 4 to 2, on the 23rd. The A's had slipped to two games behind, in 3rd place. Vickers lost another close one, 3 to 2, to close out the series on Monday the 25th.

The Tigers came to town for the first time in 1907 on the 26th. Eddie pitched and gave up only three singles, none to Cobb or Crawford. Unfortunately, the Athletics couldn't score and lost 1 to 0. On the 27th, the A's got a little revenge, winning 5 to 4 with two runs in the bottom of the 9th. Eddie Collins pinch-hit for pitcher Harry Krause, making his first major-league start. Collins hit a single and scored the tying run later in the inning. The win pulled the A's to within a game of 1st place. Jimmy Dygert was ripped in the next game, the A's losing 10 to 2.

On May 29th, the Athletics were in New York to face the Highlanders, trailing by only a game. They split a doubleheader, Vickers losing the morning game, 6 to 5, while Schlitzer won the afternoon, 1 to 0. Eddie had a pinch-hit double in the first game. The A's stayed a game back. The game on the 30th was canceled due to rain and the teams were off on Sunday the 31st.

The A's finished May at 20-18, only one game behind New York and Detroit, and a half-game behind St. Louis, in 4th place. Eddie was now 2-2 on the season, pitching less frequently than in season's past.

On Monday, June 1st, Washington was in town. Eddie won easily, 6 to 1. Dygert dropped the game on the 2nd, 5 to 2. Chief won the third game handily, 11 to 5, with Eddie Collins in center field and Coombs in right. The win tied the Athletics with Cleveland for 1st place.

The A's were off on the 4th to travel west to St. Louis. Cleveland beat New York to push the A's back a half-game before they arrived in the Gateway City. Rain prevented the game on the 5th, the A's slipping to a game back with another Cleveland win. Finally, on the 6th of June, Eddie took the mound and was brilliant, hurling a three-hit shutout, defeating the Browns 2 to 0.

The A's were back in 1st place by percentage points. It was their high-water mark for the season. The next day, Powell two-hit the A's, Schlitzer taking a 1-to-0 defeat. The A's fell a half-game back. The team lost the next game 10 to 0, Rube Waddell crushing his ex-mates, though Socks Seybold was back in the lineup.

At Chicago on the 9th of June, the A's lost again 10 to 0, Walsh beating Bender. The White Sox swept the next three, making it a four-game drubbing. Though only 5 1/2 back, the A's were now in the second division, in 6th place.

After a 2-to-1 loss to the Tigers on Saturday the 13th, the losing streak finally ended on the 14th. Vickers won 5 to 3 in relief of Schlitzer. But, the A's lost the final two to the Tigers, dropping three of four.

The A's were next in Cleveland, losing the first two games of the series before pulling out a 9-to-2 win on the 22nd, Plank picking up the win. The westward road trip ended with the A's at 25-30, nine games behind in 5th place.

The A's began their homestand on June 23rd with a 9-to-6 win over the Highlanders.

The next day, former President Grover Cleveland died and New York and Philadelphia tied 6 to 6. The A's then split a doubleheader, Plank beating Orth 3 to 0 on the morning of the 25th. Bender lost the second game on an error by Eddie Collins, who was playing shortstop. The A's took another from the Highlanders the next day, making it three of four.

Dygert beat Washington 6 to 0 on the 27th. Vickers followed with a 4-to-0 win on Monday the 29th. The A's finished the month with a 3-to-1 win on the 30th. Plank won in relief of Coombs. Also this day, Cy Young pitched his third and final no-hitter, beating New York, 8 to 0.

For the month of June, the A's went 11-13 and were now 31-31, six games behind in 5th place.

The A's beat the Senators on July 1st, 2-0, Dygert hurling the shutout.

Boston was in town on the 2nd. Bender picked up a win, 4 to 1. After rain on the 3rd, the teams played a doubleheader on Independence Day, each winning one. Vickers threw a two-hit shutout in the morning game, winning 2 to 0. Eddie lost the afternoon game, 4 to 3.

The Highlanders were next in town on July 6th. The A's won 6 to 5 behind Coombs in relief. At 35-32, the Athletics had crept to 4 1/2 games back in 4th place.

This day, Robert Peary began to sail for the North Pole.

Next, the A's dropped three of four to St. Louis, the only win coming on the 8th when Bender shut them out 2 to 0. This was followed by three losses in five games against the White Sox. Plank won 5 to 1 on the 13th. Dygert won 7 to 2 on the 15th. The team then split four games with Detroit. Plank beat them on the 16th, 5 to 3 and Dygert on the 18th, 11 to 5. The homestand ended with the A's taking 2 of 3 from the Naps. Vickers won 4 to 2 on the 21st and 1 to 0 on the 23rd.

The team then headed west, playing the White Sox on the 25th in Chicago. Plank was knocked out early, and then Schlitzer was hammered, resulting in a 12-to-2 loss. The A's fell to 42-42, ten games behind in 5th place. While they briefly went above .500 a couple days later, they ended July 44-46, twelve games back in 5th place.

In late August, Eddie took a vacation at home in Gettysburg and then returned to Philadelphia to shut out the Tigers 1 to 0. It was one of the few highlights during the remainder of the season.

One of the lowlights was Chicago White Sox Frank Smith's no-hitter of the Athletics September 20th, defeating Eddie Plank.

Over in the National League, on September 23rd, during a key game in the vicious pennant race between the Chicago Cubs and New York Giants, young Fred Merkle of the Giants made a base-running blunder forever known as Merkle's Boner. By failing to touch second in the bottom of the 9th inning, he was ruled out via force, disallowing the winning run for the Giants. The game ended tied 1 to 1 in what has been called "the most controversial game in baseball history."

The first Model T was produced by Henry Ford on September 27th.

On October 2nd, Addie Joss pitched a perfect game, beating Ed Walsh 1 to 0, who had struck out 15. It was perhaps the finest pitcher's duel in baseball history. Walsh would lead the league with 40 wins and 269 strikeouts. Joss would lead with a 1.16 ERA.

On October 8th, the Cubs won the makeup game for Merkle's Boner, winning the National League pennant.

The rest of the way, the Athletics struggled on the road and went 24-39 to finish at 68-85, in 6th place, twenty-two games back of 1st place Detroit. Eddie, now thirty-three, finished the season 14-16 with a 2.17 ERA. He only started 28 games. Rube Vickers was the ace of the staff, going 18-19, 2.21. Dygert was 11-15. Bender was 8-9.

At the plate, Eddie Collins led the team with a .273 average, trailing Ty Cobb at .350. Cobb also led the league with 108 RBI, greatly surpassing Danny Murphy with only 66. Harry Davis led the team with 5 home runs, trailing Detroit's Sam Crawford, who had 7. Topsy Hartsel led the team with 73 runs.

Socks Seybold, who had been injured in the spring, finished with a .215 average and no home runs in only 130 at-bats. It would be his final big league action.

Jimmy Collins, who had recovered from his knee surgery and looked so promising early-on, finished his big-league career with a .217 average.

Ossee Schrecongost was sold to the White Sox late in the season, and closed out his long career, hitting only .222 in his final season with the A's.

Waiting in the wings was a young third baseman named Frank Home Run Baker, who had 9 hits in 33 at-bats the final month. Another youngster, only twenty-years-old, named Shoeless Joe Jackson had been called up by Connie. Jackson had only 3 hits in 23 at-bats in his debut.

In the World Series, the Chicago Cubs defeated the Detroit Tigers in five games, ending on October 14th.

The song "Take Me Out to the Ballgame" was introduced by singer Billy Murray on October 24th. The song was written by Albert von Tilzer and Jack Norworth, who had never seen a game.

On Tuesday, November 3rd, Republican William Howard Taft was elected President of the United States, defeating Democrat William Jennings Bryan.

Three days later, on November 6th, Butch Cassidy and the Sundance Kid were supposedly killed in Bolivia, after being surrounded by a large group of soldiers. There were many rumors to the contrary, however, and their gravesites were unmarked.

The November 18th *Gettysburg Compiler* reported a 130-pound buck was received by the Adams Express Company from Fort Kent, Maine, consigned to Eddie Plank. Plank, who was hunting in Maine, sent his quarry home.

On December 28th, a strong earthquake in southern Italy killed between 75,000 and 200,000 people.

Farewell to Monte Cross, February, 1908.

Farewell banquet for Monte Cross in 1908.

The A's leaving for spring training in 1908.

Cartoon from spring training 1908.

Eddie on Opening Day,
1908.

Eddie warming up.

Eddie cartoon about his contract in 1908.

Eddie with Danny Murphy.

Eddie Plank with friend Ed Walsh.

1909:
STINGY AS HETTY GREEN

EDDIE AND BROTHER Ira were always very competitive. While Eddie had the upper hand in their baseball careers, Ira being in the Connecticut League while Eddie had become a star in the majors, it did not stop them from competing at a game of duckpin bowling, per the January 9th *Gettysburg Times*. "At the insistence of a number of Hanover friends, the Plank brothers have been persuaded to bowl for the duckpin championship of Straban Township, Adams County, on the Albaugh alleys Saturday night at 8:30."

The *Gettysburg Times* on the 12th was kind enough to report the results. The boys did make it to Albaugh's in Hanover and held their contest before dozens of onlookers. "The ten wooden men they faced each round were at several stages of the game as difficult to dispose of on the alleys as nine men on the turf diamond. They called into play out and in-shoots, uppercuts, and snake curves, but they all looked alike to the wooden men. When time was called, Eddie "the tall" Plank had Ira, his short brother, by a total of five pins." The *Philadelphia Inquirer* that day also mentioned the contest and added the score: 415 to 410. There was no mention of any wagering or prize.

Meanwhile, in Antarctica, British explorer Edward Shackleton believed he had reached the magnetic south pole on the 16th of January. Shackleton had led the Nimrod Expedition about the ship *Nimrod*.

During the first week of February, Eddie held his annual oyster roast at his home. The *Gettysburg Times* reported, "... it was greatly enjoyed by many from town and nearby who attended."

That same day, February 4th, one of the great early pitchers of the game passed away—John Clarkson—at only forty-seven years of age. Clarkson had won over 325 games, at one time a

National League best. He had six 30-win seasons including an incredible 53-win season in 1885. He pitched for Chicago, Boston, and Cleveland over the course of his career, twice exceeding 600 innings pitched in a season.

During the early months of 1909, the American Tobacco Company began contracting with players to produce a series of small baseball cards to be inserted into cigarette packs. The set was produced over three years, from 1909 through 1911 and was later identified by collectors as the "T206" series. The Honus Wagner card became the most valuable baseball card due to its scarcity. While the exact reason for this is not known, it has been suggested that Wagner did not want to promote smoking or he felt he was not properly compensated. Likewise, the "T206" Eddie Plank card is the second rarity in the set. It is said to be almost as rare as the Wagner, but, again, there is no explanation for it. Some have suggested the printing plate was broken, but this would likely affect several cards, and not just Plank's. Eddie did not smoke, but there was nothing reported about his objection to the cards.

Connie planned to have his pitchers go to New Orleans ahead of the team, as had become customary. Dygert and Schlitzer had spent the winter in New Orleans. Connie expected Eddie and Jack Coombs to join them the last week of February, but Eddie did not go.

On March 4th, William Howard Taft was inaugurated as the 27th President of the United States. Due to an ice storm in Washington, D.C., the inauguration was held indoors in the Senate Chamber. Meanwhile, Eddie had left Gettysburg for Philadelphia, where he was to meet the train leaving for spring training in New Orleans. The players arrived in the Crescent City on March 11th.

Eddie's first game action of the spring was on the 18th against the local New Orleans club. He hurled a few innings of a 2-to-1 win. Frank Baker hit a tremendous home run that turned a lot of heads.

On March 21st, Eddie was one of the pitchers in action in New Orleans, as the A's beat the local team 6 to 3. The Cleveland Club was in attendance, watching the game, including Napolean Lajoie and Cy Young. The team then began its trek north, stopping in Mobile, Montgomery, and Birmingham. Baker's hot hitting continued.

Back in Philadelphia on the 28th, the Athletics and Phillies began their annual inner-city series. Eddie started the second game and had three hits at the plate, but was the losing pitcher.

On April 6th, Robert Peary, Matthew Henson, and four Inuit explorers, Ootah, Ooqueah, Seegloo, and Egigingwah, came within a few miles of the North Pole. At the time, Peary claimed to have reached the pole, but this had been disputed ever since.

Opening Day was very special in 1909, it was the grand opening of the new Shibe Park. Over 35,000, a new attendance record, attended the game. Thousands more were turned away and watched from afar. Everyone were blessed with a sunny day, interrupted but briefly but an occasional crisp breeze.

The *Philadelphia Inquirer* described the scene before the gates opened:

AND WHILE THEY WAITED patiently, they invested in lemonade, peanuts, and popcorn until the vendors, who swarmed around them, doing a land-office business, were compelled to depart for fresh supplies. The hawkers of flags, bearing the magical emblem of the "White Elephant" garnered their share of dimes and quarters until they, too, went away empty-handed.

Then came the maddening moment when the big gates swung open amid the gleeful shouts of thousands and sixteen turnstiles began to click-click with marvelous rapidity as the invaders swarmed through them. Pausing for an instance as they entered, the faithful, as though dazzled by the first glimpse of the splendid appointments of grandstand and bleachers, were unfolded to them, then eagerly sought the most desirable seats. They were at a loss to single out the latter, however, for the upper tier of ideally arranged seats rose before them, affording an unobstructed view of every part of the diamond, no matter how they were situated."

American League President Ban Johnson surveyed the new ballpark and declared it "the greatest place of its character in the world." He shared he believed the packed house was "the largest crowd that ever witnessed a ballgame."

As dignitaries, former players, and even some of the Phillies took their seats, the Athletics and Red Sox concluded their warm-ups and lined up on opposite sides of the field. At that point, the crowd rose as vocalist James McCool sang "America." This was followed by the raising of the stars and stripes at the flagpole as the band played "The Star-Spangled Banner."

Then, the players took the field and catcher Doc Powers turned towards the mayor's box to receive the first ball. This was followed by umpire Tim Hurst shouting "Play ball!" for the first time at Shibe Park.

Powers tossed the ball to Eddie on the mound, who then delivered the first pitch to young Amby McConnell, the Boston second sacker, who was beginning his second season in the big leagues. Plank put him down and the next two, and the new season was underway on a positive note. In fact, Eddie and the Athletics had little trouble this day. Danny Murphy had four hits and helped stake Eddie to a 4-to-0 lead by the bottom of the 5th. Boston scored a run in the 6th, but the A's added-on, winning 8 to 1.

The only negative on the whole day was the gastritis that catcher Doc Powers began to suffer by the 7th inning, apparently in intense agony. Powers managed to bat in the 8th and even scored a run, but the old backstop suffered through the rest of the game and was near collapse. He was immediately taken to Northwest General Hospital where it was expected he'd miss a few games. It was initially thought some sandwiches he had eaten before the game led to the problem. No one seemed overly worried.

The A's weren't as lucky the next day. Jack Coombs lost 4 to 2 on a sloppy field.

Rain then interrupted the schedule and it was learned that Doc Powers was in serious condition with gangrene in his intestines following an operation. His chances of recovery were stated as an "even chance."

Finally, the club was back on the field on the 16th when the Highlanders were in town. However, the result was no better, Vickers losing 1 to 0. In fact, the Highlanders took two of three.

Eddie's next assignment was in Boston on the 21st, but it did not go well. Boston scored five in the 5th, knocking Eddie out. The A's lost 6 to 2. Coombs followed the next day with a brilliant one-hit shutout. Helped by a Frank Baker home run on the 24th, Eddie was back on the winning side in Boston, 4 to 1.

The A's were then off to Washington to face the Senators on the 26th. Chief Bender had his way, winning 3 to 1, but the victory was hollow. Back in Philadelphia, Maurice R. "Doc" Powers passed away. Connie Mack returned to Philadelphia by train, leaving the team in Washington. Said Mack, "Powers was the most popular man of the Athletics, and his loss is felt keenly by his teammates individually and collectively. To me, his death comes as a great personal shock. He was the only player left of the team which opened the first American League championship season at Columbia Park, and there existed between us a bond of friendship that makes the separation double hard to bear."

The *Philadelphia Inquirer* continued about "Mike" Powers, lauding his value to the team, his positive attitude, and his ability to throw out runners. "With the possible exception of Criger and Young, there never was a better-mated battery than Plank and Powers. Just what this battery did toward landing the pennants of 1902 and 1905, only Manager Mack can tell. Plank has pitched well with other catchers, but it is with reliable 'Mike' that he really did his best work. His death will be a sad blow to all the members of the club, but particularly so to Plank. They were the last of the original team."

The A's lost an empty game in extra innings, 3 to 2, on the 28th.

Back in Philadelphia, on the 29th, over 10,000 attended the funeral of Dr. Powers at St. Elizabeth's Roman Catholic Church. Eddie and several teammates were pallbearers for a very solemn service. The remains were then taken to the New Cathedral Cemetery where they were placed in a vault until Mrs. Powers could make final arrangements.

After the funeral, Eddie took a train home to spend time with friends in Gettysburg over the weekend.

Subsequent stories about Powers dying from food poisoning or due to injury during the game are unfounded. The attending physicians explained in detail that Powers had died from an intussusception, or obstruction, of the intestines. The "bad sandwich" story was initially floated as a cause, but not plausible. Powers' intestine was found to be gangrenous during the operation, clearly not a result of food poisoning. The subsequent legend that he was somehow injured during the game is also unlikely. There was no account in the paper of Powers doing anything remarkable that might have caused such an injury. It was mentioned he was in pain by the 7th inning, perhaps having aggravated his existing situation through his physical activity. But the infection that was discovered later in the operating room was likely there for a while, and Powers was likely suffering for days before Opening Day.

Regardless, one of Eddie Plank's best friends, and his battery-mate since coming to the major leagues was gone.

The Athletics ended April at 5-5, 3 1/2 games back in 5th place. They did not play again until Monday, May 3rd when the team dropped the first of three to the Highlanders.

Eddie was back on the mound at home against the Senators but lost a close one, 4 to 3. Finally, Chief put a stop to the losing streak on the May 6th thanks to a walk-off 2-to-1 win. Coombs followed with a scoreless battle against Walter Johnson, ending with another A's walk-off victory courtesy of Danny Murphy. Young Harry Krause took his turn and equaled Coombs, also beating Washington 1 to 0. Suddenly, the A's were on a winning streak.

Connie Mack loaded the boys on the train and headed to St. Louis to face the Browns, the new home of Rube Waddell. Eddie Plank had the honors to face his old mate and was the better pitcher this day. He even struck out more—seven to Rube's five. Baker had three hits to lead the offense, Eddie and the A's winning easily, 5 to 1.

Jack Powell ended the winning streak the next day, throwing a two-hitter at Philadelphia in a 2-to-0 win, but Bender returned the favor, 1 to 0, the next day.

The next stop on the westward trip was Chicago. On the 15th, the headline read "Plank Outpitches Smith …," Philadelphia winning a tight one. Said the *Philadelphia Inquirer*, "Eddie Plank's southpaw benders again mystified the White Sox giving the Athletics the first battle of the series today, 3 to 2. The side-wheeler had his full assortment of twisters going in perfect style and allowed the Sox but four hits …"

Coombs faced Walsh the next day, battling for nearly thirteen scoreless innings until the deciding run was tallied in that frame by the A's. Krause was again on top of his game for the next one, also winning 1 to 0. Little Jimmy Dygert made it three shutouts in a row with a 5-to-0 win to complete the sweep.

Next to Detroit, Chief was the beneficiary of an offensive explosion against the Tigers on May 19th. Bender won easily, 10 to 2. Murphy had three hits, including a home run.

On the 20th, the Tigers got to Eddie early for three runs in the 1st. Plank was pulled for Vickers, but Philadelphia could not overcome the deficit, losing 5 to 3.

Murphy was again the hitting star the next day, and Coombs was the winning pitcher, 8 to 4.

Eddie tried again on the 22nd. This time Plank was stellar, throwing a shutout until the 8th, at which point he already had a seven-run lead. The A's won 7 to 1.

After dropping the first game in Cleveland, everybody but Murphy was hitting in the second game on the 25th. Bender held the Indians at bay, winning 13 to 2. Coombs then dropped the third game, handing the series to the home team.

On the 28th, the A's were back at Shibe Park. Dygert won 3 to 1 against Washington.

On the 29th, Boston was in for a doubleheader and dropped both. After Krause won the morning game 3 to 2. Eddie was on for the afternoon. Eddie Collins was the hero with the stick in that one, Plank winning 4 to 2.

Boston was back on their game on the 31st, taking two for themselves.

The Athletics ended May 21-14, three games behind Detroit, in 2nd place.

Boston and the A's split a doubleheader to begin the month. Then the White Sox came into town and split a couple games. After several offdays, Cleveland was next, on May 7th, catching Eddie's turn. The Indians prevailed 3 to 1 and again the next day.

Rube Waddell and the Browns were in town on the 11th to have a rematch with Eddie. Rube was winning in the 8th inning, 1 to 0, when the A's tied the score. They ultimately won 2 to 1 in thirteen innings. Plank got a no-decision.

The A's then took two of the next three.

Against Detroit, they won two of three games but lost three in a row against Boston, including a 6-to-5 loss by Eddie on the 21st of June.

On the 22nd, the Senators were a welcome sight for Bender, who won 3 to 1. Krause threw another shutout the next day, 3 to 0.

New York was next on the 24th at Shibe Park. Cy Morgan won the opener, 5 to 3. After a 12-to-2 thrashing, the A's swept a doubleheader from the Highlanders on the 26th, Bender and

Coombs doing the damage. Morgan then lost the next one on a wild pitch, 2 to 1.

Krause beat the Red Sox easily, 9 to 1, on the 29th. That day, the *Gettysburg Times* reported Eddie's pointer dog was lost. "If returned to Brady Sefton's barber shop the finder will receive a suitable reward."

The A's ended the month with a doubleheader sweep against Boston at home. Eddie won the first game, 8 to 4. Baker hit a home run to aid the cause. Coombs beat former mate Schlitzer in the second game, 6 to 2.

The Athletics finished June at 36-25, 5 1/2 games back of the Detroit Tigers, in 2nd place.

After Bender dropped the next game to Boston on July 1st, Krause was back to throwing zeros, beating the Red Sox 1 to 0, the game won on Eddie Collin's blast off the flagpole.

The boys snagged a doubleheader in New York on the 3rd and another on the 5th. July 4th was on Sunday this year, so the A's were off. Eddie won the morning game on Monday. Said the *Philadelphia Inquirer,* "Eddie Plank and his cross-fire bothered the Highlanders, who got only seven hits, three of which were in the final period." Eddie won 7 to 2.

The A's finished the sweep of New York the following day.

Next, the Athletics were in Detroit to battle with the 1st place Tigers. Two-and-a-half games back when the series started, Krause won the first game on the 8th to inch closer.

Eddie was next on the mound and did not disappoint. "There never was an interval when Plank was in danger," reported the *Philadelphia Inquirer.* Eddie won 2 to 0 and helped himself with three base hits. The A's were only a half-game behind.

The teams split the next two, Krause winning his tenth straight, and the teams remained separated by the slimmest of margins.

On the 13th, in Cleveland, Cy Morgan lost to Addie Joss and the Naps 1 to 0 in ten innings. Coombs didn't fare much better the next day, losing to Cy Young, 4 to 3. Bender made it three in a row, losing 6 to 5 on the 15th. Morgan's luck turned on the 16th, though, as he shut out the Naps 3 to 0, salvaging a game in the series. However, the A's were now three games behind.

Off to St. Louis on Saturday the 17th, Eddie dropped the morning game of a doubleheader, 2 to 0. The team only mustered four hits, and Eddie had one of them. The A's then dropped the afternoon game and Boston caught them for second place. Both teams were 4 1/2 back of Detroit.

The A's took two of the next three and headed to Chicago.

Eddie took his next turn on Thursday the 22nd against the White Sox. He fell behind 2 to 1 in the 1st inning, and it was the margin of victory, as Chicago won 4 to 3. Eddie then headed home for the weekend, ahead of the team. He was at the farm north of town, taking a break for a few days. The team lost three more to the White Sox while he was gone, falling to 7 1/2 games back.

Eddie next headed to Washington to rejoin the team on Tuesday the 27th. The A's swept a doubleheader that day. They repeated this performance the next day, Eddie winning in the morning, 7 to 1, and Krause in the afternoon, 6 to 0. The four wins in two days pulled the A's back to 6 1/2 out.

Finally, the A's were home again on the 29th for a twin bill against the Naps. The A's won both games, making it three doubleheader sweeps in a row!

The A's won again on the 30th and then split the doubleheader on the 31st, their winning streak finally coming to an end.

The Athletics ended July 56-38, four games behind Detroit, in 2nd place.

The White Sox were in town on August 3rd. The A's swept the doubleheader, Eddie winning the first game 2 to 1. Detroit lost two, so the A's crept back to two games behind.

Both teams split doubleheaders on subsequent days, nothing more being resolved about the standings.

On August 6th, those Tigers came to town for a head-to-head series. Krause got the call for the first game and lost 3 to 1.

Next, it was Plank's turn to keep them close, and he did so with both his bat and his arm, getting a key hit and pitching effectively, 5 to 3.

On the 9th, Krause was called again, and this time he won, 5 to 1. Baker hit a home run for the home team, and Cobb was held to two singles. The A's were now only a game back.

Mack tapped Plank to pitch the critical game on the 10th. What followed was recapped by the *Adams County News*, containing accounts from several newspapers:

The Philadelphia Press: Edward Plank caused staid men to ruthlessly destroy their headgear and pound vigorously on the anatomy of their next-door neighbor. It was a sight which will never fade from the memories of the 19,080 to see that sphere go bounding gracefully over the head of Killefer, the Detroit center fielder, while Eddie ran around the paths and finally crossed the plate with a home run to his credit. Even the women and girls—and there were hundreds of them there—forgot propriety and screamed and danced about as if crazed.

While Mack's veteran southpaw was credited with the most spectacular stunt of the historical day in hitting the home run, his name will go down in the archives of the Athletics not so much for that feat as for the steadiness which he displayed in critical periods. Thrice were three Tigers on the paths pleading for succor. And in each instance, Plank settled down and retired the side amidst the plaudits of the multitudes.

The North American: If any man ever survived the situations the red-blooded Plank had to face yesterday afternoon, he must have been one of the ancient Stoics. In three of the four concluding innings, the big Gettysburg port-sider gave the most remarkable exhibition of recuperative pitching, when within a hair's breadth of disaster, that he has done since the year Connie brought him out of obscurity.

Four times in this period Detroit filled the bases yet only one run was produced. Three times the big Plank with his blinding cross-fire stopped the rally of his opponents and sent them to the field unhanded.

Philadelphia Inquirer: When it came down to the crucial moments when only the most skillful kind of strategic pitching would avert disaster, Plank showed up superbly and pulled himself out.

When the reliable Eddie Plank seemed to have dug a pit for his teammates and himself out of which all luck in the world could not pull them, the enemy found his benders impossible to connect with.

Eddie had won and hit a home run to boot. The A's were now tied for 1st place with the Tigers.

The A's next took three of four from the Browns, including another win over Waddell. The homestand over, they remained tied with Detroit as they headed to Washington.

In the nation's capital on the 16th, Harry Krause beat Walter Johnson to move the A's unto 1st place by half-a-game.

The next day, Johnson was back and went thirteen shutout innings to win 1 to 0. Bender took the loss, not yielding a run until that final frame. Fortunately, the Tigers also lost, so the lead was preserved.

On the 18th, "Plank was at his best," and the A's won 2 to 1 to increase their lead.

Out to Cleveland, the A's swiped four in a row and held steady at a one-game lead heading to Detroit.

Harry Krause was handed the ball for the first game against Detroit on the 24th. The Tigers used a four-spot in the bottom of the 6th to overcome the A's 7 to 6. The pennant race was all knotted-up again.

The next day, Eddie literally "bet the farm." He wired home to friends that he would "wager my farm near Gettysburg against any odds, that if I am given decent support I will defeat Detroit this afternoon." Reported the *Gettysburg Times*, "Eddie was mistaken this time, but still owns his farm."

In the game, Eddie led 2 to 1 going into the bottom of the 8th, when Detroit rallied. They ended up winning 4 to 3 and took a one-game lead.

The series concluded with another Detroit win.

The A's next took two of three from the Browns in St. Louis, including another victory over Waddell.

They closed the month in Chicago. Eddie threw a three-hitter on the 30th, winning 5 to 0. "Plank enjoyed one of his exceptionally great days, and for eight cyclonic innings the great flinger kept the Sox at bay," reported the *Philadelphia Inquirer*. In the second inning Eddie was involved in the offense, knocking a two-run single that chased in Davis and Oldring. When Hartsel reached on an error, Eddie took third. He then stole home on a double-steal, Topsy taking second while Eddie surprised everyone in the ballpark, sliding across home plate. A steal of home is a relatively rare event and such thefts by pitchers are even more rare. It has only happened forty times since 1900, and has not happened since Curt Simmons did it on September 1, 1963. Eddie's swipe was the only instance a Philadelphia player has succeeded at it and the only time an Athletics player has done so—Philadelphia, Kansas City, or Oakland.

Krause dropped a 2-to-0 game on the 31st, Eddie's thirty-fourth birthday. The A's finished August 74-47, now 3 1/2 games behind the hot Detroit Tigers, in 2nd place.

Chicago took another from the A's before they headed to Washington.

For the opening game against the Senators on September 3rd, Plank got the call. Said the *Philadelphia Inquirer*, "... it would have taken some mighty tight pitching and grand fielding to beat the visitors. Eddie Plank was as stingy with his hits as Hetty Green is with her coin." The A's won handily, 10 to 3.

The A's took another and headed home to meet the Senators at Shibe Park. They were still 3 1/2 games back.

At home on the 6th of September, the A's took two from the Senators, Plank registering a no-decision in the first game that went into extra-innings. Due to Detroit's sweep of the Browns, the standings did not change.

The A's next took two of three from the Highlanders and then welcomed Boston to town.

Eddie pitched the first game of a twin bill on Saturday, September 11th. He was sensational, winning 1 to 0. "So effective was the pitching and so clean the fielding that in the full nine innings, the Bostonians got but one man past first," reported the *Philadelphia Inquirer*.

Krause lost the second game by the same score, and the A's were 4 1/2 games out.

The A's then took three of four games against the Highlanders and found themselves four games out when play ended on the 15th. Detroit was next on the schedule.

Eddie and the A's won the first game of the series, 5 to 2. One of the highlights was with Cobb at the plate and the bases loaded. "... gloom as black as the clouds over the field settled down over the vast assemblage, especially when Cobb strode to the plate. The league's leading hitter failed to impress Plank, who quickly proceeded to fan him to the frenzied enthusiasm of the crowd," reported the *Philadelphia Inquirer*. Plank had also struck out Cobb earlier in the game on a ball over his head. The A's were now three games back.

Detroit won on the 17th, 5 to 3, but the A's got one back, 2 to 0, on the 18th. Bender threw a brilliant three-hitter.

Plank was back on the 20th and his "Cross-fire Baffled Tigers," read the headline in the *Philadelphia Inquirer*. The A's won 7 to 4, but the game was not without incident. Ty Cobb spiked Philadelphia shortstop Jack Barry so badly he had to leave the game. Cobb acted as if the situation was an accident, but the team felt otherwise. Barry was replaced by eighteen-year-old Stuffy McInnis, who filled in adequately. The A's had climbed back to two games out.

Next in, the A's split two with the Browns before Eddie took the mound on the 23rd. With a 3-to-0 lead going into the 4th, it looked like a sure win. But Eddie faltered, yielding two runs, and was replaced by Krause, who finished the 6-to-2 victory.

On Saturday, the 25th, the A's swiped two from the Naps, who did not score. Detroit took two from the Highlanders, keeping the margin 2 1/2.

The teams were off on Sunday the 26th, and then both lost on Monday, followed by both winning on Tuesday. Like two wrestlers, locking arms, the teams could get no closer.

The last week of September, Eddie was back in Gettysburg for a few days' respite.

The White Sox were in town on the 29th and split a doubleheader with the A's. Eddie lost a tough one to Ed Walsh, 2 to 1, in ten innings. The A's then crushed in the next game, 10 to 1, backing Bender, but Detroit swept two from Boston and inched up to 3 1/2 ahead. Time was running out.

On the 30th, the A's dropped two to the White Sox while Detroit also lost. The pennant was over. The Detroit Tigers had won.

The A's finished the 1909 season 95-58, in 2nd place, just 3 1/2 games behind the Tigers.

Eddie finished the year 19-10 with a 1.72 ERA. Bender and Krause were both 18-8. Cy Morgan won 16, and Jack Coombs 11. George Mullin had 29 wins to lead the league. Krause's 1.39 ERA topped the Junior Circuit.

At the plate, Ty Cobb won the triple crown: .377, 9 HR, 107 RBI. Eddie Collins hit .347 for the A's. Danny Murphy led the team with 5 home runs. Home Run Baker had 85 RBI.

On October 13th, while the World Series was underway, Connie had arranged for the Athletics to travel to Danville to play the Susquehanna League champions in an exhibition. Eddie pitched a few innings, and the A's won 7 to 0 against a nine that included three Coveleskis: Harry from the Phillies in right field, Frank on the mound, and John in left. Stan did not play.

Everything was not perfect for the Tigers in the World Series. In the seventh game, on October 16th, the Pittsburgh Pirates defeated them, 8-0, to win four games to three. The Tigers had won three consecutive pennants but lost the World Series each time.

Ty Cobb was off to other things. Next up was the National Highway automobile run from New York to Atlanta, which stopped in Gettysburg on the 26th of October. There was much anticipation about the arrival of the athlete, as expressed in the *Gettysburg Times* from the prior day:

> TY COBB, THE FAMOUS baseball player will be one of those who will accompany the National Highway automobile run which will arrive in Gettysburg Tuesday afternoon to spend the night here before proceeding on their way from New York to Atlanta. Cobb will drive an 80 m.p.h. Chalmers Detroit car.
>
> Considerable interest will be manifested here in Cobb as there was intense feeling aroused in Gettysburg during the past Summer against the man on account of his alleged un-sportsmanlike playing in various games with the Philadelphia Athletics, the pet team of all Gettysburg baseball fans.
>
> Cobb is generally considered one of the best players in the business and proved to be one of Detroit's prominent factors in their successful struggle for the pennant. The feat of Eddie Plank striking him out twice in one game only served to deepen the regard in which the Straban Township twirler is held by Gettysburg baseball followers.
>
> It is safe to say, that in Gettysburg at least, Cobb will be the most interesting party in the entire crowd of automobilists, about 400 strong.

Eddie and the A's spent most of the fall on a barnstorming tour of the west, playing against a group of National League players. The *Philadelphia Inquirer* reported on their return just in time for Christmas.

On December 8th, for mound opponent, William "Buffalo Bill" Hogg died suddenly in New Orleans of Bright's disease. He had been a pitcher for the New York Highlanders from 1905 through 1908. He was only twenty-seven.

Eddie warming up.

Opening Day line at the new Shibe Park on April 12, 1909.

Eddie on the mound on Opening Day.

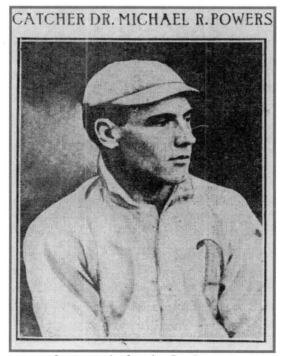

Last portrait of catcher Doc Powers.

*BEARING CASKET INTO THE CHURCH. THE
PALL BEARERS ARE SIMON NICHOLS - DAN MURPHY,
EDDIE PLANK - HARRY DAVIS - IRA THOMAS AND JACK
COOMBS MEMBERS OF THE ATHLETICS TEAM*

Eddie as a pall bearer for Doc Powers.

*CONNIE MACK AND BEN SHIBE LEADING PROCESSION OF BASE BALL
PLAYERS THE ATHLETIC - WASHINGTON - PHILADELPHIA NATIONALS
AND BROOKLYN TEAMS*

The line at Doc Powers' funeral.

Crowd outside the church for Doc Powers' funeral.

Plank American Tobacco Company card.

Plank Philadelphia Caramel Company card.

*Plank American
Caramel card.*

Eddie on the mound.

Portraits of Eddie Plank.

The famous Plank T206 card.

Harry Krause pitching in July 1909.

Packed house in August of 1909.

Eddie hitting a home run on August 10, 1909.

Pennant race cartoon from August 1909.

Caricature of Eddie Plank from late 1909.

Athletics cartoon from September 1909.

1910:
RATHER A FREAK

T HE *PHILADELPHIA INQUIRER* on February 4th announced Eddie Plank had signed a contract with the Athletics for the upcoming season:

THE OTHER TWO PLAYERS to send their contracts on to accompany that of Thomas' were Eddie Plank and Anthony Walsh, a youngster who was secured from the coal regions, and who is anxious to beat out Harry Davis and Ben Houser for the job of holding down sack No. 1. Plank in his letter states that he is in fine condition, not much overweight, and is as hard as nails. Eddie lives on his father's farm at Gettysburg, Pa., during the winter months, and being a great lover of outdoor life, farm life, and an admirer of horseflesh, he gets plenty of good healthy exercise to keep him in the best of shape. While Plank is an exceedingly hard man to catch, the success of both Ira Thomas and Paddy Livingston made behind the bat last summer with Eddie on the slab was deserving of much praise. Now that Plank is thoroughly accustomed to both catchers, he should be able to cut loose that famous cross-fire right off the reel when the campaign opens in the spring.

On Wednesday, the 16th, Eddie held his annual oyster bake at his home, attended by many friends.

The next night Eddie and Ira Plank chaired a meeting of the potential Adams County baseball league at the Hotel Gettysburg.

Eddie was off to spring training on February 28th. He met with Harry Davis and many veteran players who rode the 7:28 PM *Fast Flying Virginian* to Hot Springs, Virginia, where the older players would "get the benefit of the springs" for twelve days before joining the rest of the squad. With Davis and Plank were Rube Oldring, Ira Thomas, Jack Barry, Eddie Collins, Frank Baker, Paddy Livingston, Danny Murphy, Chief Bender, Jack Coombs, and Topsy Hartsel. Ben Shibe and others accompanied them. Cy Morgan was picked up in Washington, D.C.

On March 1st, after arriving, Plank, Davis, Coombs, Collins, and Bender golfed on the course previously used by President Taft. Davis then set about a routine of twice-a-day hikes, followed by a "scientific course of spouts of the baths, from which great results are confidently anticipated."

On March 12th, the well-rested men left Hot Springs to join Connie and the rest of team in Atlanta, Georgia.

Eddie was eased into games, facing the Atlanta Southern League team a few times until, on March 28th, the A's were in Greenville, South Carolina. Eddie went the distance and even hit a triple. Said the *Philadelphia Inquirer*, "He was there with the goods at all times and when he had to let loose, he whizzed the ball across the plate with mid-season speed and used an assortment of curves that had the Greenville swatters swinging blindly. Although there were four hits registered off him, two of these were infield taps, and they did not figure in the scoring. He fanned six men and did not issue a pass or hit a batsman."

Eddie was quoted in the *Gettysburg Times* on April 5th, stating he was going to play at least two or three more years and would not go to the minors to extend his career. "We all get old and then I guess that farm down in Gettysburg will be all right for me," he concluded. This followed his stellar performance in the inner-city series with the Phillies. Eddie and the A's won 11 to 0 at Shibe Park. The Phillies won the series this year, though.

The season opened on Thursday, April 14th, in Washington, D.C. Walter Johnson was tapped by the home Senators to face Eddie Plank from the Athletics. President Taft was on hand to throw out the first ball. He was the first President to ever do this. Johnson proceeded to throw a no-hitter until there were two outs in the 7th inning. Frank Baker hit a double off Johnson, the only hit of the day. Meanwhile, Eddie was knocked around for thirteen hits and held the opposition to only three runs, thanks to the defense of Eddie Collins. The final score at League Park was 3 to 0 in favor of Washington. The A's and Senators split the next two.

The A's finally opened their home season on the 20th, after a couple rain cancellations. Chief Bender was magnificent, winning 7 to 0 against New York. The A's dropped the next game 1 to 0.

In the sky that evening, Halley's Comet achieved perihelion. It had been visible to the naked eye for the last ten days.

On the 21st of April, a great American, Samuel Clemens, best known as Mark Twain, passed away in Danbury, Connecticut. "Give me my glasses," were the last words he wrote on a pad to his daughter, Twain too weak to speak. Carlyle's *French Revolution* lay by his side. The great author was 74. Curiously, he had been born in November of 1835, the last time Halley's Comet was seen.

Philadelphia was next in Boston on the 22nd. Harry Krause opened the series with a five-hit shutout, winning 3 to 0.

Facing Eddie Cicotte on the 23rd, Plank went all eleven innings to win 5 to 3. The A's took another from Boston and then headed to New York where they split the first two games.

The April 27th *Gettysburg Times* included an item about a pig taken in by Eddie. "Eddie Plank sent home to his farm this week a young pig by express. It was a baseball trophy presented to a member of the Athletic team. He did not know what to do with his trophy and accepted Eddie's offer to send it to his Gettysburg farm."

The Athletics ended April 6-4, in 2nd place, one game behind the Detroit Tigers.

Eddie was back on the mound against Boston at Shibe Park on May 2nd. He did not pitch particularly well and fell behind Ed Cicotte 5 to 2 going into the bottom of the 9th. A pinch-hitter was sent up for Plank, and the A's rallied for five runs, knocking out Cicotte and winning in walk-off fashion.

Krause threw a two-hit shutout the next day, winning 2 to 0. The Senators then came to town for the 5th. The A's swept them over four games, Eddie winning the final game of the series on May 9th, 10 to 2.

On May 6th, Edward VII, the King of England died. He was the son of Queen Victoria. He was succeeded by his son, George V.

Cy Morgan and the Naps' Addie Joss battled to a 1-to-1 tie after twelve innings on May 10th. The next game, on the 12th, the "Naps Were Helpless Before Big Injun," per the *Philadelphia Inquirer*. Chief Bender hurled a no-hitter, winning 4 to 0. He would have had a perfect game if not for one base on balls.

The A's also won the final game of the series, completing the two-game sweep.

The White Sox were next in town on the 14th. Eddie battled to a 3-to-3 tie through regulation in the first game of the series before Coombs relieved and snagged the win, 4 to 3.

The A's completed a four-game sweep on the 18th, winning for the thirteenth time in a row.

That day, the earth passed through the tail of Halley's Comet. Some were afraid the cyanide gas present in the tail would poison all life on earth. Gas masks, comet umbrellas, and comet pills were sold for protection, though most scientists felt the gas too dispersed to have any effect.

Detroit ended the winning streak, blasting the A's 14 to 2 on the 19th. The Tigers had 19 hits in the game, most of them against Krause.

Eddie was on the mound the next day to stop a potential losing streak. He won 5 to 2. The *Gettysburg Times* from May 21st summarized the various news accounts of Eddie's performance:

> *Philadelphia Inquirer:* Plank had the Tigers swinging like a flock of beer signs in a forty-knot gale when anyone was roosting on the sacks.
>
> *North American:* The Tigers outhit the Quakers, getting ten safe blows to the Mackmen's eight, but Eddie Plank was a very subtle distributor of the cross-fire when Royal Bengals were languishing around the paths. He had six strikeouts to his credit, which is no staggering total, but each one came at a time when an ordinary infield out might have proved disastrous.
>
> *Philadelphia Press:* Edward Plank, who learned the art of cross-fire pitching with other trivial subjects at Gettysburg College, invariably makes sorry subjects of Jennings' heavy swatsmen, and yesterday was no exception. The Tigers hit the sphere into vacant spots ten times, but the Gettysburgian steered the pennant craft through the shoals safely.

The A's split two more with Detroit.

Last-place St. Louis arrived on the 24th and promptly defeated the A's 6 to 1. Eddie made an appearance to mop up in this one. The A's then swept the next three from the Browns.

The Athletics began their road trip at the Huntington Avenue Baseball Grounds in Boston on the 28th. Eddie won easily, 9 to 3, and hit a double. The teams split doubleheaders on Monday and Tuesday.

The A's concluded May with a 26-9 record, two games ahead of New York, in 1st place.

Third-place Detroit was their next opponent. The teams tangled on June 3rd at Bennett Park following a couple days of sitting idle at the hotel due to rain. Eddie started and was knocked out after giving up three in the 1st inning. The Tigers won 6 to 1. The A's then lost two more and fell into a 1st place tie with New York. After the Highlanders won on June 6th, they were in 1st place by half-a-game.

Off to Cleveland on the 7th, the A's lost again and were now 1 1/2 games out of 1st. The next day, Bender led them back, winning handily, 13 to 1.

On June 11th, the A's were in St. Louis. Eddie was back in good form, winning 6 to 1. The A's then took two of the next three to take a one-game lead over New York.

In Chicago, on the 15th, Eddie pitched the first two-thirds of an inning until Cy Morgan was ready to go. The White Sox' Ed Walsh won the day, however, 4 to 3, Morgan taking the defeat.

The A's followed with two losses in three games, including Eddie's 4-to-2 defeat against Walsh on the 19th.

On the 21st, in New York, the A's swept a doubleheader from the Highlanders. Cy Morgan won the morning game 7 to 4. Eddie Plank was masterful in the afternoon, winning 7 to 1. The Highlanders had only three hits in the game. This knocked New York two games behind and put the A's a half-game ahead of Detroit.

Coombs and Bender led the sweep of another twin bill the next day, and the A's began to pad their lead.

New York snagged the last two games of the series.

At home against Boston on the 25th, the A's benefited from "Masterful Pitching by Old Reliable Eddie Plank," per the *Philadelphia Inquirer*. Eddie won 2 to 1, scattering seven hits.

The teams split the next four games to close out the month. At the end of June, the A's found themselves at 38-21, one game ahead of New York, in 1st place.

As fate would have it, the Highlanders were next to visit Shibe Park. Jack Coombs won the morning game, 2 to 0. Eddie was on the mound in the afternoon. He built a 4-to-2 lead, but was shaky in the 8th, when Bender was called to hold them off. The A's won 4 to 2.

The A's then won two games on the 2nd of July and split the doubleheader on the 4th, increasing their lead to five games.

Meanwhile, in Reno, Nevada, African-American boxer Jack Johnson defeated James J. Jeffries, also known as "The Great White Hope," in a bout of heavyweights. Author Jack London reported on the match, "Once again, has Johnson sent down to defeat the chosen representative of the white race, and this time the greatest of them." After the fight, in cities across the country, there were race riots and violent incidents. In Philadelphia, whites pursued blacks on the streets, throwing bricks and causing injuries. "Negro" paraders were dispersed by whites in Germantown. In Washington, D.C., there were hundreds of arrests and the mounted police charged into mobs. Two whites were fatally stabbed.

Amid the turmoil, the Athletics headed to Washington to play the Senators on the 5th. Eddie Plank faced Walter Johnson. Going into the 7th, the Senators led 2 to 0. The A's then scored single runs in each of the final three innings to nip Johnson 3 to 2. Meanwhile, the mayors of Baltimore and Washington discussed banning "moving pictures" of the Johnson fight, concerned the showing would incite further unrest. Mayor Reyburn of Philadelphia stated he would allow such pictures to be exhibited.

The A's and Senators split the next two games.

The Tigers came to town on the 8th. The A's took the opening round 4 to 3. It was then Eddie's turn on the 9th. As reported in the *Philadelphia Inquirer*, "To place the credit for the splendid victory and give honor where honor is due, first I am going to hand the lion's share of that to Mr. Eddie Plank, a young gentleman from Gettysburg, who drinks his coffee from the wrong side of his plate. Mr. Plank was taking care of the hurling end of the game for us yesterday, and in addition to pitching shutout ball and never giving the Tigers a smell of a chance to score, Eddie put the game in the ice box right off the reel by lamming out an extremely healthy and respectable hit that scored two runs in the second inning. Of course, as things turned out, we would have copped anyway without those two runs, but gee whiz it's blamed hard on the nerves to sit around all afternoon with only a one-run lead so that those runs that Eddie lammed home were mighty thankfully received at the time." Eddie won 5 to 0.

After the game, Eddie headed home to Gettysburg on Sunday.

The A's followed with two more wins against Detroit on Monday and Tuesday.

The Browns visited on the 13th and fell to the A's. Eddie took the mound on the 14th, well-rested from his respite in Adams County. Unfortunately, the A's dropped a close one, 5 to 4, helped by a miscue by Plank and catcher Ira Thomas, who did a "Little Alphonse and Gaston stunt" on a bunted ball in the 8th inning, meant to be a sacrifice. Both ran for the ball, arriving in ample time, but thought the other was going to act. Neither did, and everyone was safe. The Browns then scored two runs to take the lead.

The A's took the next two from St. Louis.

The White Sox visited on the 18th. Jack Coombs picked up a 5-to-2 victory. The next day, Cy Morgan shut them out 6 to 0. Meanwhile, in Washington, another Cy with the last name Young threw eleven innings in the second game of a doubleheader, giving his Naps a 5-to-2 win. It was the 500th of Cy Young's career.

The A's split the next two, Plank losing to Walsh, 3 to 2, on the 21st.

After splitting two with the Naps to end the week, the A's and Cleveland played a doubleheader on Monday the 25th. In the morning game, Eddie faced Cy Young, who notched his 501st win, beating Plank 4 to 2. Cy Morgan won the afternoon game 4 to 0.

The teams split another doubleheader the next day.

Washington was next in town, splitting four games. Eddie picked up a save of Bender's win on the 30th. Chief had been leading 7 to 0 going into the 9th, but faltered, giving up five runs, before Eddie stopped the bleeding.

The A's ended July 60-30, six games ahead of Boston, in 1st place.

The Athletics began August in Chicago. After dropping the first game of the series, the A's held on to a 3-to-2 win on the 2nd thanks to Eddie's save. Plank came on in the 8th when the White Sox were threatening.

The A's took another and then were locked in a sixteen-inning scoreless tie that Jack Coombs worked.

Off to St. Louis, Eddie faced the Browns on the 5th and led 9 to 1 into the bottom of the 8th. He was slapped for four runs but held on 9 to 5.

The A's swept three more from the Browns including another shutout by Coombs. Their lead over Boston expanded to 8 1/2 games.

Eddie was next on the mound at Bennett Park in Detroit on the 9th of August. He held Ty Cobb hitless and beat the Tigers 3 to 1.

The teams split two games before Eddie was back on the rubber on the 12th. Plank fell behind, 3 to 1, early in the game, but the A's rallied back for a 7-to-4 win.

The team was off to Cleveland on the 13th. The A's won four of the six games, including an 18-to-3 blow-out.

The A's were back home against Chicago on the 18th, pulling out a 2-to-1 win in ten innings. The next day, Eddie pitched a strong game, winning 6 to 1. Plank was in his "Old Time Form" per the headline in the *Philadelphia Inquirer*.

They then completed the three-game sweep the next day. The lead was now thirteen games over Boston. A three-game sweep of Cleveland followed. The A's then took two of three from St. Louis. On the 25th, second baseman Danny Murphy hit for the cycle in the 9-6 loss.

Eddie struggled in his start against Detroit on the 29th. "To begin with, Eddie didn't appear to have anything when he started save the best wishes of some fifteen thousand or so of our home folks who had gathered within the enclosure, and he didn't even have these very long. They were merged into one long drawn out wail of 'take him out' before Eddie had finished his third inning." Reported the *Philadelphia Inquirer*. Plank lost the game 7 to 4.

The teams split the next two games. Philadelphia ended the month of August, 82-37, eleven games up on Boston. Eddie ended the month thirty-five years old.

The A's began September taking two of three from Washington. They next headed to New York, where they split a doubleheader on the 5th. Eddie pitched a bit in relief of Cy Morgan in the middle of the morning game, a 5-to-2 loss.

Eddie started the next day and dropped a close 3-to-2 decision. Reported the *Philadelphia Inquirer*, "The Highlanders' parting 1910 shot at the Philadelphia White Elephants, coming champions of the American League, at the Hilltop today took the form of a 3-to-2 victory. Birdie Cree, who was born in Khedive, one of the Keystone State hamlets, being entirely responsible for tally No. 3 garnered by the locals. The forestry expert, with the score tied in the seventh inning, slammed one of Eddie Plank's curves down into the hollow in right field and thus gained himself the applause of the bugs and a pair of shoes."

The A's were next in Boston on the 7th. They swept all three games, knocking Boston back to 3rd place, 14 1/2 games out. New York was now in 2nd place.

Back home against the Senators on the 10th, the A's won all three games, increasing their lead to 15 1/2 over both Boston and New York.

Eddie was finally back on the mound on the 15th at Bennett Field in Detroit. "Just to show them he was in World's Series form, Eddie Plank conducted the one-time ferocious Tigers through nine innings of diamond sport today with only six of them hitting the warpath," reported the *Philadelphia Inquirer*. Plank won the game 7 to 1.

Jack Coombs followed the next day with a two-hitter, winning 10 to 0. The teams split the remaining two games. In the game on the 17th, Tigers pitcher Ed Summers hit two home runs off Harry Krause in a 10-to-3 win. These were the only home runs in his career.

After dropping the first game in Cleveland on the 19th, Eddie took the ball for the A's on the 20th, winning 6 to 3. The next day, Jack Coombs tangled to a scoreless tie in ten innings as the Highlanders lost. This clinched the pennant for the A's.

On the 25th, in Chicago, Eddie battled with Ed Walsh to a 1-to-1 tie through nine innings. Jack Coombs then relieved and picked up the win in extra-innings.

Eddie pitched his final game of the season on October 5th, hurling a few innings in a 7-to-4 loss to New York at Shibe Park.

On October 9th, Ty Cobb stayed out of the lineup to preserve his league-leading .383 average. Meanwhile, Cleveland's Nap

Lajoie went 8-for-8 in a doubleheader, including six bunt singles. Lajoie finished at .384, edging Cobb. There were rumors that the Browns deliberately played too deep, allowing Lajoie to get the hits. Ban Johnson later investigated and found no wrongdoing.

The A's had ended the season 102-48, 14 1/2 games ahead of New York.

Eddie Plank's record in 1910 was 16-10 with a 2.01 ERA. Jack Coombs was 31-9, 1.30, leading in wins, but narrowly losing the ERA title to Ed Walsh at 1.27. Walter Johnson led the American League with 313 strikeouts. Chief Bender was 23-5, 1.58, while Cy Morgan was 18-12, 1.55. Thus, Eddie was only the fourth best pitcher on the team at year's end.

At the plate, Eddie Collins led the team with a .324 batting average, trailing Lajoie's circuit-leading .384. Oldring and Murphy each had four home runs, trailing Jake Stahl. Eddie Collins' team-leading 81 RBI weren't even close to Sam Crawford's 120.

Suffice to say, the strength of the A's was their pitching.

On October 11th, in an exhibition game, the All-American stars routed the A's 8 to 3 at Shibe Park. Eddie pitched three innings in the game, as did Coombs and Bender.

Also, this day, Theodore Roosevelt became the first former president to ride in an airplane.

The Wednesday, October 12th *Gettysburg Times* contained a lengthy interview with Eddie Plank where he talked about his start in baseball:

"THEY ALL SAY I got my start the day of the Battle of Gettysburg, but they exaggerate somewhat," said Eddie Plank. "I was born in Gettysburg in 1875, and that gave the boys a chance to say things. I admit the 1875 without trying to get away and scalp a half dozen years off my age as some of them do.

"At any rate, I think I am rather a freak as a baseball player because I seldom have heard of any case anything like my own.

"As I told you, I was born in Gettysburg and I played some baseball around there in an amateur way, and without giving the game much thought. You see, I had other things to do, and down in Gettysburg, we regard baseball as a Fourth of July and Saturday amusement rather than a business. Honestly, I never even read the scores or knew who played in the big leagues until

I was 20 years old. Gettysburg looked big enough for me, and when I could play ball I played because I liked the running and the throwing and everything else. I didn't know a squeeze play from third base hardly. All I wanted to do was beat the other fellows.

"I started to college about the time most other fellows are getting enough. I was 25 when I began pitching for the Gettysburg College team and I was big and strong and fast and wild and inexperienced and everything else that goes to make up a college pitcher. I simply shut my eyes and cut loose and most of those who didn't strike out got bases on balls, and I have suspected since that a lot of them struck out just to escape from standing up there at the bat.

"Seriously, I think the real reason for my start was that I was older, stronger, and better developed than the average college man. That made me stand out among them and it attracted the attention of professional clubs. I had not thought of baseball as a profession at all until offered a job, after school closed, knowing about as much about major league baseball as I know about who will make a three-base hit in the morning game next Decoration Day. I started right out to pitch the way I did at school; just wait till I saw the whites of their eyes and then shoot. I must say I got away luckily especially after wounding a flock of ballplayers. Suddenly, I saw there was more to it than throwing as hard as possible and curving them. I saw I would have to do some thinking and I began to study the game. Queerly enough, I went wrong right away. I was guessing wrong, but luckily for me, I had enough speed and shoots to hang on by sheer power until I learned more. I worked and studied hard at the game, watched the other pitchers, picked up their tricks, and began to pitch with much less exertion and strain and still get results. If I had gone on the way I started, I would have been out of it in two seasons, and I'm still here. On the other hand, if I had known as much when I started about pitching, I'd be here a long time. This is a frank confession, but you say you want it for the benefit of young players, and no one needs to be told more than the new pitcher does, even if it is only to keep him from throwing his arm away."

The A's and All-Americans played another exhibition this day. The All-Americans won again, 5 to 1, against the same three pitchers—Bender, Plank, and Coombs.

The World Series opened at Shibe Park on Monday, October 17th. The Chicago Cubs, champions of the National League were in town. The Cubs had gone 104-50, cruising to a twelve-game margin over McGraw's New York Giants. Two dominant teams were about to clash.

In the first game, Chief Bender was tapped to defend the home turf. Orval Overall, only 12-6 in an injury-shortened season, was asked to take the mound for Chicago. Overall had won 20 games the year prior, plus two against the Tigers in the 1908 series.

The big Chief was dominant, leading 4 to 0 into the 9th when he was nicked for a run. Frank Baker led the offense with three hits. The overflow throng in Philadelphia was ecstatic.

That night, Eddie Plank, Jack Coombs, and Mr. and Mrs. Shibe attended *The Old Homestead* at the Chestnut Street Opera House.

Unbeknownst to Eddie, his father David Plank had traveled to Philadelphia hoping to see Eddie pitch and win in the World Series. This was not to be. Game Two, on the 18th, pitted Jack Coombs against Mordecai "Three-Finger" Brown, who had won 25 games for the Cubs. The A's offense heard none of this, raking for fourteen hits and nine runs, routing Brown, 9 to 3. Eddie Collins had two doubles. Coombs pitched well enough to win easily.

The teams then transferred via train to Chicago to play at the West Side Grounds. On Thursday, the 20th, Coombs was again tapped to start. Ed Reulbach, 12-8 on the season, started for Chicago and didn't last long. Reulbach was pulled after two innings, trailing 3 to 1. His replacement, Harry McIntire fared worse, yielding five runs while only getting one out in the 3rd. Baker ripped him for a triple, and Danny Murphy hit a home run. The A's won easily, 12 to 5.

Rain interrupted the series on the 21st. On Saturday, the 22nd, Bender faced King Cole, 20-4 with a league-best 1.80 ERA, at the West Side Grounds. The A's had a 3-to-2 lead going into the bottom of the 9th and could have clinched the series. But, the Cubs scored a run and then another in the 10th inning to win 4 to 3. Mordecai Brown entered the game after the 8th and prevented the A's from scoring. Brown was the winning pitcher.

The next day, Sunday, October 23rd, Jack Coombs was called again, this time to face Mordecai Brown. The A's scored a run in the 1st inning. Topsy Hartsel had led off the game with a single and then stole second. Eddie Collins drove him in on a single. The Cubs tied it in the second with a run off Coombs. The game remained tied until the 5th.

In that inning, Danny Murphy reached on an error. Jack Barry bunted him to second. Jack Lapp then singled him home.

The score remained 2 to 1 until the top of the 8th. The A's scored five in the frame thanks mainly to doubles by Bris Lord and Eddie Collins.

Frank Chance singled in a run in the 8th to pull within 7 to 2.

In the bottom of the 9th, Harry Steinfeldt and Joe Tinker both took Coombs to center field, where their balls were run down by Bris Lord, the latter a deep drive. Jimmy Archer, batting 8th in the lineup, touched Coombs for a single to keep the game alive. Johnny Kling was then called to pinch-hit for Brown. He tapped a ball to Barry at short, who stepped on second to force Archer.

The A's were World Series champions! Jack Coombs had won three of the four games.

The November 2nd *Gettysburg Times* mentioned Eddie Plank "is shortly to wed an old schoolmate." It appears nothing more came of this, and no mention was made of the name of the young lady, though, per Eddie Plank III, it was Anna Cora.

On November 4th, Eddie left Gettysburg for Philadelphia to participate in the A's celebration. After rain delayed the festivities, the parade occurred on the evening of November 5th. Thousands of fans cheered on Broad Street, between Montgomery and Wolf Streets. Eddie rode in a car with Coombs and Morgan. A banquet followed at the Bellevue-Stratford Hotel.

On November 26th, many of the A's, including Eddie, left on a vacation trip to Cuba. Eddie was home by December 28th. Meanwhile, Connie Mack, a widower for eighteen years, got married and went on a three-month honeymoon in Europe.

Lines at Shibe Park.

President Taft threw out the first pitch in 1910.

Harry Davis in May of 1910.

Eddie in July of 1910.

Portrait of Eddie in 1910.

Frank Baker in May of 1910.

Boxer Jack Johnson.

Philadelphia Inquirer headline announcing the World Series victory.

Cartoon for the Athletics vs, Cubs World Series.

Athletics and Cubs fraternizing at the World Series.
Plank is on the left and Harry Davis on right.

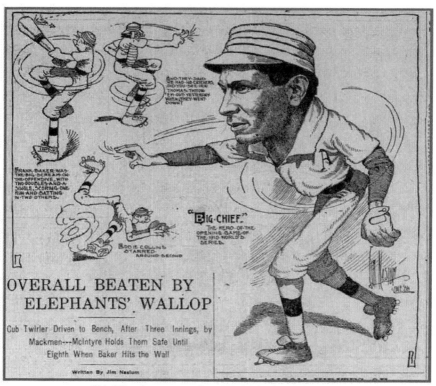

Chief Bender cartoon from World Series Game One.

PITCHERS COOMBS, PLANK
AND MORGAN

*Pitchers Plank, Coombs, and Morgan during the
World Series parade.*

The Athletics barnstorming in Cuba in December of 1910.

1911:
OLD WAR HORSE

N JANUARY 28TH, the *Philadelphia Inquirer* reported on the return of Mr. and Mrs. Mack from Europe. The Macks had been to Italy, Switzerland, France, England, and Ireland. Connie mentioned that "all thoughts of baseball were abandoned" when he left, but he was "very eager to gain the latest news of what transpired during his absence."

Apparently, Connie wasted little time to start firming up the 1911 Athletics. The February 9th *Philadelphia Inquirer* reported Eddie Plank was among four who have yet to sign: Bender, Coombs, Plank, and Russell.

Two days later, the paper reported the plans for spring training. Once again, Harry Davis was to take a cadre of the veterans to Hot Springs, Virginia, on March 1 "where a two weeks' steaming and flesh reducing stunt will be gone through. With the winter's laziness boiled out of their bones, the entire squad will be in Savannah, Georgia, two weeks later to join the young and aspiring Mackies."

The February 25th *Adams County News* announced the results of a shooting match held at Eddie Plank's farm on Washington's Birthday. "... thirty clay birds were awarded each contestant. The scores made were: Eddie Plank 26, Ira Plank 19, Robert Bell 20, and Norman Storrick 17.

Eddie signed-on again in late February and made the trip to Hot Springs as planned. He dabbled in golf while there, though he was grouped among the amateurs, and appeared not to have the abilities of Bender or Coombs at the sport.

On the 14th, he was in Savannah, pitching a couple innings against the Southern League team.

On March 23rd, Eddie and Adams County native Roy Clunk met on the diamond in Charleston, South Carolina. Reported Eddie

Collins to the Philadelphia press, as covered in the *Gettysburg Compiler*:

"DURING ALL OF THIS time Plank and Collamore were mowing the Southerners down as fast as they came to the plate. Connie's great left-hander worked the first four innings and the first man to hit was the only individual he allowed to reach first. As time goes on, more impressive does the excellent condition of the pitching staff become. Any talk of Plank being all-in would have been shamed today if the 'knockers' could have observed the hoop on his fast one and snap to his benders. Watch this old warhorse this coming season. The forebodings are bright for the Gettysburg farmer."

In New York City, on March 25, a fire at the Triangle Shirtwaist Factory fire killed 146, mostly young women who were working as seamstresses and were trapped due to the exits and stairwells being locked by management to prevent unwanted breaks. The factory was located at in the Asch Building at 23–29 Washington Place in Greenwich Village, occupying the eighth through the tenth floors. This building, now known as the Brown Building, still stands today.

During the last week in March, on the way to the Savannah Grounds, Eddie and Jack Coombs discussed Plank's future, per the *Adams County News*:

"TWO MORE YEARS," SAID Eddie, "this year and next—and back to the farm to stay the rest of my life. I shall quit the game in 1912 and all I ask is that I have two more good years. I have earned this long rest. In 1912, I will have a dozen years in the game as a pitcher. I started with Connie Mack and I want to quit with him. Most of the fellows who sit in the bleachers and roar at you when you have a bad day think that all you have to do is travel around the country and work a couple hours a day. I want to tell them that there is more work, actual work, in twirling one game of baseball then there is in two days' work on the farm. I get up at sunrise and work until sundown in the country and then sleep like a baby. But let me pitch a game of ball and my arm aches. I'm sore all over and can't sleep for pain. Two years more for me and then I'm through. If I haven't enough to live on then, I never will have if I stick in baseball twice as long."

The A's were back in Philadelphia on the 29th of March, ready to play the Phillies in the annual inner-city series, won this year by the A's, three games to two.

Opening Day for the defending World Series champions was April 12th, at Shibe Park. Chief Bender had the honor of starting against the Highlanders, who won 2 to 1.

Coombs lost the second game on the 13th, 3 to 1.

During the offday, word came of the unexpected passing of Cleveland ace Addie Joss from a brief bout with pleurisy and meningitis. Joss, only thirty-one, won 20 games four times, led the American League in ERA twice, and had a career ERA of only 1.89. He pitched a one-hitter in his major-league debut, a no-hitter, and a perfect game during his career.

Harry Krause took it on the chin on the 15th, 7 to 4. The A's had lost three in a row to open the season.

Finally, the A's got a win on the 17th against Boston at home. Eddie pitched brilliantly, winning 1 to 0. He scattered seven hits. However, they dropped the next one to the Red Sox.

On to Boston for a game on the 21st, the A's were drubbed 13 to 4. Coombs was hit hard.

Krause lost another on the 22nd, 4 to 3, the team now 1-6, in last place.

"Eddie Plank Stops Toboggan Slide" read the headline in the *Philadelphia Inquirer* about the game the next day. Eddie won 5 to 1, his second win of the season, and the team's as well.

The A's headed home to meet the Senators for a series beginning on the 25th. The A's won three of four.

On the 29th, the A's were in New York to face the Highlanders. Eddie started and was roughed up, but held on for a 10-to-6 victory.

The Athletics ended April 6-7, six games back of the hot 13-2 Detroit Tigers, tied for 5th place.

Chief lost a close one to the Highlanders in New York on May 2nd, 2 to 1. Coombs benefited from thirteen runs of support on the 3rd, winning 13 to 4.

The A's were then off to Washington. After Krause won the opener, 6 to 2, on the 4th, Eddie was on the hill on May 5. He was brilliant, winning easily, 9 to 0. Rube Oldring had a three-hit game at the plate.

The A's dropped the final game of the series. Eddie was then home with his parents on Sunday, May 7th.

In St. Louis, on the 10th, Bender was pulled in the 9th, leading 8 to 6. Eddie got the call and earned a save. After two more wins against the Browns, including a 17-to-13 win, Mack turned to Plank for the game on the 13th. "Plank was apparently as good as ever," reported the *Philadelphia Inquirer*. St. Louis mustered only four hits, twice as many as Eddie had at the plate. The final score was 7 to 0.

Meanwhile, in the National League, the New York Giants were setting records on their way to a 19-to-5 win over the St. Louis Cardinals. The Giants scored a major-league record 10 runs before St. Louis got an out in the 1st, 13 total in the inning; Fred Merkle drove in six of them. Giants manager John McGraw pulled starting pitcher Christy Mathewson after the 1st, saving him for another day. Rube Marquard then entered the game and set a record for relievers with 14 strikeouts in his eight-inning relief appearance. The record has since been broken.

On the 14th, the A's were in Chicago to face the White Sox. The A's dropped all four games in the series.

During this series, on May 15, the U.S. Supreme Court declared Standard Oil to be an "unreasonable" monopoly under the Sherman Antitrust Act and ordered the company to be dissolved.

Going into Detroit on the 18th, the A's were already ten games behind the flying Tigers. Plank, who had been saved by Mack for this series, did not pitch well in the first game, losing 9 to 4. The A's took two of the remaining three to split the series and were still ten games back.

The A's next beat the Naps on May 22nd in Cleveland, 9 to 3. Eddie was back in the winning column on the 23rd, 9 to 1. "Eddie Plank in Ye Olde Time Form Ties Up Crippled Ohioans with Steel-Bonded Knots," read the headline in the *Philadelphia Inquirer*.

The A's then took two more from Cleveland.

New York was in town on the 27th for a doubleheader. The teams split, Eddie winning the morning game 8 to 1, after which Coombs lost the afternoon, 8 to 3.

On May 30, the first Indianapolis 500 auto race was held. The winner was Ray Harroun, from Spartanburg, Pennsylvania, driving the Marmon Wasp.

The A's won the next three in a row to close out the month 23-16, in 2nd place, seven games back of Detroit.

June started with a 14-to-8 bashing of the Naps in Cleveland. Eddie followed on the 2nd with a rain-shortened 5-to-1 win. Plank allowed only three hits before the weather ended the game after the 7th.

The A's finished a three-game sweep the next day.

Detroit came to Philadelphia on the 7th with a 6 1/2 game lead. In the first game, the A's trailed 3 to 2 with two on and two out in the 9th. With two strikes on Rube Oldring, he smacked a ball deep into the outfield to score the winning runs. Jack Coombs got the win.

On the 8th, the game was tied at two into the 7th, when the Tigers put up three consecutive two-spots on Eddie Plank. The final score was 8 to 3.

The A's took the last game of the series on the 9th, pulling to within 5 1/2 games.

After winning the first two games against the Browns at home, Eddie was on the hill for a match on the 13th. Plank scattered six hits to win 6 to 0.

The A's took two of three from the White Sox, and then the Senators came to Shibe Park on the 19th. The A's swept all four games from Washington.

Meanwhile, on June 18th, the Tigers overcame a 13-to-1 deficit after 5 1/2 innings, to make the biggest comeback in Major League history. They ultimately beat the Chicago White Sox, 16 to 15.

The A's played two in Boston on the 23rd of June, and lost both, Coombs 7 to 3, and Plank 6 to 4. The A's then took the next three, making it four of five.

After the Boston series, Eddie spent a few days at home and then took his mother with him to Philadelphia.

In Washington on the 28th, the A's split a doubleheader with the Senators. Eddie gave up three runs in the 2nd inning of the morning game and lost 4 to 3. But, the bats were raking in the afternoon in support of Jack Coombs, 16 to 9.

The A's and Senators split the last two games of the series. At the end of June, Philadelphia was 42-22, only one game behind the Tigers, in 2nd place.

The *Adams County News* of July 1st included an item about wagers between Jack Coombs and Eddie Plank the prior season:

PLANK AND COOMBS WERE sitting together conversing when a reporter sauntered along. Remembering the bet of last year, he said, "Going to make any bets this year?"

"Bets, nothing," snorted Coombs, "Why you know last year if I lost I was going to give Plank one of my fine Guernsey cows. Well, I won. He went out and paid $12 for a beef critter and wanted me to take that. It would cost me only $24 to take her to Maine and I could have gone out and bought one like her for $8. No, sir, no bets this year with Plank."

"Rats," said Eddie in his own defense, "there was no kind of cow specified and no amount set for her price. What are you kicking about? I'll win more games than you will and I'll make you any bet that you want."

That day, Coombs beat Washington 13 to 8.

In New York on July 3rd, the A's swept a doubleheader. Eddie started the morning game but exited with it tied. Bender picked up the win in extra-innings, 8 to 7. Krause won the afternoon game 5 to 1. The A's had pulled to within a half-game of Detroit.

Smelling blood, the A's took two more by lopsided scores, 7 to 4 and 11 to 0, to take the lead in the pennant race on Independence Day.

However, the next day, the A's lost and the Tigers won, putting Detroit back in front.

The A's split four games with the Naps and slipped to a game behind by July 9th.

The A's came into Detroit on the 11th, 1½ games behind. Coombs was roughed up and lost 14 to 8.

The next day, Krause was no better, losing 9 to 0. The Tigers had expanded their lead to 3 1/2 games.

Bender lost a close one, 8 to 7, on the 13th to make the deficit 4 1/2.

Coombs lost again on Friday the 14th, 6 to 1, the Tigers soaring to 5 1/2 up.

Off to face the last-place St. Louis Browns on the road, Eddie was in top form, ending the losing streak with a 2-to-0 win. The Browns had only six hits in the contest.

The A's swept three more from the Browns to make it four in a row. Unfortunately, it did not make a dent in the lead.

Playing for the Vernon Tigers of the Pacific Coast League on July 19th, former circus acrobat Walter Carlisle completed an unassisted triple play. With the score tied at 3–3 in the sixth inning, and men on first and second base, Carlisle made a spectacular diving catch of a short fly hit by Roy Akin. Carlisle ran to step on second to retire Charlie Moore, who had strayed from the bag and then tagged George Metzger who was running from first. Carlisle is the only outfielder ever to make an unassisted triple play in organized baseball.

At Chicago on the 20th, Cy Young picked up the save in a 4-to-3 White Sox win.

The next day, Eddie led the A's to victory. "Mr. Plank allowed the Sox to whittle off but seven swats. He managed to string the home talent along on a lone clout in each round, the only exception being the eighth inning when three wallops resulted in the lone Sox counts of the matinee." Eddie won 10 to 2.

The A's also dropped the last game of the series.

On July 24th, an American League All-Star team—including Walter Johnson, Hal Chase, and Smoky Joe Wood—played the Cleveland Naps in Cleveland to raise over $12,000 for the widow of Addie Joss. The All-Stars won, 5-3.

Cleveland met the Athletics at Shibe Park for a twin bill on the 25th swept by Philadelphia.

Eddie and the A's won the next one, 6 to 5, but the Naps salvaged the final game of the series.

Philadelphia had crept to 3 1/2 games back in time for the 1st place Tigers to come to town.

On the 28th, the A's won two from the Tigers. Chief went eleven shutout innings to beat Summers 1 to 0. In the afternoon, Coombs won 6 to 5. The margin was now only a game-and-a-half.

The next day, the A's bats were hot, backing Eddie to an 11-to-3 win. Eddie Collins had four hits to Cobb's one. The margin was down to a half-game.

But, the Tigers staunched the bleeding, winning the final game of July. The A's finished the month 60-33, only 1 1/2 games behind the Tigers.

The series continued August 1st, the Tigers winning again, 13 to 6, to add some cushion.

The A's took three against the Browns, including a double-header on August 4th. In the morning game, Eddie threw a four-hitter, winning 5 to 1. "Plank was eminently successful in foiling the malignant machinations of the foe," wrote a reporter for the *Philadelphia Inquirer,* "allowing no more than one hit in any one inning, but fast fielding by Jack Barry saved him on no less than two different occasions." The A's moved into 1st place by a half-game. Cy Morgan won the afternoon game, 5 to 2, putting the lead at a full game.

The A's lost the final game of the series, coupled with a Detroit win, put the teams in a virtual tie on August 5th, the A's leading by percentage points.

This same day, former pitcher and umpire Bob Caruthers passed away at the age of 47. Caruthers had compiled the highest career winning percentage in major league history with at least 250 decisions. In both 1885 and 1889, he led American Association with 40 victories, pacing St. Louis and Brooklyn to pennants.

The White Sox were at Shibe Park on the 7th. The A's swept a doubleheader. The next day, Eddie started and had a no-decision, rookie Dave Danforth came in and picked up the win, 4 to 1.

Per the *Gettysburg Times*, there was a humorous exchange between first baseman Stuffy McInnis and Ping Bodie of the White Sox after Bodie had singled against Plank.

"WHAT DID YOU HIT, Ping?" asked Stuffy.

"A spitball," said the fence buster.

"Ed Plank never threw a spitter in his life," said McInnis.

"Well, then, it was a straight one," said Ping.

The White Sox and A's split the next two.

The A's and Red Sox split a doubleheader at Shibe Park on the 11th.

The next day, Eddie drove in three of the six Philadelphia runs, winning 6 to 1. He scattered eleven Red Sox hits. He then headed home for a few days.

The Red Sox won the final game on the 14th.

Off to Chicago, the A's played a twin bill on the 17th, winning both. The lead had increased to four over the Tigers.

The teams split the next two, Cy Morgan winning on the 19th, 3 to 1, in relief of Plank.

The A's were in St. Louis on the 20th and swept three from the last-place club.

In Cleveland, on the 26th, the A's swept a doubleheader, Eddie saving the first game for Coombs. The lead over Detroit was now 5 1/2 games.

The Tigers beckoned on the 27th. Bender dropped the opener, 4 to 3. The Tigers crept to 4 1/2 back.

Eddie took the mound on the 28th and fell behind early, 3 to 1 before the Philadelphia bats opened up for eleven more. The final score was 12 to 3. Lord had three hits to lead the offense. The margin was back to 5 1/2.

The Tigers won the next game, inching back to 4 1/2 out. The A's were 77-42 at the end of August and Eddie celebrated his thirty-sixth birthday.

This day, former pitcher Will White passed away at the age of 56. He won 229 games during his 10-year career, mostly with Cincinnati teams. He led the league in wins and strikeouts twice. He was believed to be the first major league player to wear eyeglasses on the field. Will and brother Deacon, a catcher, were a battery from 1877–79.

The A's swept two from Boston on the 1st of September on the road. Eddie played a role in both games, saving Bender's

1-to-0 victory in the morning and throwing a complete-game victory himself in the afternoon, 3 to 1.

The A's lost the third game in the series and headed home to Philadelphia.

Washington was the first team in on the homestand. Coombs won the first game of a doubleheader on the 4th. Eddie picked up the win in extra-innings in the afternoon, 6 to 5, defeating Walter Johnson, who had also been called to relieve.

The A's swept the series the next day.

The Red Sox were next in, for a doubleheader on the 6th of September. The A's won both games, Chief in the morning, 5 to 4, and Eddie in the afternoon, 4 to 3. Rube Oldring was the hot bat, with five hits in the first game and three in the second.

The A's took two of the next three, losing on the 9th, 2 to 0. Eddie gave up two runs in the 1st and was pulled. These were the only runs of the day.

On September 11th, the A's were in New York, winning handily, 12 to 5. Chief was the beneficiary of the run support.

Coombs won easily, 10 to 1, on the 12th.

That day, in the second game of a doubleheader that had been billed as a pitchers' duel, Boston Rustlers' Cy Young and the New York Giants' Christy Mathewson faced each other for the only time in their Hall of Fame careers. Over 10,000 fans were on hand, Boston's largest crowd of the year. Cy was hit for nine runs and three home runs before the third inning was complete. Given the quick, nearly insurmountable lead, McGraw pulled Mathewson to preserve him. He had pitched just two innings.

Eddie was on the slab on the 13th and made it three in a row against New York, winning 2 to 0. New York had only three hits in the game. The *Philadelphia Inquirer* called it "one of the very best games he has ever delivered in his eleven long and fruitful years with the forces of Cornelius McGillicuddy." The lead over Detroit had ballooned to eight games.

Due to the weather, Philadelphia next played on September 18, against the White Sox at Shibe Park. The A's won the morning game, 3 to 1, behind Coombs. The afternoon game of the doubleheader ended in a 1-to-1 tie, Morgan pitching all twelve innings.

On the 19th, the last-place Browns were visiting. The A's won the first game, but Eddie dropped the second game on the 20th, 3 to 2. After the game, Eddie arrived home for a few days off with friends and family.

The A's took the next two from the Browns. The A's lead over Detroit was ten games after September 22nd.

Also on that day, Cy Young pitched a shutout, defeating the Pittsburgh Pirates, 1 to 0. It was the 511th and final victory of his career.

The Tigers were in town on the 23rd to try to claw back into the race. The A's dominated them, 14 to 3, Krause picking up the win. The A's were two wins away from clinching.

The team traveled to Cleveland on the 24th. They won 5 to 3 behind Doc Martin, his first and only big league win.

On the 25th, the A's played the Tigers, needing to win one game. The Tigers did not go easily, winning 6 to 3 to extend their life another day.

In Boston, this day, the ground was broken for what was to become Fenway Park.

The next day, September 26, Jack Coombs had the honors, as the A's clinched the pennant, defeating the Tigers 11 to 5.

The A's cruised to the finish line the rest of the way, ending the season at 101-50, 13 1/2 games ahead of Detroit.

On the mound, Eddie finished the regular season 23-8, with a 2.10 ERA to lead the team, but trailing Cleveland rookie Vean Gregg's 1.80. Jack Coombs was 28-12, 3.53, leading the league in wins. Ed Walsh led the league with 255 strikeouts. Chief Bender finished 17-5, 2.16. Cy Morgan won 15 and Harry Krause 11.

At the plate, Eddie Collins led the team with a .365 average, trailing Ty Cobb's .420. Cobb also led the league with 127 RBI. Baker led the league with 11 home runs and led the team with 115 RBI. Frank Baker, .334, Danny Murphy, .329, Stuffy McInnis, .321, and Bris Lord, .310, also contributed with the bat. Even Jack Coombs hit .319 with two home runs.

In the National League, John McGraw's New York Giants were set to make a rematch of the 1905 series. The Giants had finished

99-54, 7 1/2 games ahead of the defending National League champion Cubs.

Christy Mathewson had gone 26-13, 1.99 to lead the team in wins. Young Rube Marquard, in his breakout season, went 24-7, 2.50. Doc Crandall was 15-5. Hooks Wiltse won twelve and Red Ames eleven for New York.

At the plate, catcher Chief Meyers led the team with a .332 average. Fred Merkle, the young first baseman, and Larry Doyle, the second-sacker, were the two top sluggers.

The World Series opened at the Polo Grounds in New York. Christy Mathewson was tapped to face Chief Bender.

Manager John McGraw thought he'd try to remind the visitors about their loss six years prior, reprising the all-black uniforms with white letters.

Stuffy McInnis missed the series due to a swollen wrist. Team captain Harry Davis took over duties at first base.

It was Davis, in the top of the 2nd inning, who singled in the first run, scoring Frank Baker, who had earlier singled and been moved into scoring position.

In the bottom of the 4th, the Giants evened things up, scoring an unearned run on an error by Eddie Collins.

In the bottom of the 7th, Chief Meyers and Josh Devore combined two doubles to score the go-ahead run.

It was all Mathewson would need the rest of the way. Game One went to New York.

Game Two was set for Shibe Park on the 16th of October. Eddie Plank faced Rube Marquard.

The A's got an early run for Eddie in the bottom of the 1st inning. Bris Lord led off with a single and went to second on an errant throw. Rube Oldring sacrificed him to third. While Eddie Collins was batting, Marquard uncorked a wild pitch, allowing Lord to sprint across the plate.

In the top of the second, the Giants evened things up against Plank. Buck Herzog reached on a single. Chief Meyers later doubled him home.

The score remained tied at one until the bottom of the sixth. After Eddie Collins doubled, Frank Baker ripped a two-run home run. The A's now led 3 to 1. It would be all Eddie needed. He cruised to the finish, allowing only one hit the rest of the way. The A's had evened the series.

During the game, in the top of the 8th inning, per an item in the *Gettysburg Times* of November 24:

JOSH DEVORE, THE LITTLE outfielder of the Giants, made a World's Series record in the second game at Philadelphia when he struck out four times. Eddie Plank outguessed him, serving a curve when he looked for a fastball and vice versa.

Devore was peeved. He turned to the umpire instead of the ball. When Connolly called him out the second time, he tossed his bat to show his disgust. The third time he tried to argue, but Connolly walked away. It was the same the fourth trip. Connolly ignored the kicks, but finally, Devore got on his nerves.

When the third strike was called, Devore said something and Connolly pulled off his mask. Later Connolly related the conversation.

"It is easy to see how you hold your job in the American League," said Devore.

"It's hard to see how you hold yours with the Giants," responded Connolly.

The *Gettysburg Times* from October 21 recounted how David Plank, Eddie's father, was finally able to see his son pitch and win a World Series game. "Great day for Eddie," said he. "He pitched a nice game of ball. I've wanted to see just such a thing as this for eleven years. Now I'm happy and there isn't anything that I want except–except Eddie to take another one and win the series." His deep-seamed face was illumined, the keen gray eyes flashed with a brilliant light.

For Game Three, the teams shifted back to the Polo Grounds. Christy Mathewson was again handed the ball. Jack Coombs was to pitch for Philadelphia.

The Giants manufactured a run in the bottom of the 3rd on singles by Chief Meyers and Mathewson, followed by a groundout by Devore.

The game remained 1 to 0 into the top of the 9th. With one out, Frank Baker ripped a Mathewson pitch deep to right for a home run. The game was tied.

Coombs put the Giants down in order in the bottom of the 9th. The game went into extra innings.

Mathewson mowed down Lapp, Coombs, and Lord in the top of the 10th.

Coombs walked Fred Snodgrass to start the bottom of the inning. Red Murray followed with a sacrifice bunt, moving Snodgrass into scoring position with one out. Snodgrass then tried to steal third but was caught, Lapp nailing him on a throw to Baker. After Merkle walked, he tried to steal second and was caught to end the inning.

In the top of the 11th, with one out, Eddie Collins singled. Frank Baker then hit a slow roller to third for a single. When Herzog's throw was wild, both runners advanced.

Danny Murphy next reached on an error by the shortstop, Art Fletcher, that allowed Collins to score the go-ahead run. Baker moved to third.

Harry Davis followed with a single to right, scoring Baker. Murphy was out trying to get to third. The inning ended when Davis was caught trying to steal second.

The game went to the bottom of the 11th, the A's ahead 3 to 1.

Herzog led off the bottom of the 11th with a double off Jack Coombs. After Fletcher flied out, Meyers grounded out, advancing Herzog to third. Beals Becker hit a grounder to Collins at second that should have ended the game, but Eddie erred, Herzog scoring. Becker then tried to get into scoring position but was caught stealing to end the game.

The A's now had a two-games-to-one advantage.

At this point, the weather got nasty—for days—the series not able to resume until October 24th after six days of rain. This lengthy delay was the longest between World Series games until the Loma Prieta earthquake interrupted the 1989 Series, which incidentally featured the same two franchises, albeit on the west coast.

Game Four was played at Shibe Park. Chief Bender started for the Athletics against Christy Mathewson.

The Giants jumped on Bender in the top of the 1st inning, scoring two runs by the time there was an out. Matty then held the A's until the bottom of the 4th.

In that inning, Baker, then Murphy, then Davis hit consecutive doubles, scoring two. Davis later scored on a sacrifice fly. The A's now led 3 to 2.

The A's added-on in the bottom of the 5th. Eddie Collins singled and was doubled in by Baker. The lead inched up to 4 to 2. It was all Chief needed to beat Mathewson for the second time.

The A's were on the verge of another championship, three games to one.

Once again, the teams rode trains to New York. Game Five pitted Rube Marquard against Jack Coombs.

The game was scoreless until the top of the 3rd when Rube Oldring ripped a three-run home run to deep left field. The A's could smell the championship. Coombs seemed unbeatable.

McGraw then pulled Marquard for Red Ames, until pinch-hit for by Doc Crandall in the 7th. In that home 7th, the Giants showed a little life, making a run out of a walk, error, ground out, and a sacrifice fly. The Giants now trailed 3 to 1. This score held until the bottom of the 9th.

Coombs got Herzog to ground out to start the Giants' 9th. Art Fletcher followed with a double to left and moved to third base on Meyers' groundout. The A's were now an out from another championship, and the runner on third did not matter.

Doc Crandall, who had mowed down the A's the last two innings, was the last hope for the Giants. He was no slouch with the bat, hitting .239 in over 100 at-bats for McGraw. The pitcher/utility infielder stepped in with the championship on the line against Coombs. Crandall ripped a double to center, scoring Fletcher. It was now 3 to 2.

Josh Devore was next up. With two out and the tying run on second, Devore avenged the four strikeouts against Plank by ripping a single to left, scoring Crandall. The game was tied.

Devore then tried to steal second to get into scoring position but was nailed by Lapp with Doyle at the plate.

The Giants had avoided elimination with a dramatic 9th inning comeback.

In the top of the 10th, Jack Coombs bunted for a single with one out. Davis sent in Amos Strunk to run for him. But, neither Lord nor Oldring could solve Crandall. The game remained tied.

In the bottom of the 10th, Plank was called to pitch. The inning did not go well. Larry Doyle, down to two strikes, greeted Eddie with a double over Baker's head. The New York throng roared its approval.

Fred Snodgrass, who was trying to sacrifice Doyle to third, bunted a ball to Plank on the third base side. Eddie sprinted for the ball and tried to nab Doyle heading into third. His throw to Baker was too late. Men were now on first and third with no one out.

Red Murray popped a ball to right, but it was too short to score Doyle. Murphy caught the ball near the infield.

With one out, Fred Merkle stepped to the plate. He hit a deep drive to the right-field line. Danny Murphy rushed in and caught the ball to cries of "bonehead" from the fans, who thought he had just caught a ball that would have gone foul. Doyle tagged up and headed home. Murphy spun and threw perfectly to Lapp on a line, but it was too late. However, Doyle, in his excitement, never touched home! The raucous crowd spilled out onto the field to celebrate the apparent victory, mobbing the players and umpires.

Said umpire Bill Klem, from the National League, after the game, "If Lapp had tagged Doyle, I would have called him out."

Connie Mack later said he had also noticed Doyle did not touch the plate but did nothing for fear of setting off a riot.

Regardless, the Giants were credited with the winning run, 4 to 3. Eddie took the loss, the series now getting tighter at three games to two.

The teams shifted back to Shibe Park for Game Six. Chief Bender was tapped to face Red Ames.

The Giants scored a run in the top of the 1st to take a 1-to-0 lead.

In the bottom of the 3rd, Bris Lord doubled home Ira Thomas, who had walked. The game was now tied.

The next inning, the A's scored four runs on sloppy play. The bases were loaded when Jack Barry came to the plate, the A's leading 2 to 1. Barry tapped a ball back to Ames, who threw it wildly to first, the ball bouncing off Barry's head and into right field. While the bases were clearing to the screams of the Philadelphia fans, right fielder Murray threw wildly to second base. Barry came in to score in a play that must have looked like Little League mayhem. No matter, the A's led 5 to 1.

Hooks Wiltse took over the mound duties for McGraw. In the 6th, the A's added a run on Barry's sacrifice fly.

The A's blew it open in the 7th, scoring seven runs on seven hits. The lead was now 13 to 1, and Bender was cruising.

The Giants finally scored again in the top of the 9th. Fletcher came in on Herzog's groundout. It was the second out in the inning and the bases were empty, the A's leading 13 to 2.

In a gesture of sportsmanship, captain Harry Davis then called for Stuffy McInnis, who had been injured the entire series, to take over at first base and play in his first World Series game.

Art Wilson batted for the Giants. He hit a shot to Baker at third, who threw across the diamond to McInnis for the final out. The A's were champions for the second consecutive season, the first American League team to do so.

The next day, the boys split up the loot at Shibe Park. Each player received $3654.58. Most of the team quickly left town, not wanting to stick around due to the extended series schedule.

From Cleveland, it was announced that Harry Davis would leave the A's to become the pilot of the Naps in 1912.

On October 31, Eddie Plank and Eddie Collins arrived at the Gettysburg farm in Plank's new automobile. The two planned to spend several days there, taking advantage of the opening of hunting season.

Chevrolet officially entered the automobile market on November 3rd, its aim to compete with the Henry Ford's successful Model T.

On November 12th, the *Philadelphia Inquirer* reported that Connie Mack had selected Danny Murphy to be the new team captain to take the place of Harry Davis.

The next month, Connie sold Topsy Hartsel to Toledo of the American Association and Paddy Livingston to Cleveland, where he would play with Harry Davis.

The 1911 Philadelphia Athletics.

The Athletics take the field for the 1911 World Series.

Bender, Coombs, and Plank in 1911.

EDDIE PLANK
Who Pitched Athletics to Victory.

Eddie Plank was the winning pitcher on October 17, 1911.

Eddie pitching.

The champions raise the flag on Opening Day at Shibe Park in 1911.

Portrait of Eddie in 1911.

RUBE OLDRING, HOME RUN HITTER

Rube Oldring with the bat during the World Series.

503 PLANK P
PHILA ATHLETICS A. L.

Eddie on the mound in 1911.

Cartoon of Stuffy McInnis.

Athletics in the pennant race.

Cartoon lauding Eddie's hitting.

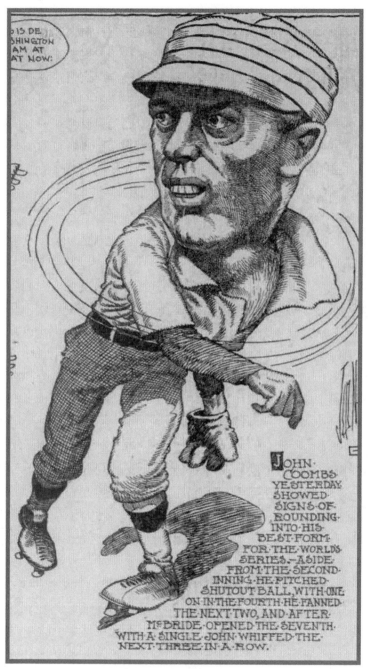

Cartoon of Jack Coombs.

Cartoon of Eddie Collins.

CONNIE AND THE SAME OLD ELEPHANT

Connie clinches another pennant.

The Athletics are World Series champions.

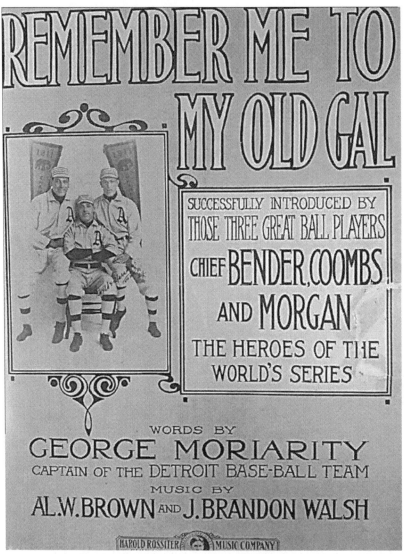

Bender, Coombs, and Morgan selling sheet music.

"DANNY" MURPHY,
NEW CAPTAIN OF
THE ATHLETICS.

Danny Murphy became the new team captain in
November 1911.

1912:
AN OLD MASTER

DDIE PLANK BEGAN the year with his annual oyster bake at the farm north of Gettysburg. The *Gettysburg Times* from January 4th recounted the evening:

EDDIE PLANK'S ANNUAL SURPRISE party has become such a regular event that it would surprise Eddie to find it a week late some year. For a number of years past, a few of the Plank boys' friends have gathered each winter to celebrate their prowess in the baseball world. The Plank farm, about three and one-half miles north of Gettysburg is improved with a brick and concrete building ordinarily used as a laundry or outhouse. This building contains a large low stove especially adapted for roasting oysters. Consequently, the 'piece de resistance' of the party is roast oysters. Other things to eat and drink are there as a matter of form.

Some twenty or more people, including a string orchestra, left the Hotel Gettysburg Wednesday evening in a big Holtzworth and Hoffman, proceeding to the Plank farm where the festivities began about eight o'clock. Songs were sung and stories told until the weaker voices gave way. C.S. Duncan, Esq., gave a short résumé of the Plank boys' baseball career, deploring the tendency of the younger generation abroad to associate with Gettysburg the name Plank, instead of the battle which formerly accounted for the town's fame. Mr. Duncan cleverly expressed the appreciation of the assembled guests for the opportunity to honor both Ed and Ira Plank. Dr. E.H. Markley also expressed the general sentiment of the crowd in a few well-chosen words. Among those present were C.K. Gilbert, Paul Martin, J.D. Swope, Esq., C.B. Tate, D.J. Forney, Dr. J.P. Dalbey, Clyde Daly, C.W. Holtzworth, J.H. Holtzworth, C.H. Wilson, Dr. E.H. Markley, J.G. McIlhenny, W.L. Hafer, J.A. Holtzworth, N.S. Heindel, Wm Weaver, John Brehm, C.W. Troxel, C.S. Duncan, Ira Plank, and Ed Plank.

A few days later, New Mexico became the 47th state on January 6th.

On the 9th, Eddie and Ira participated in a bowling contest against Chambersburg. The Gettysburg men won narrowly, 1466 to 1454.

That day, Connie Mack announced spring training plans for San Antonio, Texas. The young players would report first, followed by the veterans, a week later. The squad would remain together this year, with no special trip to Warm Springs, Virginia.

An article reprinted in the *Gettysburg Compiler* on January 10, compared the accomplishments of Christy Mathewson and Eddie Plank, the former receiving more praise. The article also reiterated that Plank planned to retire after the 1912 season.

Over 200 people turned out to watch the rematch of the bowling tournament, this time at the Monarch alleys in Gettysburg on the 17th. Once again the Planks and their Gettysburg teammates won, 1410 to 1382.

In late January, due to a meningitis outbreak in the San Antonio area, the Phillies offered to share their facilities at Hot Springs, Arkansas, with the Athletics. Apparently, Hot Springs had become a favorite spot for the major-league clubs, the Phillies were among five planning to use the facilities this year. Mack thanked Fogel, the Phillies' owner, and replied he would consider it should the outbreak not subside by the time the A's were planning to head south.

An offer also came in from New Orleans for the A's to move their training camp there, near where the Cubs would be training. In the end, the plans to train in San Antonio remained intact.

The newspapers ran a story featuring the re-signing of the Athletics lauded infield to contracts for the upcoming season. Said the *Butte Daily Post* on February 12th, "Connie Mack's $100,000 infield gave him little or no trouble getting in line. McInnis, Collins, Barry, and Baker, all well under the 30-year mark, have been signed at big increases in salary."

On February 14, Arizona became the 48th state in the union.

Six days later, the Plank boys and their Gettysburg team won another bowling match, this time in Hanover.

In late February, Connie received an offer from Giants' manager John McGraw to hold a three-game replay of the World Series in the south via exhibition games between the clubs. McGraw mentioned their willingness to travel to San Antonio, Texas, where the A's were training.

A few weeks later, when the veterans were set to arrive, Connie agreed to play two games in San Antonio with New York on the 16th and 17th of March. However, McGraw backed out of the proposition, concerned his team had not had a chance to get into shape, given the rainy weather this spring.

The team broke camp in late March and began its trek back to Philadelphia, stopping for an exhibition in Houston on March 24.

In a gesture of friendship between Japan and the United States the Mayor of Tokyo, Yukio Ozaki, gave 3,000 cherry blossom trees to be planted in Washington, D.C., on March 27.

In the first game ever played at Fenway Park, the Boston Red Sox defeated Harvard University in an exhibition game played in a snowstorm at Fenway Park, the first game ever played there on April 9.

The next day, the RMS *Titanic* left Southampton, England on its maiden voyage to New York.

Meanwhile, in New York on April 11, the local Highlanders, the predecessor of the New York Yankees, wore pinstriped uniforms for the first time in their opening game at Hilltop Park against the Boston Red Sox.

The Athletics opened their season at Shibe Park against the Washington Senators with great fanfare, as befitting the World Series champions. Mayor Blankenburg threw out the first pitch to umpire Silk O'Laughlin, who relayed it to Jack Coombs on the mound. Coombs faced Walter Johnson and beat him 4 to 2.

Cy Morgan won the next game on the 12th, 3 to 1.

This day, Clara Barton, passed away in Glen Echo, Maryland, at the age of ninety. Barton was the founder of the American Red Cross following her work as a nurse during the Civil War.

On Monday, April 15, Boston was at Shibe Park to open a series. In his first action of the year, Eddie Plank won 4 to 1, helped by the hot bat of Frank Baker.

The headlines in the newspapers that afternoon and the next day were all about the sinking of the RMS *Titanic* off the coast of Nova Scotia. Just before midnight, the luxury liner struck an iceberg. It sank at 2:20 in the morning, ending the lives of over 1500 people including businessman John Jacob Astor IV, presidential aide Archibald Butt, mystery author Jacques Futrelle, businessman Benjamin Guggenheim, painter, sculptor, and writer Francis Davis Millet, owner of Macy's department store Isidor Straus, and bibliophile Harry Elkins Widener. Miraculously, Milton Hershey, the chocolatier, was not on the ship. He had written a check to White Star Lines to cover the tickets, but due to extenuating circumstances, changed his plans and left Europe the week prior aboard the German steamship *Amerika*.

The A's dropped the next game to Boston on the 16th.

On April 18, the RMS *Carpathia* arrived in New York City carrying 706 Titanic survivors.

The next day, Walter Johnson shut out the A's on three hits in a game played in Washington.

On the 20th, Jack Coombs and the A's beat Washington 6 to 3, but Coombs had to be carried off the field, suffering from a torn ligament in his side.

Elsewhere in the American League both Navin Field in Detroit and Fenway Park in Boston hosted their first official major league games.

The A's next traveled to New York to face the Highlanders on the 23rd, losing the first game.

The following day, Eddie was on the mound and the headline in the *Philadelphia Inquirer* read "Veteran Flinger Holds Kilties to Four Hits." Eddie won easily, 7 to 0.

The A's won the final game of the series and moved on to Boston.

Playing in Fenway Park for the first time on April 26, the A's dropped the game to the Red Sox, 7 to 6. During the game, Hugh Bradley of Boston became the first player to hit a home run over the Green Monster.

The teams split the next two games, Eddie winning 7 to 1 on Monday the 29th. Boston took the final game on the 30th.

The Athletics ended April 7-6, 2 1/2 games back of the Chicago White Sox, tied for 4th place.

After dropping the first two games against the Highlanders at Shibe Park on May 1st and 2nd, the A's won a wild one, 18 to 15, on the 3rd. Plank came in to get the last couple outs for the save.

The next day, Plank was back on the slab, pitching a complete game in the A's 10-to-5 victory. Eddie yielded fifteen hits, but it was good enough to win. After the game, he headed home to Gettysburg to spend a few days.

The A's next played on the 10th of May in Cleveland against Harry Davis's Naps, where they lost the only game of the series, the others being canceled by rain.

The game on May 11th was one of Eddie's ugliest of his career. Leading the White Sox and Ed Walsh 5 to 1 going into the bottom of the 8th in Chicago, Eddie gave up a run. In the 9th, he was wracked for seven more, losing 9 to 5.

The A's lost the next two, and then Eddie snagged a win in relief in an 8-to-6 game on the 15th.

On May 17, the A's were home to face Detroit. The A's won the game 6 to 3. Ty Cobb did not play due to being suspended indefinitely for going after a fan in New York the prior week.

The next day, the Tigers threatened to strike in protest. The owner of the Tigers promised to use replacement players to avoid a forfeiture to the A's and a stiff fine. A team was quickly recruited from the coaching staff and local colleges. When the Tigers took the field, with Cobb, and he was not allowed to play by the umpire, the Tigers' players exited the field. Quickly, Jennings and the coaches called in the substitutes, signed them to contracts, and gave them the uniforms off the backs of the real Detroit Tigers.

The lineup that day for Detroit, facing Jack Coombs, was:

Jim McGarr, 2b—age 22 from Philadelphia, went 0 for 4 in his only big league appearance.

Billy Maharg, 3b—age 31 from Philadelphia, went 0 for 1. He later played another game for the Philadelphia Phillies in 1916.

Ed Irwin, 3b & c—age 30 from Philadelphia, went 2 for 3 in place of Maharg in his only big league action.

Allan Travers, p—age 20 from Philadelphia, went 0 for 3 in his only big league appearance. He also pitched all eight innings, yielding 24 runs, 14 earned, walking seven while striking out 1. The A's had 26 hits against him.

Dan McGarvey, lf—age 25 from Philadelphia, went 0 for 3 with a walk and hit-by-pitch in his only big league action.

Bill Leinhauser, cf—age 18 from Philadelphia, went 0 for 4 with three strikeouts in his only big league action.

Joe Sugden, 1b—age 41 from Philadelphia, went 1 for 4. Sugden, a coach on the Tigers, had a 13-year career in the majors, last playing for the St. Louis Browns in 1905. He had played for Connie Mack on the Pirates in the 1890s.

Deacon McGuire, c—age 48 from Youngstown, Ohio, went 1 for 2. McGuire had been a veteran of over 20 big league seasons. He had played only sparingly since 1906. He had been a manager in recent years and was the current Detroit pitching coach.

John Joseph Cofey, 3b—age 18 from Oswayo, Pennsylvania, fielded two putouts and an assist. His name appeared as "Coffee" in the box score, but he was going by the name Jack Smith. Cofey was his name at birth.

Vincent Maney, ss—age 25 from Batavia, New York, went 0 for 2 with a walk, hit by pitch, and two strikeouts in his only big league action.

Hap Ward, rf—age 26 from Leesburg, New Jersey, went 0 for 2 with two strikeouts and a caught-stealing in his only big league action.

Hughie Jennings, ph—age 43 from Pittston, Pennsylvania, went 0 for 1, pinch-hitting for Travers. Jennings was the manager of the Tigers and had a Hall of Fame career.

The A's won the game 24 to 2. Boardwalk Brown relieved Coombs early in the game, when the outcome was assured, and pitched most of the game.

The A's next played on the 21st of May against the Browns at home. They took two of three in the series.

Off to Boston on May 24th, the teams split the first two games. On the 27th, Eddie went about half-way in a 12-to-6 win before giving way to Boardwalk Brown and then Bender.

The Sox took the last game of the series.

In New York on the 29th, the A's won two days in a row to end the month of 17-16, 7 1/2 games out in 3rd place.

Joe Dawson won the second Indianapolis 500 on May 30th. Ralph DePalma's Mercedes broke down within sight of the finish, allowing Dawson to skate past for the win.

Also on May 30, Wilbur Wright, age 45, half of the Wright Brothers of aviation fame, passed away from typhoid in Dayton, Ohio.

The A's split four games with the White Sox in Chicago to start the month of June. Eddie pitched on the 3rd and won 7 to 4.

On June 5, United States Marines landed in Cuba to protect U.S. citizens and pacify a rebellion.

That day, the Browns came to Philadelphia and put a spanking on Boardwalk Brown, winning 13 to 1.

Bender won 7 to 2 on the 6th. Eddie followed on the 7th with a 9-to-4 victory. The Browns took the last game to split the series.

On the 9th, the A's were in Cleveland to face Harry Davis's team. The A's swept all four games, including an 8-to-7 win by Eddie Plank in relief of Morgan on the 11th.

The *Gettysburg Compiler* on June 12 reprinted an article from the *North American* recounting Plank's, longevity, career, and many accomplishments. Regarding Eddie's good health, the reporter wrote, "The answer to Plank's success is easy. He is the most careful of livers. He regards baseball as a lucrative business and conducts his existence in such a way as to conserve his physical resources to the limit. He owns a big farm property in Gettysburg, Pa., scene of the famous battlefield, and spends the winters there. He is a bachelor."

Eddie next started against the Tigers in Detroit on June 13th. He won the game 4 to 3. The August 13th *Gettysburg Times* recounted the pitching prowess of Plank against the Tigers that day:

TO PLANK AND PLANK alone belongs the credit for the Athletics' victory over the Tigers in the opening game of the series.

Time and again when a hit would have meant a run, Plank stood in the center of the road to victory and turned back Jennings' players. He forced such players as Crawford and

Gainer and Moriarty to drop back when thousands cheered them on.

In the eighth inning, with one run in, Cobb on third, one man up and Crawford at bat, Plank seemed the least concerned. Occasionally, he would bluff to hold Cobb at third, and when he did pitch, he didn't use speed, he used nothing but a slow bending curve over the outside of the plate.

Instead of giving Crawford a ball that Sam was likely to hit far into the outfield, Plank, cool to the point of extreme self-confidence in his position, would carefully measure Crawford with his eye and then pitch.

The games are few and far between when a man like Crawford will fall in the wake of an opposing pitcher's curves. Sam can, at least, be depended upon to send out a sacrifice fly, but Thursday, in the pinches, he would do nothing but pop weakly to Collins.

Plank is an old master at the art of pitching. He hasn't the speed of a score of other pitchers in the league. He hasn't the curves of many more.

But he has the head. He knows the batters. And he utilizes every speck of his knowledge.

When Vitt came to bat for Onslow in the ninth inning, Plank hesitated.

He didn't know Vitt. He had never seen him in an actual game.

The Athletics' twirler involuntarily, perhaps, glanced towards the bench, where his leader, Connie Mack, was sitting. Then he straightened and sent a low, nasty curve over the outside of the plate. Vitt did not move.

"You don't know that boy," yelled a spectator.

Plank worked about, then sent across a strike. And still, Vitt didn't move.

Plank sent another and this one Vitt met and the ball sped on a line to Collins.

Vitt was out.

Then came Louden. Plank knew or thought he knew more of Louden than of Vitt, and he sent across a high straight one.

And Louden didn't move.

Then Plank resorted to his famous cross-fire and Louden singled.

With Bush at bat and Louden on first, Plank shot across a straight ball, Bush met it and lined it to Barry.

The game was over.

And Plank's strategy had won it.

It wasn't his support because Athletics' errors let in two of the Tigers' three runs.

The Tigers and A's split the next two and then Eddie was back on the mound on the 16th. He survived an 8-to-6 win, his second against Detroit in four days.

Washington was in town for six games beginning on the 19th of June. The A's took the first four, sweeping two doubleheaders, before dropping the final two. Eddie pitched the morning game on the 20th and won 5 to 0. "Slants of Southpaw Plank are Thrillers" read the headline in the *Philadelphia Inquirer.* "The visitors failed to get a safe swat off Plank until the sixth, and in six of the nine innings but three men to an inning faced the veteran southpawer."

New York was next at Shibe Park starting on the 24th. The A's took three of four games.

On June 28th, the great Christy Mathewson of the New York Giants became only the eighth pitcher to record 300 career wins.

The A's took the train to Washington to start a series that day. Coombs and Pennock picked up wins as the A's swept the doubleheader.

The next day, the 29th, Eddie faced Walter Johnson, winning 2 to 1. Jack Coombs picked up the save.

The A's ended June 38-25, six games behind the Boston Red Sox in 2nd place.

The Athletics started July splitting two with the Senators to conclude the series.

First-place Boston was next in to Shibe Park for six games. This was an opportunity for the A's to make up ground. Unfortunately, they dropped four of six. Plank had one of the wins in the morning game of the doubleheader on July 4th, defeating Smoky Joe Wood, 4 to 3. Coombs won the other on the morning of the 5th. The A's slipped to eight behind.

The A's next dropped a doubleheader to Cleveland on June 8th, and then Chicago came to town for four games.

The A's took three of four from the White Sox, Eddie posting the only loss on June 10th, 4 to 3. Eddie was winning 3 to 0 into the 7th inning when the Sox tied the score. They walked off in the 9th, scoring the deciding run.

The A's next played five against Cleveland through June 16th. Eddie did not figure in any of them. The team won three of the five.

In the first game of a doubleheader at home against Detroit on the 17th, Eddie was ripped for four runs in the 2nd and was soon pulled. He was the losing pitcher in a lopsided 13-to-1 loss. After getting a few hours' rest, he was back out there for the second game in relief of Bender and picked up the win in the 11th inning, 5 to 4.

The teams then split doubleheaders on the 19th and 20th. Eddie won the morning game on the 20th, 4 to 3. Wrote a reporter in the *Philadelphia Inquirer*:

BUT, THANK HEAVEN, Ty Cobb is out of town now, and things will once again settle down to the even tenor of their way, with the home team winning a game every now and then and still managing to keep their toenails dug into the first division turf, at least. During the four days in which he tarried with us, this Cobb person did everything but tear down the outfield fences at Shibe Park and steal the grandstand, and it was probably only because he had no earthly use for such commodities in his regular business that he did not do this.

After having ripped off two home runs, three triples, three doubles, and eight singles out of twenty-three times at bat during the five games that preceded the final affair yesterday, during this farewell engagement, he introduced a novelty just by way of showing up a little and letting us see that he possessed further perquisites by galloping all the way from first to the plate on a throw to second that never even went out of the infield, and thereby scoring a run that was just the margin his team eventually won by. Well, this Cobb person is gone now, and we have nothing but ordinary human beings to contend with for a while. That ought to help some.

Eddie spent some time off at home in Gettysburg. The St. Louis Browns came to town and dropped three of four. After the last game on the 24th, Eddie returned to Philadelphia.

The A's loaded up the train and headed to Detroit for a series against the Tigers. Plank pitched the opener on the 27th and picked up a 9-to-5 win. The A's scored three in the 1st, but the Tigers responded with five. After that, Eddie was not scored on and the A's rallied for six more. Cobb had three more hits.

Coombs lost 8 to 4 on the 28th. Eddie was called again on the 29th to end a rally. Plank closed-out the game in relief of Brown, giving up just one single in over two innings of work to pick up the win in a 7-to-6 game.

The month ended for the A's with a loss to the Tigers on the 30th. The Athletics were now 55-41, 11 1/2 games back of Boston, in 3rd place. Washington was now in 2nd place, seven games behind the Red Sox.

Coombs and Bender each won games of a doubleheader in Cleveland on August 3rd.

Eddie pitched the opener in St. Louis on the 4th, winning 8 to 3. He also added two hits with the stick. The A's took three of four in the series.

Meanwhile, on August 5th, there is a schism in the Republican Party between those supporting President Taft and those supporting former President Theodore Roosevelt. The Roosevelt splinter started the Progressive Party which also came to be known as the Bull Moose Party.

Starting on the 9th, the A's took three of four at Chicago. Eddie won a rain-shortened game on the 10th, 8 to 0. Said the *Philadelphia Inquirer*, "Eddie Plank, grizzled and boasting all his fool stuff, opposed the locals and halted them with four singles in five sessions."

On the 14th, the A's were home to play four against Cleveland, sweeping them all. Eddie pitched the afternoon game of the doubleheader that day, beating Steen 2 to 0. Eddie scattered eight hits in logging the shutout.

After the series, the A's had crept to 8 1/2 games behind.

Chicago then came to town on the 18th. Plank faced Walsh. The A's outhit the White Sox 15 to 8 but lost the game, 5 to 4. The Sox swept the three games dropping the A's to 11 1/2 behind.

St. Louis was a welcome respite on the 22nd and 24th, providing doubleheaders at Shibe Park. Eddie won his game on the

22nd, 3 to 1, scattering nine hits. The A's swept all four games and gained a game back in the pennant race.

Around this time, The *New York Press* included a tribute to Eddie:

THERE IS AN OLD left-hander in the game who, though he is not as spectacular as Marquard, is still one of the greatest pitchers of the day. He is Eddie Plank of the Athletics, who is nearing his thirty-eighth birthday. Plank has been the steadiest of Mack's gunners this season. Twice he lost games when the White Sox got to him in the ninth inning. On the whole, the Gettysburg cross-fire artist has been the most reliable pitcher in the Mack camp and has done better work this year than Coombs or Bender.

Plank is like wine, he improves with age. Mathewson is the only pitcher now in the game who has scored more victories than Plank. Eddie started in to pitch about the same time that "Big Six" entered the National League, and like Matty has fallen only once under the .500 mark. Eddie is five years older than Mathewson. He was twenty-five when he joined the Athletics fresh from college. Plank is a grand old warrior and is a shining example of what the simple life can do for a ballplayer.

Detroit was next into town. The A's took two of three from the Tigers, but could not gain ground.

The month ended with a series in Boston commencing on the 29th. Eddie was tapped for the first game and was knocked out in the fourth, trailing 5 to 0. The A's lost the game 8 to 1. They then dropped the next two.

The A's ended August 73-50, 13 1/2 games behind Boston in 3rd place. Eddie Plank celebrated his thirty-seventh birthday.

As the Athletics entered September, it looked very unlikely the team would repeat. Every time they got some momentum, the Red Sox were playing just as well. Every time the two faced off, the Red Sox were dominant.

The A's started September winning two of three in Washington. Plank beat the Senators 3 to 2 in the first game of a doubleheader on the 2nd. Eddie scattered six hits, and Bender came in for the save. The A's split the other two. Unfortunately, they lost another half-game in the standings.

The A's moved on to Hilltop Park to play five against the Highlanders. Philadelphia won four of the five games, Eddie picking up two wins.

On the 5th, "Ed's Cross-fire Mowed Them Down in Deadly Style" was the headline in the *Philadelphia Inquirer*. "In the second game, New York had very little chance with Plank. The veteran fork-hand slinger had his deadly cross-fire working to perfection." Eddie won a shortened contest 5 to 2, the Highlanders not scoring until the 6th inning.

Eddie picked up a win in relief on the 7th in a game that went into extra-innings. The A's won 10-8 in the 11th.

Despite the victories, no ground was gained on Boston.

The A's were in Detroit from the 10th to the 12th, winning two of three, but losing another game in the standings. Eddie picked up a save on the 11th in a 9-to-7 game.

The next four games were at Cleveland, starting on the 13th of September. The A's lost the first three games. Eddie took the mound on the 16th with the team nearing elimination. "Plank never pitched a better game in Cleveland," wrote a reporter from the *Philadelphia Inquirer*. Eddie held the A's to only four hits in shutting them out 8 to 0.

In Chicago on the 18th and 19th, the A's dropped two of three and were eliminated from the pennant race.

The rest of the way, Eddie beat the St. Louis Browns on the 22nd of September, 8 to 2. He was greatly helped by Eddie Collins who had four hits and stole six bases.

In Philadelphia on the 27th, Eddie faced Walter Johnson in one of the most remarkable games of his career, though it did not start out that way. Eddie got behind 4 to 0 by the end of the 2nd inning. "The Gettysburg farmer then shifted his wad over into the gable end of his mouth, which restored his equilibrium, and permitted but eight widely-separated hits in the following seventeen innings, holding the foe scoreless for sixteen consecutive rounds." Washington's Bob Groom, a 24-game winner in 1912, started for the Senators and held the lead until the bottom of the 9th when the A's scored three to tie. He was then yanked for Walter Johnson, who proceeded to hurl ten shutout innings. So, while the Nats threw their two best at the A's, Eddie kept chugging along all by himself, trading zeros with Johnson until the top of the 19th, when Washington finally got a run. In the end, Eddie lost 5 to 4, but no one felt that way. It was the most remarkable pitching performance in a losing cause that anyone could recall.

The Athletics finished the season 90-62, fifteen games behind the Boston Red Sox, in 3rd place. The Senators were one game ahead of the A's, nabbing 2nd place, thanks to that 19-inning Walter Johnson victory.

Eddie finished the season the ace of the staff at 26-6, 2.22. Smoky Joe Wood led the circuit in wins with 34. Johnson led the league with a 1.39 ERA and 303 strikeouts. Jack Coombs was 21-10, 3.29. Bender and Brown each won 13.

At the plate, Ty Cobb won the batting title at .402. Eddie Collins led the A's with a .348 average. Home Run Baker tied with Tris Speaker for the home run lead with 10. Baker also led the league with 130 RBI. Baker also hit .347.

McInnis had a great year at .327. Oldring hit .301. Captain Danny Murphy hit .323 in limited duty.

In the end, the A's pitching, besides Plank, was not as strong as prior seasons.

On October 9th, in the *Gettysburg Compiler*, Eddie predicted the Boston Red Sox would beat the New York Giants due to their pitching staff. "Boston has five men she can trust," said Eddie. "New York two and a youth who has just shown himself."

In the first game of the World Series, the Red Sox beat the New York Giants, 4 to 3. Smoky Joe Wood picked up the win.

Mathewson was on the hill for the Giants in the second game and battled for eleven innings to a 6-to-6 tie.

Back at Fenway Park on the 10th, Rube Marquard was on his game, winning 2 to 1.

On Friday, the 11th, at the Polo Grounds, Wood won his second game of the series, 3 to 1.

At Fenway on the 12th, Hugh Bedient defeated Christy Mathewson, 2 to 1. Boston was now within one win of the championship.

The series shifted to New York on the 14th. Marquard was again dominant, winning 5 to 2.

That day, in Milwaukee, Wisconsin, while campaigning as the Bull Moose Party candidate, Theodore Roosevelt was shot by a would-be assassin. Though the bullet was still in him, Roosevelt delivered his speech on schedule. Upon completion, he checked into a nearby hospital, where it was deduced that the speech lodged in his breast pocket had saved his life.

On the 15th at Fenway Park, Smoky Joe Wood finally fell, losing to the Giants 11 to 4. Momentum seemed to be with the Giants.

In the final game at Fenway Park on the 16th, Mathewson and Bedient battled to a 1-to-1 tie through seven innings. Wood then replaced Bedient. The game remained 1 to 1 until the 10th inning.

In the top of the 10th, with one out, Red Murray doubled off Wood. Fred Merkle followed with a single to drive home the go-ahead run. Wood then escaped without further damage.

All that remained for the Giants was for their ace, Mathewson, to shut down the Red Sox for one more inning.

Clyde Engle led off for Boston and hit a Mathewson offering to Fred Snodgrass in right-center field. Fred called off Murray and camped under the ball, only to have it bounce out of his glove and onto the ground. Engle hustled into second on the error.

Harry Hooper then drove a ball deep to center, but Snodgrass tracked it down. One out.

Steve Yerkes was next up and drew a walk. There were now men on first and second.

Tris Speaker was the next to bat. He ripped a Mathewson offering to right field, scoring Engle. Yerkes and Speaker advanced on the throw to the plate.

With the game tied and the winning run at third base, Christy then intentionally walked Duffy Lewis to load the bases and set up a force at any base.

Larry Gardner was next up. He hit a fly to right field deep enough to score Yerkes, who tagged up and ran across the plate with the walk-off win.

Boston went nuts! The Red Sox were champions. Wood won his third game of the series.

Eddie pitched for Hanover against Shrewsbury on the 17th. The game went twelve innings without a run before it was called because of darkness. The *Gettysburg Times* reported, "Plank's work was up to its usual standard and there is hardly a doubt he would have pitched a no-hit game if he would have been able to let out. The four hits were made in four different innings and came when Plank eased up to give the catcher some rest. Plank had the situation in hand at all stages and did not issue a pass. He retired the side in the ninth on nine pitched balls."

Eddie invited York Springs hurler Jim Myers to stop by for a visit on the 19th. There was talk that if Eddie was impressed, Myers might get a contract with the Athletics.

Vice President James S. Sherman died in office on October 30, a few days before the 1912 presidential election.

Eddie and several players headed to Cuba on the November 2nd. Plank was back in early December.

On Tuesday, November 5th, the Governor of New Jersey, Democrat Woodrow Wilson won in a landslide over Republican incumbent William Howard Taft, whose support had been split by Theodore Roosevelt's Bull Moose Party. Roosevelt finished ahead of Taft in the electoral vote.

On December 18th, amateur archaeologist Charles Dawson claimed that he had discovered the "missing link" between ape and man at a presentation to the Geological Society of London. After finding a section of a human-like skull in Pleistocene gravel beds near Piltdown, East Sussex, Dawson contacted Arthur Smith Woodward, Keeper of Geology at the Natural History Museum. The two discovered more bones and artifacts at the site, which they connected to the same individual. These included a jawbone, more skull fragments, a set of teeth, and primitive tools. It took 41 years until this find, known as "Piltdown Man" was debunked as a hoax.

An item in the December 30th *Gettysburg Times* reported that Eddie and Ira Plank were riding with Allan Holtzworth, returning from Hanover to Gettysburg when their car broke down near Brushtown. The men walked back to town to procure some help. After a lot of work, the men were on their way, arriving the next morning.

Eddie in 1912.

PICTURE SHOWS FANS IN THE "SUN PARLORS"; JACK COOMBS, THE VICTORIOUS PITCHER, ON THE LEFT, AND MAYOR BLANKENBURG, WHO THREW OUT THE FIRST BALL

Opening Day in 1912.

MANAGER HARRY DAVIS, OF THE CLEVELAND CLUB

Harry Davis as manager of Cleveland in May of 1912.

Cartoon of Eddie Plank from July 1912.

Another Plank cartoon from 1912.

1913:
THE CY YOUNG OF
SOUTHPAWS

N EARLY JANUARY, the Plank brothers were on the local bowling circuit, defeating Hanover at the Monarch Alleys on Tuesday, January 7th, 1468 to 1402. Eddie had the highest score of all ten players at 309.

The January 16th *Gettysburg Times* included an item announcing that Ira Plank was to train the Gettysburg College team this season and brother Eddie was to help. Despite having one of the best seasons of his career, it appeared Eddie was going to hold to his promise of retiring after 1912.

The Plank brothers' roles were further elaborated in an item the following week. Ira was to be the coach while Eddie helped during the "early spring."

On the 21st, the Plank brothers both attended the surprise dance party at the home of Mr. and Mrs. Lewis Storm. It was a large affair with over fifty attending.

The January 29th *Gettysburg Times* repeated items from the Philadelphia press concerning Eddie Plank and Chief Bender:

TWO VETERAN PITCHERS OF the Mack corps—Charles Albert Bender and Edward Plank—are the only players belonging to the Athletics who have failed to affix their signatures to contracts for the 1913 season. Bender is in Atlanta, Ga., and will undoubtedly sign his contract when he returns. Plank is on his Gettysburg farm and it might be that he has not gone to town recently and the ink in his well is dry.

Plank hinted that he might retire after the 1912 season. However, he dislikes letter writing almost as much as he does life in a large city. So Mack is confident that the contract of his star southpaw will arrive before February 24, when the Athletics start for San Antonio. Plank finished second in the American

League last season, with twenty-six games won and six lost. It is hardly likely he would quit after making such a grand record.

The 16th Amendment to the United States Constitution was ratified on February 3rd. It authorized the Federal government to impose and collect income taxes. The year was off to a wonderful start!

On Saturday, February 8th, the *Gettysburg Times* contained an article illustrating the heightened concern about Plank and his promised retirement:

EDDIE PLANK, THE ATHLETICS' star southpaw, has not signed his 1913 contract yet, and it is feared that the great pitcher will make good his threat to retire from the game according to the *Philadelphia Press*. Manager Connie Mack admitted at his Tioga home that he was not sure Plank would be with the White Elephants when they left for San Antonio on February 24.

"I hope and expect that Eddie will change his mind and play this year," said Connie. "I will probably hear from him within the next three or four days."

"Did you have any intimation that Plank intended to retire from baseball?" Mack was asked.

"Yes, he told us last summer that 1912 would be his last year as a major-league pitcher," Connie replied. "I also heard from him recently. But you know how Eddie is about those matters. He's never in a hurry to make up his mind. He takes his time and considers a thing thoroughly from every angle. I hope that after he has given the subject consideration he will send in his signed contract.

"You know Eddie does not have to play baseball to live. He owns several farms around Gettysburg, Pa., and also has income sufficient to keep him in comfort as long as he lives. I guess he's wealthy and in that respect far more lucky than you and I. That is why if he once makes up his mind to quit it will not be a matter of money and nothing will tempt him to return to the game."

Although Manager Mack's optimism would not permit him to say that he was worried, it is plainly evident to those who talk with him that he will not be perfectly contented until he has Plank's contract on his desk. The great cross-fire southpaw finished among the American League twirlers last season, winning

26 and losing 6. Had he been missing from the Mack camp, the Athletics might have finished lower in the race.

Plank is one of the high-strung ballplayers who worry over defeat and is tireless in his efforts to win, continued the *Press*. Therefore, he has always said that he would quit when he began to feel he was going back. He has been pitching major league ball for eleven years and has always been an idol, not only in Philadelphia but in every city where he appeared.

Manager Mack said he had the signed contract of every other player and was only waiting the time to start for San Antonio.

To the relief of Connie Mack and the multitude of Athletics fans, Eddie signed his contract about a week later. Report the *Gettysburg Times* on February 17th:

SUNDAY'S *PHILADELPHIA NORTH AMERICAN* told of Eddie Plank's decision to join the Athletics for the coming season:

Connie Mack got Gettysburg, Pa., on the long-distance phone yesterday afternoon. He talked many minutes to a lisping voice on the other end. At the finish of the conversation, Connie hung up the receiver and announced that Eddie Plank, the Cy Young of southpaws, had agreed to cross-fire another year for the Athletics.

The news that Eddie was coaxed into changing his mind about retiring comes as gladsome tidings to the local baseball tongs. For a time it seemed certain that Plank would quit as he has been on the verge of retiring for several seasons.

Mr. Mack had to talk like an insurance agent to convince Plank that 1913 was no kind of a year to retire from baseball. The tall tutor drew such a vivid picture of the fallacy of any ballplayer, particularly a left-handed pitcher, quitting the game in such a year as the present one Plank began to listen attentively.

Then Mack drove the point home stronger, although the talk was costing him 75 cents for three minutes and 25 cents for each extra minute.

As Mack is a deliberate orator, he can do no more than 100 words a minute, so it is little wonder that at the finish, the phone girl told him he owed Mr. Bell's company $7.75. But who wouldn't pay $7.75 for a pitcher like Plank?

Returning to the conversation, Mack worked Plank into a corner and told him that he would be a fine type of mental bantamweight to duck the Athletics in a year when they looked like sure pennant winners. Mr. Mack also opined that the World Series check would be a handy thing for a saving man's bank account. At the words "Series check," Mr. Mack could also hear Plank's ears prick. Eddie interrupted Connie and told him that he had said enough.

"I'll put my signed contract in the mail tonight," he broke in, "and board the *San Antonio Express* at Harrisburg. Tell the engineer not to forget to stop. S'long Connie," and the rebellion of Eddie Plank ended.

The next evening, on Tuesday the 18th, Eddie held his annual oyster bake at the farm with about twenty friends. The author is certain a lengthy recounting of Connie's phone call was one of the stories told.

On the 24th, Eddie boarded the train to St. Louis as it stopped in Harrisburg. He was happy to see his good friend Harry Davis back in the fold as a coach, his tenure as manager of the Cleveland club lasting less than a season. Plank often lived at Davis's Philadelphia house during homestands.

The team arrived in Palestine, Texas, on the 25th to find Jack Coombs waiting for them in the station.

As usual, the team split into two squads, separating the veterans and the younger players. After a couple weeks of stretching and practicing, they began playing local teams.

On March 4th, Woodrow Wilson was inaugurated as the 28th President of the United States, succeeding Taft.

Three days later, on the 7th, the *Alum Chine*, a British merchant vessel laden with 343 tons of dynamite exploded in Baltimore Harbor. The blast was heard in Philadelphia and rattled windows for miles. Dozens were killed in the immediate vicinity.

Later that week, in Auburn, New York, on the 10th, 90-year-old Harriet Tubman, the former slave who helped free others via the Underground Railroad, passed away.

The A's began their circuitous trip home, stopping for exhibitions in southern cities.

There was a lot of rain that spring, especially near Dayton, Ohio, where four days of rain in the Miami Valley resulted in what became known as the Great Dayton Flood on March 25. It was the worst natural disaster in Ohio's history. Over 360 were killed and 20,000 homes were destroyed.

On March 29, Eddie was home in Gettysburg for a few days as the team arrived back in Philadelphia to kick off the inner-city series.

On March 31, J. P. Morgan, financier and banker passed away in Rome, Italy, while traveling. He was 75 years old and one of the richest men in American history.

The Athletics opened the regular season on April 10 in Boston. Jack Coombs opposed Smoky Joe Wood. Jack lasted only five innings until the Red Sox closed to within 7 to 5. Chief was called in relief, but got into trouble quickly, yielding three hits and a run in two-thirds of an inning. Eddie was called to end the rally but gave up a couple more runs due to sloppy play. By the end of the 6th, it was A's 10, Red Sox 9. Plank pitched the rest of the way and was awarded the win.

After a rainout, the teams were back at it on the 12th. The A's jumped to a 4-to-0 lead in the top of the 1st. Coombs started again, but could not get out of the 1st inning, giving up four runs. Herb Pennock was called in, but walked two, and made no progress. For the second day in a row, Plank was summoned. It proved to be a smart move. He pitched the rest of the way, eight and one-third shutout innings to pick up the victory, 5 to 4.

Jack Coombs accompanied the team on the train back to Philadelphia after the Boston series but he was in so much pain the team sent him home to Philadelphia with what Connie called "the grippe." He was expected to get some bed rest for a few days and be back on the diamond.

Boston next came to Philadelphia for four games starting on the 17th. The A's won three of four. On the 21st, Eddie was called to get the final out for Byron Houck. The A's won 6 to 4.

Meanwhile, on April 18, former pitcher Roscoe Miller, aged 36, passed away. He had pitched for the Tigers, Giants, and Pirates. He was the first 20-game winner in Tigers history.

The Woolworth Building opened in New York City on April 24. It was the tallest building in the world for more than a decade.

The New York Yankees came to Shibe Park on April 22 for a four-game series. The A's won three of four. Eddie pitched the final game on the 25th. He threw a brilliant three-hit shutout and struck out ten.

The *Gettysburg Times* of April 26th, praised Eddie for his performance in New York the day before:

THE FEAT OF EDDIE PLANK on the baseball diamond Friday caused this morning's city papers to devote much space in praise of Gettysburg's hero. The *Philadelphia Press* says:

The polished pitching of Eddie Plank, the daddy of them all in the matter of usefulness in his particular sphere, turned New York club swingers back to the bench with the regularity of the ticking of a watch yesterday when the Athletics made it three victories out of four starts against Frank Chance and his Yankees. Score 4 to 0.

Mack's grand old southpaw—old in years as well as in point of service with the Athletics—gave the best exhibition of pitching staged in the major leagues this season with the ease of a farmer raking his potatoes. As cool as a cucumber and as calculating as a bank clerk, Plank allowed only twenty-nine men to bat against his cross-fire. This is only two more than the regulation number of nine innings. He showed that his control was true by not permitting a base on balls.

Not once did a New York runner advance so far as third base. It was considered some feat to reach second off the thirty-eight-year-old Plank who is starting his twelfth season as a member of the Athletics in an auspicious way. Three New York base runners reached the middle sack, but on all three occasions, they failed to advance any further.

In seven of the nine innings, the Yankees were retired in one, two, three order. As a matter of fact, there were only two clean bingles off the delivery of the veteran cross-fire artist.

Said Frank Chance after the game, "This is the first time I have ever seen Plank in action and I feel sure he is the greatest left-hander I ever batted against. While his cross-fire, slow ball, and change of pace impressed me greatly, to my mind his fastball is the best thing he has. It is nothing short of marvelous that a man 38 years old can have the fastball he has, for while some veteran pitchers can win games on their generalship and experience, they no longer have any speed. Plank is truly a wonder, and I can readily understand why the American League players call him the best left-hander in the country."

Eddie spent April 26 and 27 at home with friends and family. Meanwhile, Washington was in town on the 26th. The A's won 3 to 2.

After some rain, Eddie was in Philadelphia on the 30th to pitch against the Senators' Walter Johnson. The pitchers' duel went eight innings with neither side scoring, both pitchers giving clinics. Finally, the Senators got to Eddie in the 9th for two runs. The final was 2 to 0 in favor of Johnson. Eddie struck-out 12 to Walter's 10.

The Athletics ended April 9-3, half-a-game ahead of the Senators, in 1st place.

For the first of May, the A's were in New York at the Polo Grounds for a series of four games. The A's swept all of them. Eddie pitched the get-away game on May 5th. The A's led 1 to 0 until the bottom of the 5th when Yankees' catcher Ed Sweeney hit a home run to tie things up. It was one of only two base-runners Eddie allowed all day. The A's rallied for seven runs late, winning 8 to 1. "The Gettysburg veteran never had his southpaw flipper behaving more nobly," reported the *Philadelphia Inquirer.*

Next was a long train ride to St. Louis to play the Browns. The series of four games opened on May 7. The A's took three of four, including Plank's win on the 10th. Eddie went the distance of ten innings, giving up only three earned runs. He won 8 to 6.

Word from Philadelphia was that Jack Coombs was improving and should be back with the team soon.

The team next split two in Chicago before heading to Cleveland for four games starting on the 15th.

Dennis Coughlin passed away on May 14 at the age of 69. He was an outfielder for the 1872 Washington Nationals of the National Association and was best remembered as the only major leaguer who was wounded in combat during the Civil War.

Eddie pitched the opener against Cleveland on the 15th. He gave up to runs in the first two innings and was pulled, losing 2 to 0. The A's could not solve Cy Falkenberg and lost 2 to 0. Philadelphia took two of the next three to split the series.

The road trip concluded at Detroit for three games beginning on the 19th. The A's dropped the first two games and then handed the ball to Eddie on the 22nd. Eddie went the distance and was masterful, pitching around the tougher Detroit hitters, he shut them out, 7 to 0. Detroit managed only three hits. "Old Master Plank: Venerable Edward Confines Tigers' Heavy Artillerymen to Three Insignificant Singles, Macks Winning in a Walk" read the headline in the *Philadelphia Inquirer*.

The train dropped Eddie off in Harrisburg on its way to Philadelphia. Eddie spent a few days at Gettysburg.

Back home, Jack Coombs was not improving. He had been near death with what was diagnosed as typhoid fever which had settled in his spine. He was hanging on in the hospital but was no longer expected back anytime soon.

Washington came to Philadelphia to play five games at Shibe Park beginning on May 24. The A's won the opener and then split the doubleheader on the 26th. On the 27th, they swept a doubleheader, Plank winning, 8 to 0, in the morning and Bender, 7 to 1, in the afternoon. Plank was stingy again, being nicked for only two hits, as he went the distance. "28 Senators Faced Plank in 9 Innings" read the headline in the *Philadelphia Inquirer*.

The Yankees were next to Shibe Park for four games, all of which the A's won.

Philadelphia ended May 28-10, half-a-game up on Cleveland, in 1st place.

The A's briefly went to Washington for a doubleheader on June 2nd. They won both games, including a win over Johnson by Boardwalk Brown.

Ty and the Tigers next came to Philadelphia for a four-game set. Eddie pitched the opener on June 3rd. Plank went the distance, giving up only two earned runs on five hits, winning 7 to 3. Cobb and Crawford both tripled in the game, but Eddie Collins hit a triple and a home run. The A's promptly swept the next three.

On June 5, Chris von der Ahe, brewer and former baseball executive died at 61. He had owned the St. Louis Browns of the American Association (and National League) from 1882 to 1898 and was credited with greatly developing the entertainment aspect of the sport with fan-friendly promotions and ballpark attractions. He also presided over the first team to win four straight pennants—the St. Louis Browns from 1885 to 1888. These Browns later became the St. Louis Cardinals.

The American League St. Louis Browns, related in name only, were in town for four games on the 7th of June. The A's took three of four. Eddie notched a save, pitching the final three innings of a 10-to-4 win on the 10th.

Cleveland was next on the schedule. Mack had saved Plank for the opener on the 12th. He did not disappoint. Facing a team with Shoeless Joe Jackson and Napolean Lajoie in the lineup, Eddie held them scoreless into the 9th, winning 6 to 1. The Naps managed only five hits. The only Cleveland run was a 9th-inning home run by Jackson. "Plank again was the old master," said the *Philadelphia Inquirer.*

After splitting the next two, Mack went back to Plank for the last game of the series. Once again, Eddie was up to the task, holding the Naps to only six hits, three by Lajoie, en route to a 3-to-2 victory over Falkenberg. The win was Eddie's 10th of the season.

The White Sox were in town from the 17th to the 19th for three games. Philadelphia won two of them, including a brilliant four-hit shutout by Boardwalk Brown.

Last year's champions, the Red Sox, visited on the 20th for three games. They won the first two and lost the last one 13 to 4.

Now on the road, the Athletics made the short train ride to Washington for a six-game marathon starting on June 25. The A's won the opening round, defeating Walter Johnson 14 to 2.

Eddie pitched the morning game on the 26th. Plank cruised to an 11-to-2 victory. He again yielded on five hits. The teams split the remaining four games.

Next, to the Polo Grounds, Eddie opened the series against the Yankees on June 30th. The A's won easily, 6 to 0, New York getting only three hits. "A Mere Waltz for Sir Edward Plank" read the headline in the *Philadelphia Inquirer.* "Plank saw to it that New York never got very frisky with his offerings. His cross-fire was whistling through with the speed of a Bender and he mixed a change of pace so skillfully that the Gothamites were breaking their backs all day long. Three scattered hits were all that the Kilties were able to garner off the great left-hander and these were so sparsely scattered that they had absolutely no charm."

The A's ended June 48-17, 8 1/2 games ahead of Cleveland, in 1st place. The Yankees were 19-46, already twenty-nine games behind in last place.

The A's opened the month of July sweeping the next three games.

Marking the fiftieth anniversary of the Battle of Gettysburg, thousands of Civil War veterans from both sides converged on Gettysburg on July 3rd.

The A's were at Fenway Park for a doubleheader on Independence Day. The A's lost the morning game, 13 to 6. Eddie had the ball in the afternoon and won 5 to 3.

The A's won on the 5th and then split a doubleheader on Monday the 7th. Eddie pitched the afternoon game and lost 8 to 3. He was pulled after two ineffective innings.

The A's next stopped in Cleveland on July 9, winning two of three, the only loss, 4 to 1, Plank losing to Falkenberg on the 10th. Eddie pitched well, yielding only two runs in seven innings.

Detroit was next on the schedule for five games starting on the 12th. The A's won a wild one, 16 to 9, to open the series. Eddie pitched the final inning-and-a-third and was awarded a save despite yielding four runs.

The A's then lost the next three before Plank started the getaway game on the 15th. Eddie went the distance, scattering nine hits as the A's won easily, 7 to 0. "The only thing to be regretted was that Ty Cobb was not in the lineup, for when Plank and Cobb indulge in a battle of wits, humorous situations arise for the delectation of the populace," opined the *Philadelphia Inquirer*.

The Chicago White Sox played host to six games starting on July 16th. The teams each won three.

Jiggs Donahue, aged 34, passed away from syphilis on July 19 in Columbus, Ohio. He had been a key member of the 1906 White Sox that beat the Cubs in the only all-Chicago World Series ever played.

Eddie opened the series in St. Louis on the 20th with an 8-to-0 shutout. He scattered six harmless hits en route to his 15th win of the season. The A's won two of the next three and took the long train ride home. Eddie stopped off at home for a few days.

The Tigers came to town on the 25th. The A's won the first game, 4 to 0, and handed the ball to Eddie on the 26th. Eddie pitched eight innings but lost 6 to 2.

Boardwalk Brown threw a shutout the next day, winning 8 to 0. The A's had taken two of three from Cobb's crew.

St. Louis was next in Shibe Park to start a series on the 30th. The A's won the first game 2 to 1, but Eddie dropped the game on the 31st, 4 to 3. He led most of the way, but three runs in the 6th were is undoing.

The A's ended July 67-29, eight games up on Cleveland, in 1st place.

August began with the A's splitting two against St. Louis at home.

The Naps were then in for four games. Philadelphia took three of them, losing only Eddie's game, 5 to 0, on the 5th. Plank only pitched the 1st inning, giving up three unearned runs. He was pulled at that point, and the A's couldn't overcome the deficit.

That same day, Jack Coombs was back in uniform working out with the team. He was back at his normal weight, having spent several weeks on his farm in Kennebunkport, Maine, to regain his health. However, it was apparent he was not close to being ready for a game. Coombs would miss the rest of the season.

On August 8th, Honest John Gaffney, "The King of Umpires" passed away in New York City at the age of 58. He was the first umpire to wear a chest protector and was a good friend of Connie Mack. Connie later arranged for an exhibition game to cover the cost of Gaffney's monument.

Also that day, the White Sox came to Philadelphia for a four-game series. They took three of four games.

The A's' westward swing began on the 14th of August with a stop in Cleveland. Once again, Eddie was not very effective, losing the game 6 to 2. He lasted only five innings. The A's dropped three of the four games.

Connie tried Eddie again for the opener against Detroit on the 18th. Eddie pitched much better in this game, taking a 4-to-4 tie into the bottom of the 9th. The Tigers scored a run in the inning to walk-off with the victory, 5 to 4. The A's recovered to win the next two in Detroit.

At Chicago on the 21st, the A's opened a three-game series with the White Sox. The A's took two of the three and Eddie made a positive contribution with a save in the 2-to-1 win on the 22nd.

The A's next enjoyed their stop in St. Louis, outscoring the Browns 20 to 1 in a three-game sweep. Boardwalk Brown and Eddie Plank threw shutouts, Plank's occurring on the 25th. Eddie won 3 to 0, scattering five singles and striking out 11 en route to the victory. "Eleven Brownies Fanned by Plank: Mack's Grand Old Man Discovers His Cunning and Missourians Punch Holes in Atmosphere Trying to Hit" was the humorous headline in the *Philadelphia Inquirer*. Wrote the reporter, "All doubts about the decline of the venerable Edward Plank were removed today. Hostiles up and down the league have written unkind pieces to the public print alleging that the Sage of Gettysburg is a back number. Forget it. Athletics 3, Browns 0. Cause, Plank."

In the game, Eddie was having difficulty with umpire Bill Dineen's pitch calls. The disagreement became heated in the 8th inning, Plank barking at him angrily. Dineen replied in kind. "I don't care what you do," yelled Eddie. Teammates settled down the matter.

That same day Frank L. "Red" Donahue, the former Phillies and Browns pitcher, passed away at age 40 from tuberculosis. Donahue won 20 or more games three times with the Phillies and Browns and collected 164 career wins.

The A's were next at the Polo Grounds in New York against the Yankees. They lost two of three to the last-place club.

The Athletics finished August 81-41, seven games ahead of Cleveland, in 1st place. Eddie finished the month by turning thirty-eight.

As September began, it appeared Eddie was nursing a sore arm, or Connie was saving him. Eddie did not pitch in the home-stand against Washington that began on September 2nd. The A's took three of four.

Boston came to town and swept a doubleheader on September 4th. Connie tapped Eddie to pitch on the 5th. He lost 6 to 3 but was victim of some sloppy fielding, half of the runs were unearned. The loss dropped the A's lead over Cleveland to 6 1/2 games. The Athletics salvaged the final game of the series.

Chicago was next in town, splitting four games on the 9th to the 12th of September.

Cleveland visited Philadelphia on September 13th for a three-game series. Chief Bender figured in the decisions for the first two games, losing to Falkenberg, but winning the next game, on the 15th, in relief. Bender was now 21-10 on the season.

That day, Frank Hough the long-time sports editor for the *Philadelphia Inquirer* passed away at his home in Germantown at age 56. Connie Mack, the Shibes, and captain Danny Murphy attended the funeral a few days later. Hough was laid to rest in West Laurel Cemetery.

The next day, Eddie was called in the 7th inning to pick up in a game tied at four. He threw four hitless innings, walking two and striking out six. Eddie picked up the win when the A's scored a run in the 10th. He was now 17-10.

Cleveland was now 9 1/2 games behind and the pennant was nearly won.

The A's split two games with St. Louis at Shibe Park on the 17th and 18th.

Late in the season, Eddie had breakfast with the writer Norman Beasley. Thinking about Bender and Coombs, he wondered, "How much longer would the big chap last if he looked after himself with the same care the frail fellow does (referring to Plank)."

"Plank stood American League batters on their heads for nearly a dozen-and-a-half years while giants flashed for a time and were heard of no more."

Beasley asked Plank at breakfast, "What is the real reason for your long life in the big leagues?"

Eddie answered quickly, "Taking care of myself. If I had the physique of a youngster who reported to our club a day or so ago, I would go on for another ten or fifteen years. Guess it is the way nature equalizes things. The big fellows have so much physical strength, they don't pay any attention to it. They burn themselves out.

"It makes me sick sometimes to think of the way I have been cheated physically. But, probably, had I been a husky bird, I wouldn't have paid any more attention to the rules of nature than some of those other fellows."

The *Gettysburg Times* on September 20th contained an article about Connie Mack's plans for the upcoming World Series:

THAT EDDIE PLANK IS to figure prominently in the coming World's Series is the plan of Connie Mack who expects to work the Gettysburg boy and Bender as his principal pitchers.

Mack is not so optimistic of ultimate victory as he was when his team opposed the Giants two years ago. In discussing the club's chances he said:

"I intend to rely on my old standbys—Eddie Plank and Chief Bender, presuming, of course, that we win the American League pennant. That we accomplish this little detail I am certain. This pair of hardy twirlers have stood me in good stead for a number of years, and they are surely not going to throw me down now.

"I have four good young pitchers—Shawkey, Houck, Bush, and Brown—but Plank and Bender will shoulder the brunt of the work on the minaret for the Athletics when we meet the Giants for the third time.

"I will not go on record as saying that we will outhit McGraw's horde. My club can hit equally as hard as that of McGraw, but in an abbreviated series, such as the World's Series, calculations cannot be very dependable. My players are more reliable afield, and that will prove a big advantage in our favor.

"While Plank and Bender are not rated very high in the pitchers' records, they are as reliable a duo of hurlers as I have ever had. Both are at their best in pinches, and in a short series, I can recommend them to be anything in sight.

"But it must be remembered that Plank and Bender are cold weather pitchers, and that is why I look to them to carry the Athletics through to another world's championship."

Analyzing the foregoing, it is found that Mack makes the reservation that if Plank and Bender are in their top form, this team had a good chance of victory. But should those veterans fail him—or should even one of them be unable to come up to the mark—Mack will be forced to call upon his youngsters and jeopardize his club's chances.

The Detroit Tigers came to Shibe Park on the 20th of September. The A's won the first game 4 to 2.

The A's then swept a doubleheader on Monday the 22nd. Joe Bush won the morning game, 4 to 0. Eddie got the ball in the afternoon in relief of Herb Pennock in the 3rd. Eddie threw seven scoreless to pick up the victory, the A's winning 1 to 0. "Old Master Ed Plank in Great Form" read the headline in the *Philadelphia Inquirer*. The A's had clinched another pennant.

With the pennant in hand, the A's offense went nuts the next day, beating Detroit 21 to 8 on the 23rd. The team had 25 hits in the ballgame.

The A's closed out the season 2-8 as Connie rested Plank and Bender. Eddie spent some time at home at the end of the month. The Athletics finished the season 96-57, 6 1/2 games up on Washington.

Eddie Plank finished the regular season 18-10, 2.60. He also had four saves. Chief Bender was the ace of the staff, going 21-10, 2.21, with 13 saves. Boardwalk Brown was 17-11, Bullet Joe Bush 15-6, and Byron Houck 14-6. Jack Coombs pitched five innings all season.

In Washington, Walter Johnson won the "triple crown" of pitching with 36 wins, a 1.14 ERA, and 243 strikeouts.

Eddie Collins hit .345 to lead the A's, trailing Ty Cobb's .390. Frank Baker hit .337 and led the league with 12 home runs and 113 RBI. Stuffy McInnis hit .324.

The October 7th *Gettysburg Times* previewed the World Series from a local perspective:

INTEREST IN THE WORLD'S Series baseball games is perhaps in a higher pitch in Gettysburg than in any small town in the country. The home of Eddie Plank is watching keenly every development in the greatest event in America's sporting circles, and on every side is the hope expressed that "Eddie" may figure prominently in the games and may have a share in bringing the championship honors to the Athletics.

All predictions for the first game were to the effect that Bender would be used against Mathewson and this was somewhat disappointing to Gettysburg fans who want, more than anything else, to see Plank pitch against the New York wonder and to win. It is possible that he may be given the opportunity before the end of the series.

Many Gettysburg people are planning to see one or all of the games and some of them are already on the ground. Others expect to go on the special train Wednesday when it is confidently believed they will have a chance to see Eddie in action. Those who stay at home are making arrangements to receive the news of the games, play by play, as was done two years ago. Every ball pitched will be announced a few minutes afterward in the Square in front of Stallsmith's News-stand and no small degree of satisfaction will be had in this way.

Betting on a small scale is going on here as in other years and, from the odds offered, it is found that the general sentiment named the New York Giants as the winners of the first game, with the Athletics winning the second on their home grounds.

No matter how the series goes, it is now the plan to give Eddie Plank a complimentary banquet soon after its close. Efforts are on foot to get Connie Mack and Ban Johnson here for the occasion and the event, which is to be held at the Eagle Hotel, will attract a hundred or more admirers and enthusiasts.

The first game of the 1913 World Series was held at the Polo Grounds in New York. Once again, the Athletics were to face Muggsy McGraw's New York Giants.

The Giants had run away with the National League pennant by 12 1/2 games over the Philadelphia Phillies, winning 101 games and losing only 51.

Christy Mathewson led the team with a 25-11 record. Rube Marquard was 23-10, and Jeff Tesreau, 22-13.

Catcher Chief Meyers led the team with a .312 average in less than 400 at-bats. Nobody else topped .300 and Larry Doyle led the team with 71 RBI.

It's clear the Giants won the pennant because of their pitching.

Bender and Marquard were summoned to pitch the opening game before 36,291 fans.

The A's got out to a 5-to-1 lead in the 5th, thanks to Baker's two-run home run. This knocked Marquard from the game.

Bender had trouble in the bottom of the 5th, giving up three runs, the lead narrowed to 5 to 4.

The A's added a run in the 8th off Doc Crandall on three consecutive hits including McInnis's double.

Chief held them the rest of the way, winning 6 to 4.

The second game was set for Shibe Park on the 8th of October. Eddie Plank faced Christy Mathewson. The two masters traded zeros for nine innings.

Eddie retired the first seven Giants in order, a streak that ended with Fred Snodgrass and Christy Mathewson singling back-to-back in the 3rd inning. But, Eddie wiggled out of it.

Meanwhile, in the bottom of the 1st, the A's had runners on second and third and one out for Baker, who struck out. McInnis then hit a fly to left, ending the threat.

Mathewson put the A's down in order in the 2nd and 3rd.

In the top of the 4th, Tillie Shafer reached on an error by Collins but was caught stealing during the next at-bat.

Mathewson again got in trouble in the bottom of the 4th. With one out, Baker singled. McInnis then grounded out, moving Baker into scoring position. Mathewson countered by intentionally walking Strunk to get to Jack Barry. It proved to be a winning strategy, as Barry grounded into a force at second base.

In the top of the 5th, Eddie allowed two base-runners on a single and a walk but got Herzog to ground out to end the frame.

In the bottom of the 5th, Plank singled off Mathewson but was stranded at first, Eddie Murphy and Rube Oldring unable to move him.

Eddie then retired the Giants in order in the 6th and 7th. Mathewson retired Collins, Baker, and McInnis in order in the 6th, but was nicked by Lapp for a single in the 7th. It proved harmless.

In the top of the 8th, Eddie again retired the batters in order.

Mathewson quickly got two outs in the bottom of the 8th, but Collins and Baker followed with singles. McInnis was up with another chance to knock in a run but again grounded-out to end the threat.

In the top of the 9th, Eddie retired Doyle on a fly to deep center. Fletcher then singled, and George Burns walked. The Giants had two men on and one out. Plank retired the next two on flies to the outfield—the threat was thwarted.

Things got exciting in the bottom of the 9th. Amos Strunk led off with a single to center field against Mathewson. Jack Barry, tried to bunt him over. The ball slipped past Mathewson between first and second base, and Jack was safe at first. Doyle ran in and grabbed the ball, but threw wildly to first. Strunk and Barry kept running, each gaining the next base. As Strunk rounded third, it appeared he would score, but third base coach Harry Davis put on the brakes and held the runner. There were now runners on second and third with no one out. The A's were ninety feet from victory, though many in the crowd thought Davis was playing it too safe and that Strunk could have scored.

Next up was catcher Jack Lapp. He hit a grounder to Wiltse at first, who had come in for Snodgrass earlier in the game. Wiltse, normally a pitcher, fielded the ball and threw home as Strunk was sliding in. Amos was called out, but Barry moved up to third.

Now with men on the corners, and one out, it was Eddie's turn to bat. Rube Oldring, who was in the hole, momentarily motioned for Plank to return to the bench, but Eddie soon turned and went to the plate, the decision having been made not to pinch-hit for him. It was the bottom of the 9th and many in the crowd groaned, expecting a pinch-hitter. Eddie had only hit .105 in the regular season, by far the worst mark of his career. Plank's career batting mark was nearly twice as high. Everyone thought Danny Murphy would get the call off the bench. The captain had hit .322 as a pinch-hitter during the season and had won many games over the years with his clutch hitting. However, Connie stuck with Plank, who also rolled a ball to Wiltse. Hooks picked it and fired home, catching Barry in a run-down, but was finally tagged out. Lapp and Plank moved up into scoring position.

Eddie Murphy was next up with a chance to win the game. Mathewson got him to knock a ball back to the box which Christy picked and tossed to first.

The Giants had escaped disaster and there were murmurs in the crowd. Many talked about Mack not pulling Plank for a pinch-hitter.

Plank, retained in the game by Mack, took the bump in the top of the 10th, the score still 0 to 0.

Larry McLean greeted Eddie with a clean single to right. McGraw replaced McLean at first with Eddie Grant.

Hooks Wiltse was next up. He put down a sacrifice bunt that moved Grant to second.

Christy Mathewson stepped to the plate with a chance to take the lead for himself. Mathewson, a fair hitter like Plank, knocked a ball into left-center for a single. Eddie Grant rounded third and scored the first run of the game. The crowd groaned.

Herzog next reached on an error by Collins. Eddie then hit Doyle with a pitch to load the bases with only one out.

Shortstop Art Fletcher was next. He lined a ball to left that fell in for another single. Two more runs scored.

Eddie retired the next two in order, but the damage was done. It was 3 to 0 and his masterpiece had been spoiled.

Mathewson quietly retired the A's in the bottom of the inning, 1-2-3. The Giants had tied the series.

The third game on the 9th at the Polo Grounds was an easy win for the A's. They jumped to a 5-to-0 lead on Tesreau after two innings. Bullet Joe Bush could front-run with the lead and handled the Giants, 8 to 2. The A's had regained their advantage, two games to one.

Writer Cullen Cain recalled an episode before the fourth game of the series, "An idea of the Chief's temperament may be gained from an episode in the World Series with the Giants in 1913. It was Bender's turn to pitch that day, but the Chief refused to even warm up before the game. He was moody and preoccupied. Mack knew his Indian too well to insist upon his going in when he did not appear to wish to pitch. So, while it was not Plank's turn, and while Bender's matchless skill that day might mean the series, Plank was thrown into the breach."

"I went up there and began to warm up," said Eddie, and I knew I was not at my best, for I had pitched two days before. And I knew what the Chief knew. So, I watched him sit on the bench with his head down, poking at the turf with the toe of his shoe. It came on close to game time and Bender began to get nervous and fidget around the bench, and then I knew I would not pitch that day. But I kept on shooting them over.

"Mack never said a word, nor did he even look toward Bender, and then, two minutes before game time, Bender suddenly got up from the bench and came out to me and caught the ball as it was returned by the catcher and told me to 'get the --- out of here.' I headed to the bench, and the Chief began to burn them into the waiting glove. His mood shifted, he was at his wonder best, and so, of course, we won."

Chief Bender won the fourth game of the series, 6 to 5. The A's got out to a 6-to-0 lead by the end of the 5th and hung on. The Giants rallied for three in the 7th and two in the 8th, but could not tie, the Chief getting Red Murray to ground out, stranding Shafer on third. The A's now led the series three games to one.

Game Five was a rematch for Plank and Mathewson at the Polo Grounds on the 11th.

The A's finally scored off Mathewson in the top of the 1st. Eddie Murphy started the game with a single. After Oldring failed to bunt him over, grounding into a force, Eddie Collins singled to put men on the corners. Home Run Baker then popped a fly to left, deep enough to score Murphy. The A's led 1 to 0.

Eddie put the Giants down in order in the first and second. "Matty" retired the A's in the second.

The top of the 3rd inning was almost a repeat of the 1st. Murphy led off with a single. Oldring reached on an error by Doyle at second. Collins then bunted to move the runners up. Frank Baker followed with a single, scoring Murphy, and putting men on the corners. This time, McInnis hit a sacrifice fly, scoring Oldring. The score was 3 to 0.

It was all Eddie would need.

The Giants again went in order in the 3rd and 4th innings.

In the bottom of the 5th, after Burns lined out, Tillie Shafer drew a walk. Red Murray then popped a ball to Plank, who fumbled it for an error. With runners now on first and second base and one out, Larry McLean singled to left-center, scoring Shafer. But, Plank got Fred Merkle to ground into a double-play to end the threat—Collins to Barry to McInnis—three-fourths of the $100,000 infield.

In the bottom of the 6th, Mathewson led off the inning with a single, but Herzog grounded into a double-play. Eddie then retired Doyle.

Plank mowed them down in the 7th and 8th, putting them out in order.

Finally, in the bottom of the 9th, leading 3 to 1, Eddie was still on the mound with the championship in his grasp.

Doc Crandall pinch-hit for Mathewson and grounded out to Collins. One out.

Buck Herzog was next. He popped a ball deep, behind short and second. Barry ran out after it and snagged it. Two outs.

Larry Doyle stepped to the plate, the last hope for the 1913 Giants. He hit a fly to Eddie Murphy in right, who secured the ball. Three outs. The A's were World Series champions again.

There was bedlam on the field as many fans, presumably from Philadelphia, streamed onto it. "Gettysburg Eddie" was their hero, and he was lifted on the shoulders of the fans and carted about the stadium, much to his embarrassment and surprise.

A good description of the enthusiasm of the locals in Gettysburg was provided in the *Gettysburg Compiler* from October 15th:

GETTYSBURG WAS WILDLY EXCITED last week over baseball and our great veteran player, Eddie Plank. Crowds running into the hundreds gathered in the Square each day to hear the returns from the battlefields of the World Series and the news at times was received with shouts and blowing of auto horns, almost as enthusiastically as though the games were being witnessed.

The whole town and county had Eddie Plank on the brain and the games of Wednesday and Saturday were nervously and enthusiastically followed than any of the rest. Eddie Plank is the greatest American baseball star as his own people look upon him and any assertion to the contrary might have provoked a riot last week. There was, however, no such assertion, nor the shadow of one for Eddie holds a place near the hearts of our people and everyone was sorry that they could not have been part of the crowd on Saturday when after the final victory Eddie was hoisted on the shoulders of a crowd of his admirers and carried around the field.

The October 13th *Gettysburg Times* compiled the various reactions to the Athletics' victory in the final game:

BUT ONE TOPIC OF conversation was welcome in Gettysburg Saturday evening and that was Eddie Plank. Pitching one of the best games of his long career, he defeated New York in the World's Series and gave Gettysburg just what it wanted—a decisive victory over Mathewson. But everyone knows the story of the game and all they want now is to hear what the big city dailies have to say of the baseball idol.

Public Ledger: Marvelous is the word that expresses Plank's exhibition. In his long, exemplary, and even distinguished career on the diamond he never pitched a better game. He was absolutely invincible. The Giants, in name only, were as plastic as potter's clay. They were making their last stand, had been driven into their last entrenchment and they fought with the desperation of trapped tigers. But all their fierce, furious fighting spirit availed naught. Plank was master. Well has Plank been called the "Old Master." His consummate skill never merited the title more than it did this afternoon when 40,000 wild, despairing spectators, 99 out of every 100 hostile in mind, did their utmost to unnerve him through all the game. But he was immovable as the polar star. The carnage of Little Round Top would not have disconcerted him. Like the heroes of Gettysburg, he was making his last effort for a cause. And he won.

New York American: Once beaten in this series by the great Christy Mathewson, many doubted that Plank—thirty-nine years old, and thirteen years a big-league pitcher—could return after such a short rest, but the box score shows the game he pitched. Again, he was opposed by Mathewson, and again the big baseball idol of Manhattan pitched a great game, but before the snapping cross-fire of the old side-winder, the Giants hung helpless when they needed the punch.

Philadelphia Press: Plank did come back in one of the most sensationally perfect games of his career. His great and ancient rival, Christy Mathewson, on the other hand, was hit hard in the early part of the game. After the game, Eddie refused to discuss the rumors he would quit baseball with today's game. "I haven't a word to say about that now," was his only comment. The fact that he let down the desperate Giants today with only two hits, is accepted by Mack and the rest of the team as a guarantee that Eddie will be back with the Athletics next year. "The old boy will be out there winning a couple more games for us in the World's Series next October," was the laconic comment of Stuffy McInnis upon the rumor.

North American: As soon as Murphy caught Doyle's fly and the Giants, beaten in a series for the second time by the long, lean hand of Mack, had streaked for their clubhouse to hide their disappointment, the crowd rushed for Plank. Plank faced the mad mob bewildered. It might not have surprised him on the home lot, but to get this kind of greeting on a hostile field, from a crowd that out of loyalty to the home team had steadily been rooting against him from the time the first ball was pitched, seemed too much.

A bunch of strong arms grabbed him. Up in the air went Eddie and he was carried from the field, across its whole length and all along the whole way, from bench to taxicab, he got nothing but cheers, not one unkindly word coming from that crowd that had seen its team humiliated three times running on the home ground to make complete the triumph of the Mackmen. In his taxicab, the hero of the day was overwhelmed. "I don't deserve all this," he said, as he sat with bowed head while his comrades on the team fell over him in the madness of their rejoicing.

Philadelphia Record: Two hits were the entire product of the Giant attack on Plank, and he gave one base on balls, which started all the trouble in the fifth. For the rest of the time he was superb, and although the Giants swung viciously and violently, and hurled their bats angrily against the ground and yelled at the veteran from the bench and coaching line, he stood firm till the last, immovable, a regular Rock of Gettysburg.

Baltimore American: For one last forlorn and hopeless stand, today McGraw sent in Mathewson to grapple again with Plank. But even Matty, the Miracle Man, had no magic and no wizardry which might cope with the power and foe on one side and the weakness of his pals upon the other. And while the mighty Mathewson was struggling between two such fires in vain, Plank, one of the grandest of pitching veterans, worked his last and greatest game.

The big banquet which is to be given in honor of Eddie has been postponed, upon his own request, to Monday evening, November 3, and indications now are that every available seat will be sold.

When the shares were handed out for the series, each member of the Athletics received $3243.94. It was Eddie Plank's fourth World Series check.

Soon after the money was divided, word came that thirteen-year-old Harry Davis, Jr. had died at home. "Excitement caused by the World's Series was partially responsible for his death," reported the *Philadelphia Inquirer*. A funeral was held on the morning of the 15th. Eddie Plank, Chief Bender, Eddie Collins, Jack McInnis, Jack Barry, and Frank Baker were pallbearers for the son of their good friend, third base coach, and former team captain, carrying the lad from their home at 2405 West Lehigh Avenue to the waiting hearse.

It is very likely young Davis was sickly for some time. It is also very likely Eddie Plank knew him well. Plank boarded at the Davis home during the season, when the team was home.

That afternoon, Eddie was back in Gettysburg and dropped by the Eagle Hotel to greet a group of Girard College boys who had been touring the battlefield. The young men were ecstatic to spend a half hour with the baseball star, shaking hands and chatting about the recent World Series. They had no idea Eddie had helped to bury his friend's son in the morning, but the attention from the lads likely lifted his spirits.

On October 27, the official announcement regarding the banquet to honor Eddie Plank was made. The date had been moved to Thursday, November 6, and the time was half-past nine. The venue remained the Eagle Hotel.

Meanwhile, on the 28th, Eddie joined in the World's Champions banquet in Philadelphia held at the Bellevue Stratford. Over 500 players, fans, reporters, and officials gathered to celebrate. The dinner was preceded by a parade of the players in automobiles from Shibe Park to the hotel.

On October 31, the Lincoln Highway, the first automobile road across the United States, was dedicated. The Pennsylvania portion ran from Philadelphia through Lancaster and York to Gettysburg, then on to Chambersburg and beyond.

Eddie Plank picked up his Stetson hat in Carlisle, Pennsylvania, on November 1st at the store of J.A. Stambaugh. Eddie had received a letter announcing a gift from the president of the J.B. Stetson hat company for his championship. The letter permitted him to pick up a hat from any official Stetson agent.

George Stovall, former St. Louis Browns player-manager, became the first Major Leaguer to jump to the outlaw Federal League after signing a contract to manage the Kansas City Packers on November 2.

On November 4th, Eddie participated in a bowling contest in Gettysburg. Eddie Collins and Harry Davis were present in the audience.

The Eddie Plank banquet at the Eagle Hotel on the night of Thursday, November 6, was best described in the *Gettysburg Times*:

A GATHERING SUCH AS Gettysburg has possibly never seen in its history assembled at the Eagle Hotel Thursday evening to pay homage to one of the town's most honored sons, Eddie Plank.

Ministers, lawyers, physicians, merchants, farmers, mechanics, laborers, and those representing other occupations and professions attended. Members of the Good Intent team on which Eddie first played ball greeted him again, together with members of the teams that opposed him a score or more years ago when he made his first victorious tour of Adams County. There were his warm personal friends and the members of the rising generation who gave him the adoration due a hero. More than two hundred were present and of that number, many came from a distance while the portions of the county north, east, south, and west of Gettysburg all sent their delegations.

An informal reception in the lobby preceded the supper and Connie Mack, Eddie Collins, and Harry Davis numbered among the Gettysburg boy's best friends in the baseball world were eagerly sought. A stirring march played by the town orchestra as the banqueters entered the dining room which was decorated with the huge World's Championship pennant of 1910 and the pennants of the Athletics and Gettysburg College. A fine likeness of Eddie appeared on the cover of the menu card and on the various pages were extracts from newspapers giving the many complimentary names that have been applied to the "old boy" as Connie Mack frequently and most affectionately referred to him during the course of the evening.

An elaborate menu was served and the spirit of the occasion was not lost here with such delicacies as "white elephant" and "Athletic salad" to be found while Eddie Plank pennants surmounted the croquettes and the ices were enclosed in imitation baseballs. The tables were conveniently arranged for the diners and the table with the guest of honor and his friends was located in the center of the room where it was sought out all evening by the many who were anxious to talk to Eddie and to meet Connie Mack and the others.

In the opening session of toasts and speeches after the supper, Charles S. Duncan, toastmaster, spoke of the character of the gathering and said, "There is but one thing in the world that could get a crowd of this size and character together. That is the great game of baseball and Eddie Plank. Every walk in life is represented here and Eddie should be the proudest man in the country today to think that it is in his honor that such an affair has been possible. And let it be known that we do this not simply because he is the greatest southpaw in the world, but because we love him and respect him" Mr. Duncan then introduced Judge Swope who spoke of the delight of Gettysburg fans in having present Mr. Mack.

"Mr. Mack," he said, "You are the peerless leader of the peerless team of the peerless baseball association of the world. We are happy you are with us tonight when we join to do honor to our own Eddie Plank, great as a baseball pitcher and great as a man. Eddie, we are glad you were born here. You are a credit to the town. There is not a hamlet in these broad United States, however small, that does not know the name of Eddie Plank and where he is from. You are a great combination—you and Connie Mack—and I want to say that I hope you will stay together many more years (Eddie and Connie shake hands vigorously) and that finally after a continued stretch of service lasting a long time may you come back to the farm bearing the praise of your great leader whom you have served so well.

"There are many things that come to my mind tonight and one of them is the wonderful pair of pitchers, Plank and Mathewson, good as they are, and they are good only because they have led clean and sober lives. We are honoring Eddie tonight not simply for his baseball prowess but because he is a clean, sober, honorable man, a great lesson to the young men of today."

Judge Swope then presented to Plank the token of esteem purchased by the banqueters, a scarf pin with a cluster of eight diamonds. "This is a case of diamond meeting diamond," said the speaker, "you are both typical of purity, virtue, and worth."

In his characteristic brief, though sincere, fashion Eddie accepted it. "This is quite a job," he said, "for me to say a few words and I want to say that they will be very few. We have others here who will talk to you about baseball and I will simply thank you from my heart for this beautiful gift."

Connie Mack's speech was followed as closely, perhaps, as any oration from President, scholar, or orator that ever appeared on a Gettysburg platform. For twenty minutes he told of baseball—it's victories and its defeats, its happy side and its misfortunes—but through it all was the frequent, almost tender, allusion to the "old boy" whom he patted on the shoulder as he talked and told how he had put him in to save the day on so many critical occasions. The history of several World's Series was related and Connie Mack took occasion to explain thoroughly how utterly false is the rumor that becomes current every year that baseball is "fixed," that there is something crooked about the whole proceeding. Twice, he declared, the World's Series have gone for five games instead of only four because of an accident while another time six games instead of five were played for the same cause.

In speaking of Eddie, Connie Mack declared he was the greatest left-handed pitcher in the history of baseball and then called attention to his record in World's Series games. "You will notice," he said, "that Plank has won two games and lost four. Let me tell you that if we had been able to score just two runs for him at the proper times that record would read 'won five lost one.' Eddie is a man without vices, a model for the young men and boys of the present day to strive after."

Connie Mack's speech was declared by the toastmaster to be "one of the most interesting we have ever listened to in all our lives" and then Eddie Collins was called upon. He told of Plank's treatment of his teammates of his never being known to blame a defeat on anyone but himself, of his spirit when losing and of his fine qualities as a man. Harry Davis told more about Eddie that delighted his hearers and in closing said, "Everything that has been told here tonight about him is absolutely true. I know it."

William Hersh, Esq., sprung one of the hits of the evening when he produced a receipt signed by Eddie Plank for $5.00 for "one week's service on the Gettysburg baseball team." It was given to John L. Hill, treasurer of the town team in 1896 and was eagerly examined by Connie Mack and many others when it was produced. "Since then," smiled Mr. Hersh, "he has been getting $6.25 a week."

Dr. Granville closed the evening in telling how great an advertisement Eddie Plank had been for Gettysburg College and how he was both a member of the faculty and textbook in teaching the boys at the local college how to play and how to live. Shortly before two o'clock this morning the banquet came to a close and again Eddie was surrounded by his admirers, eager to grasp his hand while many sought Connie Mack to have him place his autograph on their imitation baseballs that were part of the menu.

The committee having the banquet in charge and to whom the credit for its complete success is due was composed of the following: J. Harry Holtzworth, Samuel E. Weiser, Charles W. Myers, Rufus H. Bushman, W.H. Kalbfleisch, and William E. Allison.

A later recounting of the event in the *Gettysburg Compiler* of November 12th expanded upon Eddie Collin's comments:

EDDIE COLLINS WAS NEXT called upon by the toastmaster and in opening, he said he wanted to give a nearer view of the honored guest of the evening. He had been with him every game in the last seven years. Many players when they at the washrooms after the play will knock and say if they had had support at this or that point the game would have gone different. He had never heard a word of the kind from "Bunny"—Eddie's nickname to his players. "Bunny" was never heard to blame anyone but himself for the loss of a game. He recalled a game with Washington which was lost by an error of his own but which was credited against Plank. After the game, he was in the washroom and felt chagrined over the loss he had occasioned and plainly showed his gratitude and "Bunny" came over to him and put his arm around him and said, "Don't think about it, there will be lots of other games to be played and we will win our share of them." Eddie had always been a good loser and had endeared himself to all his teammates in many acts of kindness and thoughtfulness.

Collins told of the night before the final game. He had gone to New York with "Bunny" and the party went early to bed. During the night "Bunny" had loudly gone to the back room and getting a steaming hot towel, had wrapped it around his good left arm. At Collin's inquiry as to what was the matter, came the reply, "only the old rheumatiz." A second time that night he heard Plank get a second steaming towel for that arm. When it came to warming-up time the next day, Eddie said he "dreaded it for it was going to be painful," but when the game opened he watched him swing into his well-known gait, he knew the game was as good as won. There was a time, however, when there were two on the bases and he walked to the box and said to Eddie, "Are you sure you can handle things?" and "Bunny" replied with spirit "Give me that ball and get out of here." And the balls went across the plate with that great skill of his until the inning was over and the men on base were left there.

Tragically, by noon the next day, the owner of the Eagle Hotel, Richard M. Ham, had taken his own life in his parlor at the hotel, a revolver fired into his skull. Some had noticed Ham was not his usual jolly self during the Eddie Plank banquet. Charles W. Myers had gone to the desk several times to try to settle-up on the bill but was turned away each time, the transaction never completed. On Friday morning, Ham was to meet with his attorneys William Hersh and John D. Keith. While they were arriving, Ham shot himself. The two attorneys responded to the cries of the Hams' nanny to find Ham sitting on his chair in the parlor, blood spilling from his skull. Ham died within hours. It was believed he was stressed about "imaginary financial problems" having just taken sole ownership from his partner.

Eddie and Ira were off to the Cashtown deer camp with Harry Davis on Sunday, November 9th. Everyone gathered around the fire to hear baseball stories into the night. This was Davis's last night in town before returning to his home in Philadelphia.

On November 25, Eddie accompanied Connie Mack to Harrisburg to speak before the Board of Trade.

In Dearborn, Michigan, the Ford Motor Company introduced the first moving assembly line on December 1st. This greatly reduced the assembly time for a Model T, permitting Ford to make more at a lower price. Though not the inventor of the assembly line, Ford was the first to use it on a large scale, leading to mass production.

Aaron Montgomery Ward, businessman, known as the inventor of the mail order catalog, passed away on December 7th. He was 69.

On December 23, the Federal Reserve was created by Woodrow Wilson, giving the U.S. government tighter control of the money supply.

The next day, on Christmas Eve, Louis Francis "Chief" Sockalexis, the former right fielder for the 1897-99 Cleveland Spiders, passed away in Burlington, Maine, at the age of 42. He was the first Native American to play in the major leagues.

World Series fans on a streetcar.

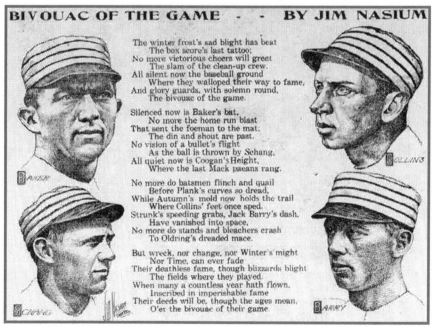

Poem about the 1913 Athletics.

The A's win the 1913 American League pennant.

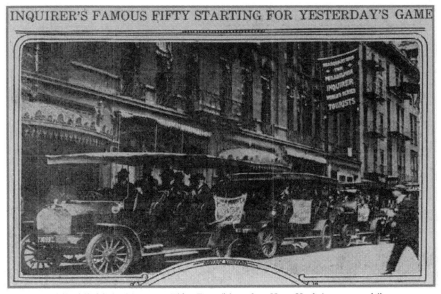

Philadelphia's "Famous Fifty Fans" head to New York in automobiles.

World Series battle at Shibe Park in 1913.

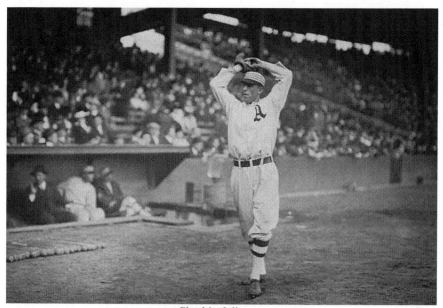

Plank's delivery.

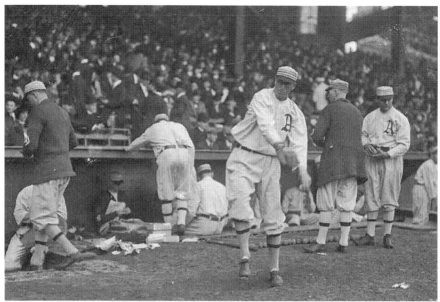

Plank's delivery.

Plank's delivery.

Rooftop bleachers during the World Series of 1913.

Game Two of the 1913 World Series.

"Eddie Plank, the Veteran Pitcher"

Cover of the program from the Eddie Plank banquet in Gettysburg in 1913.

The Athletics win the 1913 World Series with Eddie on the mound.

Eddie Plank with Connie Mack and others touring the Gettysburg Battlefield in 1913.

1914:
THE MARVEL OF
BASEBALL

T HE *GETTYSBURG TIMES* on January 14th contained an item suggesting Eddie Plank might be an investor in the Lancaster baseball club in the Tri-State League. Appeals were being made to Connie Mack to get involved.

Always competitive, Eddie took his bowling team to Chambersburg on the 21st for a match against a team featuring Pittsburgh third baseman Mike Mowrey, who was a native of nearby Brown's Mill. Plank's boys won.

The January 24th *Adams County News* mentioned the Eddie had still not signed a contract for 1914. "Last year Plank did not sign a contract until the season had almost started. At that time the wonderful southpaw announced that he was going to retire after a long and meritorious career in baseball, but Manager Mack succeeded in getting the Gettysburg graduate to sign. It will probably be the same this year. Plank is anxious to retire, and if he does it will not be in want. He is worth more than $50,000 and owns considerable farmland up-state."

Rumors had now shifted to Plank managing the Reading team in the Tri-State League or still possibly taking a stake in the Lancaster club. Said Connie upon hearing them, "There is nothing to it," he declared emphatically, "because Plank is needed more in Philadelphia than Lancaster. Plank isn't ready for the minors. He pitched better ball last season than he did in all the years he has been with me. I would no more think of letting him go than I would Collins or Baker. I think that Plank is the marvel of baseball, and I wouldn't be surprised were he pitching good ball for me five years hence. He isn't thinking of any minor-league berth. He knows he is far from being through with the majors."

As the month was ending, Eddie spent some time in Table Rock, visiting with his brother Luther. Luther later told a story about Eddie that occurred during his playing days and may have occurred around this time.

Eddie drove from the farm to the Table Rock Mill to see Luther one day. When he arrived, he said, "Lute, close the mill and come with me. I want you to drive me around a bit."

Luther closed the mill and chauffeured Eddie while he told him where he wanted to go. When they arrived at the first destination, Eddie reached into a small tin box, took out a paper, and went into the house. Not long after, he returned to the car and informed his brother of the next location.

Luther observed the same activity at the next stop and then several times more. Finally, the curiosity got the better of him and he asked his brother, "Eddie, what are you up to?"

Eddie replied, "Well, you see these are IOU slips from people I loaned money to. I am going back to each of them and marking them 'Paid in Full.' Now, just look at this young man here. He has a wife and family now and responsibilities and it would be impossible for him to get ahead enough to pay it back. I just consider them paid and that is final."

By mid-February, Eddie was still holding out for more money, having rebuffed Connie's latest contract offer. Mack was steadfast stating that Eddie would not get a raise and that he expected him to be in Jacksonville, Florida, for training later in the month. Plank was the only Athletics player not yet signed.

Finally, it was announced in the February 24th *Gettysburg Times* that Eddie would be heading south on Wednesday the 25th to Baltimore to meet the train heading to Jacksonville. Meanwhile, most of the rest of the team had headed to New York to cruise via steamer to Jacksonville. Mack had decided to go by train, uncomfortable with sailing. Bender stayed behind for a couple more weeks. So, Eddie joined Connie on the train and the two spent the long ride to Jacksonville together.

Eddie first pitched in a ballgame on March 5th against Jacksonville, exercising for a few innings. On the 12th, he worked in an exhibition against the Chicago Cubs in Tampa.

Connie and the boys began heading north later in March. Plank pitched in the game at Waycross, Georgia on the 20th and Savannah on the 23rd. Eddie then worked at Richmond on the 27th against the Virginia League team. To the delight of the 6000 fans present, Eddie did an imitation of Rube Waddell, from when he was in his prime. In the 9th inning, with the A's ahead 9 to 3, after striking out Troutman and getting two strikes on McIntyre, Eddie called in his outfield and demonstrated he was in top condition. He then finished off McIntyre. Ryan was next to bat and the umpire initially objected to the positioning of the outfielders, but then relented. Amos Strunk then took off his spikes and put on slippers and Collins threw away his glove. Eddie then fanned Ryan on three strikes, striking out the side. None of the three batters could touch his cross-fire. The crowd cheered loudly as Eddie walked off the field, pleased that he had honored the memory of his now desperately ill teammate.

On the 28th of March, the A's faced the Baltimore minor league team in Baltimore. Babe Ruth pitched. He had also faced them earlier in the spring in Wilmington, North Carolina.

On April Fool's Day, the 1st, Rube Waddell passed away in a sanitarium in San Antonio, Texas, from tuberculosis at the age of thirty-seven. Connie Mack was shocked by his passing and told the *Philadelphia Inquirer* on the 2nd of April, "He was the greatest pitcher in the game, and although widely known for his eccentricities, was more sinned against than sinner. He was the best-hearted man on our team and every man with whom he came in contact will verify my statement."

Rube was buried in San Antonio on April 3rd.

Preaching in Scranton on Saturday the 4th, Billy Sunday compared the clean living of Plank and Mathewson to the late Rube Waddell and Bugs Raymond. "I tell you, you can't beat the booze game. You have to pay the freight," he said.

Reverend Thomas Davis, the chaplain of the Athletics was not happy about Sunday's sermon, "I have known Rube for eleven years and I believe he was a sufferer of tuberculosis, which sooner or later would have caused his death. I do not believe it was caused by the use of intoxicating drinks. Waddell was a big kind-hearted fellow," he continued, tear in his eye while his voice trembled. "He was the first to help a player in trouble and the last to leave a player who had been injured on the field." Davis then went on to praise Connie Mack, who "never swears, chews, drinks, or smokes, and when Thomas is catching, Plank pitching, McInnis at first, Collins at second, Barry at short, and the mighty

Baker at third, there is the cleanest infield in the game, not a man of whom drinks, swears, or chews tobacco."

Christy Mathewson added on, writing in the *Philadelphia Free Press* that "Plank is the type of twirler who wears well because he has always taken care of himself, and he also has an easy pitching motion that does not use up his arm." Mathewson thought Plank would be around for many more years.

In Philadelphia, the inner-city series was held again. Plank beat the Phillies 6 to 1 on the 6th of April. Eddie was roughed up a bit in the game on the 10th, losing 6 to 1.

The regular season got underway on the 14th, the A's in New York against the Yankees, who won 8 to 2. Eddie's first appearance was a scoreless inning in a loss to the Red Sox in Boston on the 16th. His first victory of the season was an 8-to-2 win over the Red Sox at Fenway on the 20th. Eddie Collins had three hits in the game for the Athletics.

On April 21st, the 2300 U.S. Navy sailors and marines occupied the harbor at Veracruz, Mexico to enforce an arms embargo with Mexico, who was friendly to Germany.

Two days later, on the 23rd, Weeghman Field in Chicago opened, the home of the Federal League Chicago Whales. It would later be known as Wrigley Field.

On April 24th, rookie Rube Bressler won his first major league game, 7 to 6, against the Yankees at Shibe Park. Bressler, who would ultimately convert to an outfielder and hit over .300 during his long career, won the game in relief. Later in life, Bressler discussed Plank and Bender in *The Glory of Their Times* by Lawrence Ritter, "I used to try to get near them and listen to what they were talking about, and every question I'd ask they'd pay attention and tell me what they thought. I used to put sticks behind my ears so they'd stand out further. Boy, I wanted to hear what those guys had to say."

On April 27th, Eddie got his first save of the year, pitching the last inning of a 5-to-4 win against the Yankees at Shibe Park.

The A's ended April 5-5, in 5th place, three games behind the Detroit Tigers. Eddie was 1-0.

The Boston Red Sox were at Shibe Park on May 2nd. Harry Hooper had three hits against Plank, but Eddie scattered ten hits in winning 5 to 2.

Eddie next pitched Friday, May 8th in Washington at Griffith Stadium. He was winning 3 to 0 until he gave up four runs in the bottom of the 5th inning. Plank was yanked, the A's pulling ahead in the top of the 6th, 6 to 5, but the game ended tied at nine.

That Saturday and Sunday, May 9th and 10th, Eddie was home near Gettysburg and took in the baseball game against Villanova Saturday afternoon.

Woodrow Wilson signed the Mother's Day proclamation on May 14th. That day, at home against Cleveland, Eddie held Nap Lajoie and Shoeless Joe Jackson to only one hit in ten at bats. Cleveland managed only five hits as Eddie shut them out 1 to 0 in thirteen innings.

On May 16th, Eddie and Jack Coombs observed the college baseball game between Ursinus and Gettysburg at Patterson Field in Collegeville. The game went seventeen innings, tied 1 to 1, before it was called due to darkness. The two were scouting Ursinus pitcher Russell Conwell "Jing" Johnson, "split ball wonder" who struck out 27 in the game. Connie later signed him prior to the 1916 season.

Eddie's first loss of the season came on May 21st at home against Detroit. He gave up two runs in the first two innings and was pulled with two outs in the 2nd. The A's lost 6 to 4.

On the 28th, before only 3500 fans, Eddie pitched against St. Louis at Shibe Park. He went the distance, winning 3 to 0. Home Run Baker hit his second of the season to aid the cause.

The Athletics concluded May tied for 1st place with the Washington Senators, at 21-13. Eddie was 4-1 so far.

Eddie next appeared on June 1st, earning a win in relief against the Yankees, 9 to 8. Eddie pitched the final six-plus innings of the game, which went twelve innings.

Eddie subsequently survived two hits and three RBI from Ty Cobb at Navin Field on the 8th, as the A's topped the Tigers, 5 to 4. Baker hit his third of the season in this game.

The following day, on June 9th, Honus Wagner of the Pittsburgh Pirates got his 3,000th hit, only the second player to do so. Cap Anson had been the first to do so in 1897.

On the 16th, at Comiskey Park in Chicago, Eddie earned his second save of the season, pitching the final inning of a 10-to-7 victory by Bob Shawkey.

Two days later in St. Louis, Eddie did not have his best stuff, lasting only until the 5th inning when Boardwalk Brown took over. The Browns won 6 to 5, a late A's rally falling short.

Still at Sportsman's Park on the 22nd, Eddie redeemed himself with a brilliant 3-to-0 win over the Browns.

Austrian Archduke Ferdinand and his wife, Duchess Sophie, were assassinated by nineteen-year-old Serbian nationalist Gavrilo Princip in Sarajevo, Bosnia and Herzegovina, on June 28th, triggering World War I.

The next day, the A's put up five runs in the 1st inning to give Eddie an early lead against the Red Sox at home. He cruised to a 7-to-2 victory.

After June, the A's had begun to separate from the competition, now 39-26, in 1st place by 2 1/2 games over Detroit. Eddie was 8-2 on the season.

In the first game of a doubleheader against the Yankees at Shibe Park on July 4th, Eddie was called on to hold a 4-to-2 lead in the 8th. He was tagged for four runs, and took the loss, 7 to 5,

Four days later, Eddie was rested on the 8th to take on the 2nd place Tigers at home. He held Cobb-less Detroit to only three hits, winning 3 to 0.

Meanwhile, his former battery-mate, Ossee Schrecongost collapsed unexpectedly at a cafe on Columbia Avenue near 12th Street in Philadelphia.

The next day, July 9th, Ossee, only thirty-nine, died of uremia, a symptom of kidney failure, in Philadelphia. He had been a catcher for eleven seasons, and a teammate of Eddie's from 1902 to 1908. He twice hit .300. "Shreck" as he was known, had told friends after Rube Waddell died, "I do not care to live now. The Rube is gone and I'm all in. I might as well join him."

A service for "Schreck" was held in the city on the 11th. He was later buried at Kittanning Cemetery in Kittanning, Pennsylvania.

A rookie pitcher named Babe Ruth made his debut that day. Connie Mack had been offered the opportunity to buy Ruth and another player from the Baltimore Orioles minor league club for $20,000. With attendance down and the team in good standing, Mack passed on the opportunity, though he recognized Ruth's talent. He then recommended Ruth to the Boston Red Sox.

On July 18th, Eddie faced the Chicago White Sox and Ed Walsh at Shibe Park. Plank won 4 to 1.
A week later, in Detroit, Eddie doubled in two runs to help his cause, beating the Tigers 10 to 4.
On the 31st, Eddie pitched five innings of solid relief in a game tied 6 to 6. Eddie won in extra innings, 9 to 7.
The Athletics cruised through July, finishing at 59-33, with a comfortable 6 1/2 game lead over the Boston Red Sox. Eddie was now 12-3 on the season.
Meanwhile, in Europe, the first shots of World War I had been fired.

On August 4th, following Germany's invasion of Belgium, Great Britain declared war on Germany. The United States remained neutral.
Eddie's next start was August 9th at League Park in Cleveland. He easily beat the woeful Naps, 10 to 5. Shoeless Joe was 3 for 5 in defeat.
The August 12th *Gettysburg Times* announced the Eddie was spending several days at home.
The steamship S.S. *Ancon* became the first vessel to traverse the newly-opened Panama Canal on August 15th.

Eddie's next start was August 18th against the Detroit Tigers in Philadelphia. Eddie pitched around Cobb, walking him twice and holding him hitless in two at-bats. The A's won 2 to 1.
On the 24th, Eddie faced the Browns at home. He cruised to a 7-to-1 win.
In front of only 2000 fans on the 28th, Eddie was roughed up by the Chicago White Sox at Shibe Park. He was pulled after four innings, losing 6 to 4. The A's lost 8 to 6 in a rain-shortened six inning contest.
Eddie turned thirty-nine on the 31st. The A's were 82-38 with a healthy thirteen game lead over Boston. Plank was 15-4. Eddie

and the A's were running away with the pennant, and the fans seemed bored.

On September 1st, it was announced that the last known passenger pigeon, a female named Martha, died in the Cincinnati Zoo from old age. The pigeons had been hunted to extinction.

At Fenway Park on September 3rd, Eddie dropped a 3-to-1 decision to the Red Sox.

On the 7th, in Washington, Eddie registered his third save of the season with three innings in relief of Chief Bender. The A's won 8 to 7.

Two days later, on the 9th, Eddie started against the Red Sox at Shibe Park and went the distance, exchanging zeroes with Ray Collins into the 11th inning. Boston scored two unearned runs and won 2 to 0.

At Navin Field, in Detroit, on the 19th of September, Eddie took the mound and lost a close one, 4 to 3.

That same day, the *Adams County News* announced that Eddie had purchased two row houses in Philadelphia, 2748 and 2750 Hemberger Street, adjoining three such units purchased by Mrs. Jack Coombs. The homes were a short walk from Shibe Park.

On September 27th, Chief Bender threw a four-hit shutout, beating the St. Louis Browns 6 to 0. The Athletics had clinched the pennant. On this day, Napolean Lajoie of the Cleveland Naps became the third member of the 3000-hit club.

The A's finished September with a 96-50 record and an eight-game lead over Boston. Eddie was 15-7.

The regular season ended on October 7th with a lopsided 10-to-0 win over the Yankees at Shibe Park. Only 500 attended the game. The A's finished 99-53, 8 1/2 games up on Boston.

Eddie finished the season 15-7 with a 2.87 ERA. Mack only started him 22 times. Chief Bender, 17-3, and Bullet Joe Bush, 17-13, led the team in victories. Bob Shawkey was 15-8. Weldon Wyckoff and Herb Pennock each won 11 games, Rube Bressler 10. Eddie led the team with 110 strikeouts. Walter Johnson led the American League with 28 wins and 225 strikeouts. Dutch Leonard had an amazing 0.96 ERA.

At the plate, Eddie Collins hit .344, trailing Ty Cobb's .368. Home Run Baker hit .319 and led the league with 9 home runs.

Stuffy McInnis hit .314 and knocked in 95, trailing Sam Crawford's 104.

The first game of the 1914 World Series was held at Shibe Park on October 9th. There was great anticipation in the city. The champion Athletics were favored to win the series. Before the first game, Gene Stallings, the manager of the Boston Braves, and Connie Mack had a quarrel about Boston's use of Shibe Park to practice. When things got underway, Chief Bender faced Dick Rudolph. It did not go well for the Athletics, who lost 7 to 1.

The next day, Eddie Plank took the mound and was expected to even things up. He faced Bill James who had gone 26-7 on the year for the Braves. The two hurlers traded zeroes through eight innings. Finally, in the top of the 9th, Boston scored a run to take a 1 to 0 lead. In their bottom of the 9th, the A's got two men on and were threatening. Murphy came to the plate and hit a smash, but it was turned into a double play, ending the game. The A's had been limited to only two hits. Boston 1, Philadelphia 0. The Braves now led the series two games to none.

The series next shifted to Fenway Park in Boston on Monday the 12th. Bullet Joe Bush got the call for Philadelphia to face Lefty Tyler. The A's jumped out to a 1-to-0 lead in the top of the 1st. The Braves answered with a run in their 2nd. In the top of the 4th, Philadelphia again went ahead by a run, only to be tied at two in the bottom of the 4th. Bush and Tyler then locked things down until the 9th. In the top of the 10th, the A's scored twice against Tyler, but Bush could not close it out in the bottom of the 10th. The Braves answered with two runs of their own. The game was now tied 4 to 4 going into the 11th. Bill James was called to relieve Tyler, and he shut down the A's in the 11th and 12th. Finally, in the bottom of the 12th, Boston scored a run to win the game 5 to 4. The Braves now led the series three games to none.

The next day, at Fenway, Dick Rudolph beat Bob Shawkey, 3-to-1, the championship going to Boston on a sweep of four games for the first time in history.

The November 7th *Adams County News* reported on the surprise release of Eddie Plank by the Philadelphia Athletics the prior Saturday, October 31st. "While I have no intention of retaining the three above-named players in 1915 (Plank, Coombs, Bender), I would not have asked waivers on the players at this time but for the fact that one of the three had told me that he was talking business with the Federal League; that he was offered big money, and that he did not suppose that we would want to meet the offer."

Eddie was interviewed by the *Philadelphia Bulletin*, and provided the following:

"IT WAS A COMPLETE surprise to me, and I knew nothing about it until a friend of mine called me this morning from Philadelphia and told me he had read it in the paper. I would have thought Connie would have told me something about it, particularly since I told him a few days ago I received a strong offer from the Federal League. I was man enough to do that, and Connie might at least have done the same towards me. I gave the best I had to the Athletics and would like to be able to say the club treated me well in return. I feel that I have at least a couple years more good pitching left in my old wing, and the fact that the Athletics want to release me will not make the Federals believe that I am all in. If the Feds think that way, I don't have to worry, for I have got mine stowed away in farms and the bank, and I don't have to play ball anymore unless I want to. Even now I am not sure I will play ball with the Federals, but if I do, you can bet that I get a fat salary, and I shall give them my best in return."

At the time, Eddie was the oldest pitcher in the American League. Only he and Harry Davis remained from the initial 1901 Athletics team. Boston, New York, and Cleveland were soon inquiring about Plank's willingness to play in their cities. Former player and manager Arthur Irwin, representing the New York Yankees, even visited Eddie in Gettysburg to convince him to sign with the team rather than defecting to the new Federal League.

Many years later, in 1921, it became known that Irwin had been leading a double life, keeping families in both Boston and New York. Neither knew of the other until Irwin became gravely ill and took his own life. His wives thought he had been a model husband.

The second week of November, Eddie Collins was in town and spent some time at the Plank farm.

The U.S. troops in Veracruz withdrew on November 23rd.

On December 2nd, it was announced that Eddie had signed with the Federal League. Harry Goldman, the secretary-treasurer of the Baltimore Terrapins represented the league on a visit to Gettysburg to sign the contract. Said Eddie, "The fact that I have signed with the Federal League is everything I can say at the present time. What the length of the contract is or with which club I expect to play, I will not be able to tell my friends for some time. My contract is a general one and it is within the power of the League authorities to send me where they wish."

Later that day came a dispatch from St. Louis. Plank had been assigned to the St. Louis Terriers. The St. Louis Terriers completed the 1914 season in the basement, finishing 8th in a league of eight teams with a record of 62-89. Jack Coombs signed with Brooklyn of the National League. Chief Bender went to the Baltimore Terrapins.

The next week, the Athletics announced the sale of Eddie Collins to the White Sox for $50,000. The $100,000 infield was no more.

Eddie modeling for a Royal Tailors advertisement.

Eddie in the Sporting News *in 1914.*

Eddie following through.

Eddie on the field in 1914.

Johnny Evers meets Eddie Plank at the 1914 World Series.

Connie releases Plank, Bender, and Coombs after the season.

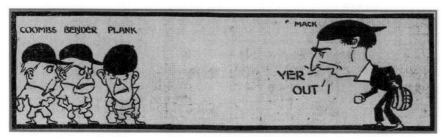

Cartoon of the release.

Word puzzle featuring Eddie Plank in 1914.

1915:
SAME OLD WIZARD

URING JANUARY, MARY Mallon, working as a cook at New York's Sloan Hospital under an assumed name, infected twenty-five people and was quarantined for life. She has since been known as "Typhoid Mary."

This same month, the U.S. House of Representatives rejected a bill that would have given women the right to vote.

On January 30th, Eddie Plank married his long-time sweetheart Anna Cora Myers, daughter of Mrs. Sarah Ellen Myers of New Oxford, Pennsylvania, in Ridgewood, New Jersey. Eddie and his bride kept it quiet locally to have more privacy. Plank was thirty-nine and his bride twenty-six.

On January 31st, Eddie and former teammate Harry Davis were in Philadelphia at the tabernacle to hear former baseball player Billy Sunday preach. Sunday, who had played for several teams in the National League in the 1880s and 1890s, including the Phillies, had become the most popular evangelist in the country. He was in town preaching against booze.

During the sermon, Eddie turned to Harry and said, "Gee, Billy's got the right dope all right. He's on the level. I want to meet him."

After the sermon, the players were taken to Ma Sunday, who then took them to her husband. Billy Sunday was introduced to the ballplayers as he wiped the perspiration from his brow. "Hello, Harry, old scout. Hello, Eddie, how's the soup bone?" he said. The three continued some small talk including some banter about Eddie going to the Federal League.

On February 8th, the film *The Birth of a Nation* (originally called *The Clansman*), directed by D. W. Griffith, premiered in Los Angeles. It would be the highest-grossing film for the next 25 years. The film is credited with inspiring the creation of the second era Ku Klux Klan which grew rapidly in popularity.

The *Adams County News* reported on February 13th that, per the *York Daily*, Eddie Plank had signed in the Federal League for a lot more money. "Plank only smiles when he is asked to name the figures in the agreement, but it is said that the veteran southpaw will receive $9,000 a year for each of two years. The sum is several thousand more than he received from the Athletics."

Fielder Jones, who had led the White Sox to the pennant in the dramatic finish against the Athletics, was the manager of the St. Louis Terriers in the Federal League. He had taken over for the final 38 games, replacing Miner Brown. The team went 12-26. Said Jones in an interview about the upcoming season, published in the February 19th *St. Louis Post-Dispatch*: "The best ballplayers don't always make the best club. Give me a couple of wise, willing pitchers who will work; pitchers who will sew the runner on first base and exercise their brains in the pinch, and surround them with a little speed and hustle, and I'll win a lot of ballgames. I'm pretty well pleased with my team for next season. I regard Eddie Plank as the best pitching bet in the league. Plank's peculiar motion—you know he faces first base when he pitches—and his eagerness to win, will make him a headliner. You can't solve Plank's delivery in a season; I couldn't in three, and during my stay in the American League, I feared him more than any other hurler—and for that reason, I expect him to win."

On February 22nd, Eddie and Mrs. Plank headed south for spring training in Key West, Florida and Havana, Cuba. Eddie announced the marriage to the public now, and it was mentioned in the February 27th *Adams County News* and *Gettysburg Compiler*. Said Eddie, "Yes, I am married. I suppose you will hear all about it tomorrow, but I wanted to keep it a secret until I left for spring training. Mrs. Plank will meet me and go along south where we train."

The Planks traveled separately on their way to Key West. Meanwhile, Fielder Jones first stopped in Jacksonville, Florida, where he met up with seven other team members. This initial group included pitchers Otis Crandall, Edward Willett, Bob Groom, and Dave Davenport; catchers Grover Hartley and Harry Chapman; infielders Ernie Johnson and Baker Borton. Said Jones of the upcoming activities in Key West, "The first and most important step will be an effort to teach the players the value of obedience."

The March 9th *St. Louis Star and Times* included an example of Fielder's discipline. Plank was not immune to it, given his status. "It sounds rather odd to hear him tell old-timers like Eddie Plank, Al Bridwell, and Ward Miller how to run to first base. 'Don't look at the ball. Never look at the ball,' calls Fielder as the men run down the line." wrote the reporter.

In the game that day against local players in Havana, Eddie threw three frames and was "the same old wizard."

Eddie was mentioned in the March 18th *St. Louis Star and Times*, telling stories about Connie Mack to the younger players. "Yes, Connie Mack is a wonderful manager," said Eddie. "He is a quiet observing man, just one would judge from a look at his pictures. He pulls in harmony with all his players and it is rare indeed that he gives one a 'calling.' Right well, I remember the first and only rebuke Connie ever directed toward my head. We were playing Chicago in 1906, and the gentleman who was umpiring the game (there is no need mentioning his name here) was calling balls on me when the mother was cutting the plate in half. I raised the Dickens with him and he kept calling them bad until the tenth inning and I flew off my guard. I took off my glove and threw it in the air and was immediately chased off the field. As I walked over to put on my sweater, Connie said in a slow, desperate way, with a piercing note of sarcasm in his voice, 'Nice work Eddie, you showed excellent judgment.' That was all, just seven words, but believe me, boys, I'll remember those seven words as long as I live. They hurt me worse than if he had lit in and cussed me until he was blue in the face. I don't retain their memory with any hard feeling toward Mack attached—far from it. I simply remember them as forming the best rebuke I ever received. It taught me a lesson I never forgot—I never lost my head to such an extent as to get myself chased for it." Eddie went on to encourage the players to "keep their heads." "My policy is to never kick on a decision," concluded Eddie, "and I have found it a very good rule to follow."

Jones wisely used Plank to help coach the crew, the *St. Louis Star and Times* referring to him as the "Kohinoor" (a famous Indian diamond) of the baseball world.

Mrs. Plank reported in a letter home to her mother, mentioned in the *Adams County News* on March 20th, that they arrived safely in Havana and were staying at the Hotel America. They reported warm weather and said only a few got seasick on the voyage. That day, in Havana, Eddie "toiled and held the ebony-hued enemy to three hits while he fanned five."

As the month of March was ending, comparisons were being made between the Federal League and the others. The young league had not picked up as many players as feared and the noteworthy ones had been released by their major-league teams. "Some of the Fed teams can't be worse than the Pirates, Reds, and Phillies now seem to be." surmised "Wray's Column" in the March 26th *St. Louis Post-Dispatch.*

The next day, the *St. Louis Star and Times* included an item about the lower gate receipts in Cuba as compared to post-season tours in the past. Eddie reminisced about the 1910 Athletics each getting $500 to play in Havana. "Every man in the party of fourteen received his $250 when he reached the city and 250 greenbacks at the end of two weeks' stay. They treated us like a passel of kings. We had all our expenses paid and enjoyed ourselves to our hearts' content without laying out a nickel."

On March 29th, the *St. Louis Post-Dispatch* included an item about Eddie. "Comes the news from Havana that Eddie Plank has a weakness for thick steaks and good coffee. There are thousands of guys with the same weakness, but without the necessary bankroll to back it up."

Jones and the Terriers broke camp in Havana on April 5th. Fielder was very optimistic about the prospects of his team. "The fans back in old St. Louis might think it a joke when I say that the Terriers will be the runners-up for the pennant this season, but when they see my squad they will be surprised. Eddie Plank, the veteran twirler, is going to win a good many games this season for us, and his knowledge of the game is going to be a great help to the younger men on the team. Plank was good enough last fall to be picked by Connie Mack to pitch in the World's Series, and if Ed is good enough for a World's Series, he will be good enough for the Terriers."

This same day, boxer Jess Willard, the latest "Great White Hope," defeated Jack Johnson with a 26th-round knockout in sweltering heat at Havana, Cuba. The remarks of promoter Jack Curley were reported in the *Evening Public Ledger* in Philadelphia. Said Curley, "Willard will take a brief rest and then will meet any white fighters. He will draw the color line. The fight was a big success. Willard deserves the thanks of the entire white race for his glorious victory, bringing back to the white race the heavyweight championship title."

The Federal League season began Saturday, April 10th. The Terriers were in Chicago at Weeghman Park to face the Whales. Weeghman would later be known as Wrigley Field. Eddie Plank was the starting pitcher for St. Louis and was winning 1 to 0 until the bottom of the 8th when Chicago rallied for three runs. Eddie lost the game 3 to 1.

Bob Groom threw a three-hit shutout the next day as the Terriers tallied their first win of the season, 3 to 0.

Charlie Chaplin's *The Tramp* was released this day in movie theaters.

On Thursday, April 15th, at Gordon and Koppel Field in Kansas City, against the Packers, Eddie relieved Dave Davenport in the 7th and pitched an inning and a third in a 4-to-3 loss.

Due to a sore arm, Eddie's next action was not until April 27th in Pittsburgh against the Rebels at Exposition Park. He beat Howie Camnitz 5 to 2 to register his first win of the season. Afterward, Eddie took the morning express train to Gettysburg. He shook some hands and hurried home for breakfast. His intent was to spend several days at home with Mrs. Plank.

The Terriers ended the month of April not much better than last season at 5-9, in 7th place, four games back of the 1st place Newark Pepper. Eddie was 2-1 on the season.

Eddie rejoined the team after the respite with Anna Cora, who was now pregnant. The Terriers were in Newark, New Jersey, to face the Pepper at Harrison Field on May 2nd. He threw a three-hit gem to beat Cy Falkenberg 1 to 0. Young Edd Roush, in his first full season in the major leagues, was held hitless.

On May 6th, Red Sox pitcher Babe Ruth hit his first major league home run off the Yankees' Jack Washop in New York at the Polo Grounds.

The next day, the RMS *Lusitania* was sunk by a German U-boat while sailing from New York to Great Britain. Nearly 1200 were killed including many Americans.

On May 8th, Eddie was on the mound in Buffalo, New York, to face the Blues at Federal League Park. He only pitched one inning, after the Terriers staked him to a 3-to-0 lead in the 1st.

He handed a 3-to-1 lead to Groom, who finished off the victory. Apparently, Eddie's arm was bothering him again.

Home at Handlan's Park in St. Louis against the Kansas City Packers, Eddie was back on the mound on May 15th. Everybody in the Terrier lineup had a hit as Eddie cruised to a 13-to-2 victory. Eddie, himself, was 2 for 5.

A rematch against Cy Falkenberg was held on the 21st at home. This time, Newark won narrowly, defeating Plank 4 to 3.

On May 29th, the Brooklyn Tip-Tops were in town. Eddie pitched the Terriers back to .500, winning handily, 11 to 0. Only three Brooklyn players had hits. Right fielder Jack Tobin was 5 for 5 and first baseman Babe Borton 4 for 5 to lead the Terrier attack. Tobin, twenty-three, was in his second year of what would be a long major-league career resulting in a .309 career batting average. Borton, twenty-six, was amid his only season as a regular player in the big leagues. He would spend most of the rest of his career in the minors.

The Terriers ended May 17-17, in 6th place, 4 1/2 games back. Eddie was now 4-2.

On June 2nd, Eddie was back in Chicago to face the Whales. He won narrowly, 2 to 1. Joe Tinker, the famous Cubs shortstop was in the lineup for the Whales, nearing the end of his great career. He had a hit against Eddie, one for four on the day.

Four days later, in Kansas City, Eddie lost a close one, 3 to 2.

On Saturday, June 12th, the Pittsburgh Rebels were in town. Eddie won his sixth game of the season, downing them 4 to 1.

Five days later, in Newark against the Pepper, Eddie relieved Bob Groom in the 7th, the Terriers leading 3 to 2, and earned a save as St. Louis held on.

Eddie was next on the hill at Washington Park in Brooklyn on June 19th to face the Tip Tops, who were named after a local bakery. He won 6 to 2 and contributed an RBI single.

The June 26th *Adams County News* reported Eddie was home for a few days and said his arm was feeling better than it has in years. "The old wing shows no signs whatever of soreness," he said. Later that day, Eddie pitched against the Baltimore Terrapins at Terrapin Park. He shut them out on three hits, 2 to 0. Former Athletics teammate Chief Bender opposed him. Eddie was happy to have a base hit off him.

The Terriers ended June at 37-25, having gone 20-8 during the month. They were now tied for 1st with the Kansas City Packers. Eddie was 8-3 on the season.

Back in Buffalo on July 1st, Eddie lost 4 to 1 but held the Blues scoreless until the 7th inning.

The July 3rd *Adams County News* attributed Eddie's success beyond age forty to clean living and hard work. Eddie, however, was still a few weeks from his fortieth birthday.

Back home at Handlan's Park on the 13th, Eddie pitched fourteen innings of three-hit ball but lost 2 to 0. The Terriers managed nine hits against the Whales, but could not muster a run.

A week later, at home, Eddie Plank and Chief Bender had a rematch as the Terriers hosted the Terrapins. Eddie went the distance and won 4 to 1. Chief dropped to 3-13 on the season, which was his worst in the big leagues.

In Chicago, on July 24th, the steamer *Eastland* capsized causing the loss of 844 lives. This same day, Eddie beat the Brooklyn Tip-Tops 4 to 2 in St. Louis. It was his tenth win of the season.

The next day, in a tight game against the Tip-Tops, Eddie pitched the final two innings to save the contest for Doc Watson, the Terriers winning, 6 to 5.

On the 29th at Handlan's Park against the Newark Pepper, Eddie entered the game tied at eight going into extra innings. He pitched two innings and gave up three runs in the 11th, taking the loss.

By the end of July, St. Louis slipped to 50-44, four games behind the Kansas City Packers, in 4th place. Eddie was now 10-6 on the season.

On August 1st, Buffalo was in town. Eddie was rocked for six runs early and was replaced by Ed Willett. Willett held the Blues scoreless the rest of the way, but the Terriers could not rally, losing 6 to 3.

Eddie was back on his game on the 5th at Terrapin Park in Baltimore. He tossed a six-hit shutout. His opponent, Rankin Johnson, gave up only one hit and lost 1 to 0.

Four days later, Eddie threw another shutout in Baltimore, beating Jack Quinn 3 to 0. The Terrapins managed only four hits against him. Eddie had two hits himself, including a double.

In Newark, at Harrison Field on the 14th, Eddie faced the Pepper. He scattered five hits and won 3 to 1.

In Brooklyn on the 19th, Eddie topped the Tip-Tops 4 to 3. Eddie had a hit, run, and RBI to help himself. After the game, he headed home to Gettysburg.

On Sunday, August 22nd, Eddie was nearly run over by a train, as he was motoring from Gettysburg to Harrisburg to catch a train west to rejoin his team. Per the *Adams County News* from August 28th, "Eddie Plank had a narrow escape from death, trying to get his automobile across the tracks of the Philadelphia and Reading Railway on Sunday when he found the subway at Rosegarden (near Grantham) filled with water as a result of the recent very heavy rains. Rosegarden is a station on the Reading between Boiling Springs and Bowmansdale. Plank was motoring from Gettysburg to Harrisburg to catch a train for Chicago, where he was to pitch this afternoon. After a hair-raising trip, in which he forded four streams from which bridges had been washed away, he found his path blocked where the road passes under the tracks at Rosegarden, and with his driver, dug a zig-zag pathway to the embankment of the railroad, up which he drove the car. Then he stalled the engine trying to cross the rails just as a fast train shot around the curve. Plank stuck with his machine and got out of the way with only a foot to spare, dug a path for his car down the other side and arrived in Harrisburg in the evening, just in time to catch his train west."

Against the Chicago Whales on August 24th, Eddie faced off against George McConnell, who was amid a 25-win season, his only season in double-digits. Eddie lost a close one, 4 to 3.

On August 28th, Eddie faced the Kansas City Packers at home. He won a close one, 3 to 2.

The Terriers finished August 66-56, 3 1/2 games back of Pittsburgh, in 3rd place. Eddie was now 15-6 on the season and forty years old.

Eddie was in Pittsburgh against the Rebels on September 4th. He fell behind 3 to 0, but the Terriers scratched back to 3 to 2. The Rebels added three late runs to finish them off 6 to 3.

Two days later, Eddie started at home against the Chicago Whales, but the game was called after five innings tied at two.

Albert Goodwill Spalding passed away on September 9th. He had been a pitcher, manager, and executive in baseball and started the A.G. Spalding sporting goods company. He published the first official rulebook for baseball.

On September 11th, Eddie faced the Newark Pepper at Handlan's Park in St. Louis. His mound opponent was veteran Ed Reulbach who had been one of the stars of the good Cubs teams the prior decade. The Terriers got out to a 6-to-1 lead by the 3rd inning and Eddie cruised from there. He even had three hits at the plate. The Terriers won 12 to 5 and Eddie won the 300th game of his career. He became the first left-hander to do so. The win also pulled St. Louis within a game of 1st place Pittsburgh.

Brooklyn was at Handlan's Park on the 16th of September, tied with the Terriers after nine innings, 6 to 6. Eddie was summoned to keep it close, but gave up two runs in the 11th and took the loss. St. Louis slipped to three games back in 3rd place.

Eddie was used in relief again, in the first game of a doubleheader against Brooklyn on the 18th. He came on for extra innings with the game tied at three. The Terriers scored a walk-off win in the 12th, and Eddie picked up the win, 4 to 3. In the second game, the Terriers got out to a 4-to-0 lead, but Doc Watson began to falter in the 4th inning. Eddie was called in to stop the rally, two runs already across. He staunched the bleeding and shut out the Tip-Tops the rest of the way, until the game was called due to darkness, the Terriers winning 5 to 2. Eddie had nabbed both wins in the doubleheader. The team was now in 2nd place, but still three games behind.

Eddie was used again in relief the next day, trying to preserve a 9-to-7 lead late in the game against the Terrapins at home. Baltimore rallied in the 8th inning, tying the game at nine and sending it into extra innings. This time, Eddie wasn't so lucky, losing in the 12th, 12 to 9.

On the 23rd, against the Terrapins, Eddie started and enjoyed an early 5-to-1 lead. He knocked three hits himself and cruised to a 10-to-2 victory. The Terriers were now a game-and-a-half behind Pittsburgh.

Eddie took the mound for the second game of a doubleheader against the Buffalo Blues at home on the 26th. The Terriers had won every game since Eddie's last start. Plank was at his best in this one, giving up only three hits while shutting-out Buffalo 5 to 0 for his twentieth win of the season. These four more wins in a row put St. Louis in a tie with Pittsburgh for the league lead.

Doc Crandall was clutch in the next game, winning his twentieth game of the year while defeating Buffalo 3 to 2. The Terriers remained tied with Pittsburgh.

The Kansas City Packers were next in town, on the 29th. Dave Davenport battled KC's Gene Packard and lost 1 to 0. St. Louis slipped to a half-game back.

Eddie faced Kansas City on the 30th, the headline in the *St. Louis Post-Dispatch* that day reading "Terrier's Hopes of Flag Depend on Plank." Under pressure, Eddie pitched a strong game, but trailed 2 to 1 going into the bottom of the 7th inning, Kenworthy having stolen home on one of Eddie's slow deliveries. But, that's when the Terriers came to life and rallied for three, giving Eddie a 4-to-2 lead which proved insurmountable. St. Louis kept pace with Pittsburgh, only a half-game behind.

On October 2nd, Pittsburgh lost a doubleheader, but St. Louis also lost to Kansas City. The Chicago Whales, who had just swept Pittsburgh, vaulted into 1st by a half-game over the Rebels and Terriers. It was to be a photo finish between three teams.

On October 3rd, Doc Crandall started for the Terriers but was pulled with a 4-to-2 lead after two innings. Eddie pitched the final seven innings and did not allow a run. He was credited with a save, though modern rules would assign him the win. The Terriers had done their part and finished the season 87-67.

Meanwhile, in Chicago, the Whales and Rebels battled in a doubleheader. The Rebels won the first game 5 to 4. This put them in a tie with the Terriers, the Whales a half-game back. In the second game, the Whales won 3 to 0. This resulted in the Whales and Terriers tying at the top, the Rebels now a half-game back.

The Terriers had gone from worst to first! Or had they? With an 87-67 record, their winning percentage was .56493. The Whales had two fewer decisions and were 86-66 with a .56579 winning percentage. The difference between the two was .00086! And that was how it ended, the Terriers coming in second by the slimmest margin in history.

Frustrated, most of the players headed for home rather than participate in a banquet for their benefit. Fielder Jones, who had promised the team would finish runner-up back in the spring was, unfortunately, very prescient. But, he vowed to come back next season, as did the players.

The October 6th *Gettysburg Times* reported Eddie was home after the baseball season. He had compiled a solid 21-11 record with a team-leading 2.08 ERA. He also led the team with three important saves. Dave Davenport led the team in wins with a 22-16 record. Doc Crandall also won 21 games.

The top hitter on the team was Charlie Deal, in limited action, at .323. Ward Miller hit .306 in 536 at bats. Ernie Johnson hit 7 home runs to lead the team. Babe Borton's 97 runs and 92 RBI were also team leaders.

On October 15th, the Boston Red Sox became World Series Champions, defeating the Philadelphia Phillies four games to one.

On Monday, October 18th, the Planks announced the birth of a son, Edward Stewart Plank, Junior. Mrs. Plank gave birth at their home in New Oxford.

On November 25th, Albert Einstein formulated his theory of general relativity.

In mid-December, the *Gettysburg Times* announced Eddie was a free agent, free to sign with any team, the Federal League's future uncertain. The Pittsburgh, Newark, Buffalo, and Brooklyn franchises had been bought out by American or National League owners. Phil Ball of the St. Louis Terriers bought the St. Louis Browns. Charles Weeghman, the owner of the Whales, was allowed to buy the Chicago Cubs. The Kansas City team went bankrupt, and the Baltimore team refused to deal.

Later in the month, on the 30th, Fielder Jones wrote an article in the *St. Louis Post-Dispatch*, discussing the potential of the newly combined Federal and American League teams in St. Louis. Discussions were under way about merging the teams. Jones discussed Plank in the article, "Eddie Plank's arm is as good as ever was," he said, "but Eddie can't move around like he used to. You know in a tight ballgame a lot depends on a pitcher's fielding. If you can turn a well-designed bunt into an out, you'll often win a close game."

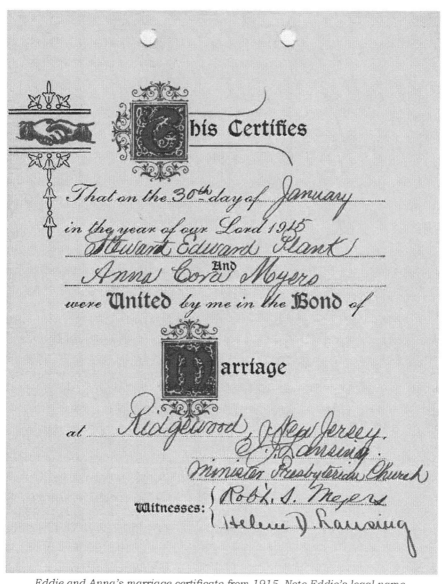

Eddie and Anna's marriage certificate from 1915. Note Eddie's legal name.

House near the incident at Rosegarden (photo by the author).

*The railroad overpass near Rosegarden along the Old Gettysburg Pike
(photo by the author).*

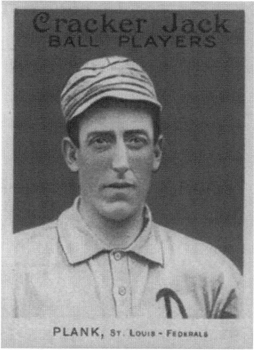

1915 Cracker Jack baseball card of Eddie Plank noting St. Louis as his team, though the photo is in an A's uniform.

Sign for the recently-built Rosegarden development near the train mishap (photo by author).

1916:
MASTER OF OLD

ARLY IN JANUARY, Eddie's status for the upcoming season was uncertain. On January 22nd, it was reported that the New York club had offered him a contract, but Eddie was not moved. Fielder Jones was also trying to re-sign him for the Browns, but Eddie did not oblige.

On February 3rd, the National Baseball Commission decided to honor the reserve clause of the Federal League teams, even if the contracts were expired. This meant Eddie Plank was the property of the St. Louis Browns. Eddie had been appealing for his free agency to no avail.

"Eddie Plank is as good as he ever was. He still got his fast one," said Fielder Jones in the February 18th *St. Louis Dispatch*.

A few days later, on the 22nd, the paper expanded on Eddie's salary predicament: "Manager Jones of the Browns was more optimistic yesterday about his chances of having Eddie Plank on hand Monday when the vanguard of Browns moves on Palestine. In a letter to Jones yesterday, Plank offered to mediate and Jones immediately indicated an answer. It is understood that Plank's salary with the Terriers last season was $8000, but a substantial slice has been cut from this figure in the new document tendered for the coming season. Plank must sign with the Browns or quit the game, as the National Commission has denied his plea for an unconditional release. Plank's annual allowance in 1914 with Connie Mack was $4000. He received a bonus of $1000 when the Mackmen won the pennant besides sharing in the World's Series melon. His portion as a member of the losing team was $2519.55, yielding him a gross income of $7519.55. The Terriers boosted this to an even $8000 to acquire his services last season, but with peace declared, such salaries no longer prevail."

The next day, Eddie sent a telegram confirming his acceptance of the terms offered.

On February 26th, Eddie Plank left for spring training with the St. Louis Browns in Palestine, Texas.

On March 8th and 9th, Pancho Villa and about 500 raiders attacked Columbus, New Mexico, killing a dozen U.S. soldiers. The U.S. 13th Cavalry drove the invaders back. On the 15th, Woodrow Wilson ordered 12,000 U.S. troops to pursue Villa into Mexico.

Eddie took the mound for the first time in a spring training game at Denison, Texas on March 20th. He pitched four solid innings.

The March 31st *Gettysburg Times* reported a heroic deed performed by Eddie at spring training. "Eddie Plank is as much a hero in Palestine these days as he is the hero of Gettysburg, a title he has borne gracefully for some years. A Texas ranger was robbed of a lot of money and jewels in the lobby of the Palestine Hotel the other night. Plank climbed out in his nightie and ran down the bandit, capturing him without assistance. The town blacksmith is making Eddie an iron cross."

The next day, Eddie provided the following interview to the *Gettysburg Times*:

EDDIE PLANK REFUSES TO be counted out. He scoffs at the idea that he won't amount to much this season and confounds his critics by the assertion that he expects to keep on pitching in the majors until he is 45—5 years more. He recently consented to talk about himself. Here is what he had to say:

"I've never had a sore arm, and when I quit the game it will be because I am tired of it. I'm 40 now, but I'm going to stick in the big leagues for five more years. At 45, then, I think I'll stay home. Pitching is a job. It must be studied by the pitcher. He must study the other fellow, the batter, and then give him what he knows he cannot hit. That's the way I've pitched for fifteen years. The fellow with the fastball will last longer than the one with the curve. I'll pitch five fast ones to a single curve or slow ball. But the winning pitcher must have the combination. He must mix 'em to the batter. Control is the biggest point. If you can point it where you want, then you'll win more games than you lose. I believe control just was natural to me. If you can keep the ball away from the groove of the sluggers, you'll win. Benny Kauff got one real hit off me last season. It was a drive over the right-field fence in St. Louis. He had me three and two and my foot slipped just when I shot the ball. It went outside and he met it. You can't fool Ty Cobb. He'll hit anything. Against Ty Cobb, I just try to get him off his stride and trust the luck of my fielders. Against sluggers like Crawford, Speaker, and Jackson they are considered easier to fool than Ty because they swing a heavy bat and hold it on the handle. Ty uses a lighter one and he swings it like a toothpick.

"I never tried for a strikeout record. You won't last long if you attempt to fan every fellow who comes up. I know that I have eight other fellows on the field with me.

"In spring training, I take my time. Never a curve until after the first week and then I start my speed gradually. I believe this system has kept my arm in shape for fifteen years."

Meanwhile, Fielder Jones was making his roster decisions and mentioned how Eddie was still "not yet right." Apparently, Eddie was easing himself through training and was not showing his full potential yet.

Per the April 8th *Gettysburg Times*, Eddie purchased the lot on Carlisle Street, across the street from the Gettysburg Academy building from Mrs. J. Emory Bair. Eddie planned to erect a home on this spot, a sixty-foot lot.

The Browns opened the season April 12th in Cleveland with a 6-to-1 win, Bob Groom picking up the win.

Eddie opened his season in Chicago on the 16th. He faced former teammates Eddie Collins and Shoeless Joe Jackson. Combined, they went 1 for 8. St. Louis got out to a 6-to-1 lead before they started to hit Plank. Ultimately, the Browns won 6 to 5.

At home against Cleveland on the 22nd, Eddie relieved Dave Davenport after eight innings, the game tied at one. Eddie proceeded to hurl seven more shutout innings, the game ending in a 1-to-1 tie.

Eddie next pitched against the White Sox at home on the 29th. He faced Reb Russell and lost 3 to 1. Jackson had three hits this time around.

The Browns ended April 5-9, 3 1/2 games back in 7th place.

Eddie's next start was a 5-to-4 win over Ty Cobb and the Tigers at Navin Field in Detroit on May 5th. Eddie was leading 5 to 1 into the bottom of the 9th and was nicked for three.

This same day, the U.S. Marines landed in the Dominican Republic and began an eight-year occupation.

After the game, Eddie headed home to rest for a few days. He worked on arranging an exhibition between the St. Louis club and Gettysburg Blue Ridge team for mid-August.

On May 10th, in Washington, Eddie dropped a 1-to-0 game to Joe Boehling.

In his return to Shibe Park, Eddie lost 5 to 4 to Bullet Joe Bush on May 15th. Said the *Philadelphia Inquirer*, "For Six Innings Plank Was Master." He led 4 to 1 into the bottom of the 7th when the A's erupted for four runs.

Eddie was at the Polo Grounds in New York to face the Yankees and former mate Home Run Baker on May 22nd. He beat the Yankees easily, 9 to 5.

Eddie next pitched at Navin Field against the Tigers on the 29th. He only lasted two innings, yielding six runs. The Tigers ran up the score, 17 to 6.

The next day, at home on the 30th at Sportsman's Park, Eddie entered a tie game in the 11th inning and pitched five scoreless innings as the Browns beat the Cleveland Indians 5 to 4.

The Browns ended May 14-24, 9 1/2 games back in 7th place. Eddie was 4-4 on the season.

On June 1st, in the second game of the doubleheader, Eddie pitched the last three innings of a 6-to-5 win over Cleveland, earning the save. Meanwhile, in the North Sea, the Battle of Jutland was being waged between the navies of Germany and England.

At home against the Red Sox on the 12th, Eddie pitched in relief of Jim Park in the 7th and shut out Boston the rest of the way. Meanwhile, the Browns took the lead and won 4 to 3.

Washington was next in for Eddie on the 15th. He dropped a squeaker, 1 to 0, losing to Joe Boehling.

On the 20th, the White Sox were in St. Louis. Eddie faced off against Lefty Williams and lost 4 to 2. Eddie was pulled in the 6th inning.

Four days later, Williams and the White Sox did it again, beating Plank 5 to 4. Eddie was chased in the 4th inning this time.

On June 28th, the Tigers were in town. Eddie held Cobb hitless and knocked in two runs himself. He pitched a complete game and won 5 to 3.

The Browns ended June 29-36, nine games back in 7th place. They had gone 15-12 on the month and were keeping pace with the leaders. Eddie was now 6-7.

On July 1st, in Cleveland, Eddie entered the game in the 7th inning when it was tied 4 to 4. He then pitched into the 11th inning when Cleveland finally scored another run, winning 5 to 4.

At Comiskey Park in Chicago on July 4th, Eddie entered the second game of the doubleheader in the 11th inning, when it was tied at six. Eddie pitched until the Sox scored in the bottom of the 13th, winning 7 to 6.

On July 7th, in Washington, D.C., Eddie faced Walter Johnson. The *St. Louis Star and Times* described him as "the master of old." It was his finest performance on the season to date, a five-hit shutout of the Senators. The Browns won 5 to 0.

An item in the July 8th *Gettysburg Times* mentioned Eddie and Mrs. Plank visiting the building site on Carlisle Street. "Eddie Plank returned today for a brief vacation before joining his team for next week's schedule. He was accompanied here from New Oxford by Mrs. Plank, and together they visited the site for their new home on Carlisle Street. The ground has been staked off for the residence which is to be a colonial in design and completely equipped in every way. Work on the new house will be started in the near future, it is expected. Eddie motored here after having pitched one of his best games of the season on Friday, taking his team to victory over Washington and Johnson, 5 to 0. His friends were glad as ever to greet him."

Shibe Park was the scene of Eddie's next start on July 12th. He faced the 18-51 Athletics and beat them easily, 8 to 3.

At Fenway Park, on the 17th, Eddie ran into Dutch Leonard, losing a tough battle, 3 to 2.

Eddie then nursed his arm for two weeks, pitching again on July 30th at home against the Yankees. He threw a four-hit shutout, beating Ray Fisher 4 to 0.

The Browns were on a winning streak, finishing July at 48-49, 7 1/2 games out, in 7th place. They went 19-13 for the month and had closed a little ground. Eddie was now 9-10 on the season.

On August 4th, at Sportsman's Park, the Red Sox were in town. Two great left-handers faced-off: Eddie Plank for the Browns and Babe Ruth for the Red Sox. It wasn't even close. Eddie tossed a two-hitter, winning 6 to 1. Eddie improved to 10-10 while the Babe dropped to 15-9. It was the Browns' 14th straight win.

Four days later, Washington was in St. Louis. Eddie did not allow a hit through eight innings and had a 9-to-0 lead into the 9th. In that frame, Rip Williams pinch hit for the pitcher and drew a walk. After Craft was retired, Eddie Foster ripped a double to score the Senator's only run. It would be their only hit as well. Eddie won his one-hitter, 9 to 1.

On August 11th, against the Indians at home, Eddie earned a save by pitching the last two scoreless innings of a 3-to-1 Browns victory. St. Louis was now 59-51, in 4th place, only 4 1/2 games out of first!

Eddie started the next day and was marvelous again. He hurled a two-hit shutout, winning 11 to 0 against the Indians.

On August 16th, Eddie was visiting his parents on the farm. He then headed to Philadelphia to pitch against the A's on the 17th. He again battled Bullet Joe Bush, the two tangling to a tie after nine, 3 to 3. Eddie got into trouble in the bottom of the 10th and was relieved by Davenport, who couldn't stop the rally. The A's scored the winning run, and Eddie took the 4-to-3 loss on his record.

Per the *Gettysburg Times*, on August 22nd, a party from Gettysburg motored to Washington in hopes of seeing Eddie defeat the Senators and Walter Johnson. Those that went included C. William Beales, Norman S. Heindel, Esq., J. Rogers Musselman, Daniel A. Skelly, Jr., C. William Duncan, Horace E. Smiley, and Clarence Epley. They went in Mr. Beale's car. Mr. Epley was chauffeur.

Plank faced Johnson the next day, on the 23rd, in the second game of a doubleheader. The game was shortened to seven innings because of darkness, Johnson winning this battle 4 to 2.

At the Polo Grounds on the 26th, Eddie relieved in the middle innings of a game against the Yankees. New York took the lead while he was in and ultimately won 10 to 6, Plank taking the loss.

In the first game of a doubleheader against Boston at Fenway Park on the 29th, Dutch Leonard was knocked out in the 1st inning after recording only one out. He allowed two runs on two hits, one walk, one hit-by-pitch and a wild pitch. The Browns won 5 to 3 behind Dave Davenport, Babe Ruth taking the loss. The Browns then won the second game behind Bob Groom, 8 to 2. At 68-57, the Browns were now in 3rd place, only four games behind.

The next day, Dutch Leonard no-hit the Browns, winning 4 to 0. What a turn-around!

At the end of August, Eddie turned forty-one. The Browns were now 69-58, four games back in 4th place. Eddie was 12-13 on the season.

On September 4th, at home against the White Sox, Eddie allowed Chicago two early runs but held them the rest of the way. Unfortunately, the Browns could only muster one run against Joe Benz and lost 2 to 1.

Three days later, on the 7th, Eddie saved a game against the Tigers as the Browns won 6 to 5. Plank pitched the last two scoreless.

At Comiskey Park on the 10th, Eddie took the mound against the White Sox. He went ten innings against Reb Russell, winning after the Browns put up a three-spot in the 10th.

At home in St. Louis against the Red Sox on the 14th, Eddie beat Ernie Shore 6 to 1. He gave up only four hits and evened his record at 14-14.

In mid-September, Pete Bigler, a local third baseman on the Gettysburg Blue Ridge team was drafted by the St. Louis Browns on Eddie Plank's recommendation. The local team received $500 in the transaction.

On September 17th at Sportsman's Park against the Senators, George Sisler, batting third, pitched a marvelous game, beating Walter Johnson 1 to 0. Young Sisler had come up as a pitcher the prior season but was showing prowess with the bat. This was his last win as a pitcher in the big leagues. He would go on to a Hall-of-Fame career as a first baseman, twice batting over .400.

The next day, Washington rookie Claude Thomas baffled the Browns, two-hitting them, winning 1 to 0. It would be Thomas's only big league win despite a long minor league career. Eddie gave up a run in the 1st inning and held them the rest of the way, taking a tough loss.

Back in Philadelphia at Shibe Park on the 22nd, Eddie faced off against young Elmer Myers. Myers, a rookie from York Springs, was touted as the latest local Adams County pitching phenom. He would win 14 games in 1916, his highest total, 55-72 on his career. Old enough to be his father, Eddie schooled the twenty-two-year-old, winning 6 to 3.

Two days later, on the 24th, George Sisler faced off against Socks Seibold on the mound. This would be the last major league start as a pitcher for Sisler, who lost to Seibold, 2 to 0. This was Seibold's first major-league win, not to be confused with Socks Seybold, with a "y", who played for the Athletics during the prior decade. Connie must have liked his "Socks."

The Browns finished September 78-75, thirteen games back in 5th place. Unfortunately, they faded this month, slipping to 9-17 down the stretch.

Eddie pitched his final game of the season on October 1st. He beat the Tigers at home 6 to 3, finishing the season 16-15 with a 2.33 ERA. The team was 79-75, in 5th place, twelve games behind.

Dave Davenport and Carl Weilman each had 17 wins to lead the Browns. Walter Johnson led the American League with 25 wins and 228 strikeouts. Babe Ruth's 1.75 ERA was tops among the Americans.

At the plate, George Sisler led the team with a .305 average, trailing Tris Speaker's .386. Del Pratt of the Browns led the league with 103 RBI. Wally Pipp led with 12 home runs, exceeding the Browns' top slugger, Pratt, who had 5.

During the World Series, held October 7th through the 12th, the Boston Red Sox defeated the Brooklyn Robins, four games to one.

The October 19th *Gettysburg Times* mentioned a dispatch from St. Louis that said, "Eddie Plank, veteran pitcher and member of the St. Louis American League club, today informed manager Fielder Jones that unless he was traded to some other club, he would quit baseball. He is dissatisfied with St. Louis, not the club."

On November 7th, Democrat Woodrow Wilson narrowly defeated Republican Charles E. Hughes to win re-election.

An item in the November 18th *Gettysburg Compiler* mentioned a hunting party consisting of Harry Davis of the Athletics and Eddie Collins of the White Sox enjoyed several days of rabbit hunting hosted by Eddie and Ira Plank at their home near town.

The United States rejected, on November 21st, the offer from Germany of 10,000 British pounds per person lost when the *Lusitania* was sunk. Tensions remained very high with Germany.

The next day, writer Jack London, aged 40, died of kidney failure at his California home. He had made a fortune writing serialized fiction in magazines. His most famous work was *Call of the Wild*.

On December 18th, the Battle of Verdun ended in France with an allied victory over Germany.

The Russian mystic Grigori Rasputin was murdered in Saint Petersburg, Russia on December 30th bringing an end to bloody 1916.

Eddie with the St. Louis Browns in 1916.

Eddie sent a postcard home to himself from spring training.

Eddie Plank art deco drawing.

Eddie Plank card from 1916.

1917:
OLD SOUP BONE

T HE YEAR BEGAN with an item in the *Gettysburg Times* suggesting Eddie was about to be sold to the New York Yankees by Branch Rickey, the Browns' Business Manager. Eddie said he knew nothing of the transaction and would be willing to play for New York provided "the salary was satisfactory." No trade was consummated, though there was a lot of talk throughout the winter.

On January 10th, William F. "Buffalo Bill" Cody, frontiersman and showman, passed away. He was seventy-one.

The next day, January 11th, a great explosion occurred at an ammunition factory at Kingsland, now Lyndhurst, New Jersey. German saboteurs were originally blamed for the fire which ignited over a half-million 76mm shells over the span of four hours. People in New York watched the spectacle with amazement.

On February 3rd, the United States broke off diplomatic relations with Germany.

Three days later, Eddie participated in a basketball game with the Gettysburg Five against Susquehanna College featuring former baseball teammate Dick Kauffman.

On February 19th, Fielder Jones, in the *St. Louis Post-Dispatch*, said he was very happy Eddie Plank had not been traded to New York for Fritz Maisel. Said Jones, "I regard Plank today as the greatest money pitcher in the game. Just put something on the game and I'd rather have Plank in there than any pitcher I know. So why would I be disappointed over the failure to get Maisel? The truth is that the Plank-for-Maisel deal never greatly interested me."

Before the end of the month, Eddie sent his signed contract to St. Louis, where it was received by Branch Rickey. On February 28th, Eddie and family moved into their new house in downtown Gettysburg, on Carlisle Street. Five days later, on March 5th, Eddie headed to St. Louis to begin training with the Browns in Palestine, Texas.

On Tuesday, the 6th, the *St. Louis Post-Dispatch* reported "Ancient" Eddie passing through town on his way to Texas. Eddie declared himself in the "proverbian pink." Arriving in Palestine the next day, Eddie said "he is down to weight and will require only sunshine to get his old left flapper to working order."

A few days later, Eddie was the subject of ribbing from some of the younger players. When he started to pitch, one was heard to say "listen to all that squeaking."

"Why don't you get an oil can out and lubricate that old soup bone," said another.

Still, another said, "Look out, Eddie, don't get too fearless or that brittle wing will fly up in the grandstand."

Talking to the press, Eddie said he had wintered in Gettysburg and it was one of the coldest on record. He said he had not been able to get any of his baseball equipment out since the prior season ended.

On March 19th, in Palestine, Eddie talked about not playing in the "bush leagues" after he retires from the major leagues. The paper surmised he had acquired a small fortune in salaries and bonuses over the years and had invested wisely.

President Woodrow Wilson asked Congress for a declaration of war against Germany on April 2nd. The United States had now entered World War I.

On April 10th, the Eddystone Ammunition Company factory in Chester, Pennsylvania exploded, killing 133. Saboteurs were suspected, and the City of Philadelphia was put under martial law.

The next day, April 11th, brother Ira Plank married Blanche Kump of Hanover at the Lutheran parsonage in Chambersburg. The newlyweds headed to New York on a wedding trip, likely passing through Philadelphia on the train.

That same day, the St. Louis Browns opened the season against the Chicago White Sox in St. Louis.

Three days later, on the 14th, Eddie Cicotte of the White Sox no-hit the Browns. It was a harbinger of things to come for St. Louis.

Eddie made his season debut in Chicago against the White Sox on April 19th. Eddie won 6 to 2, defeating Shoeless Joe Jackson and former teammate Eddie Collins, who was hitless in four at-bats. "He is a master," said Fielder Jones about Plank after the game.

On May 5th, Browns teammate Ernie Koob hurled a no-hitter against the White Sox, winning 1 to 0. The following day, Bob Groom of the Browns also threw a no-hitter, winning 3 to 0 in the second game of a doubleheader.

Eddie next started on May 18th, having pitched only three brief appearances in relief during the intervening month due to a sore shoulder that "hurt when he threw curves." He lost to the 12-16 Washington Senators, 8 to 2.

On Sunday, May 27th, Eddie made his third start of the season, battling Carl Mays and the Boston Red Sox to a 1-to-1 tie after eleven innings.

On June 5th, the U.S. Army began conscripting soldiers.

Finally, on June 20th, Eddie was back on the mound, having been unable to play due to illness. He beat the Tigers 3 to 2 in Detroit, holding Cobb, amid a hitting streak, to one hit in four at-bats. On the 24th, still in Detroit, Eddie dropped a game 4 to 2.

On the 28th, he started against Cleveland at League Park but left after two scoreless innings.

Plank was back at it on the 30th of June in Detroit, winning 4 to 3. He was now 3-2 on the season.

While the Browns were on the road, racial tensions in East St. Louis, Illinois, just across the river, were mounting. On July 1st and 2nd, the violence became deadly, resulting in over 250 deaths. The tensions had arisen in May when black workers were brought in to replace striking white workers.

The Browns were home at Sportsman's Park for a doubleheader against Cleveland on July 4th, soon after the violence. Eddie finished the second game in relief of Bob Groom, pitching the final seven innings and yielding three runs. He lost the game 5 to 3.

Ty Cobb's hitting streak was finally ended at 35 games by the White Sox on July 6th.

On July 8th, at home against the Yankees, Eddie was called upon to close out an 8-to-2 win, pitching the last three-and-two-thirds innings for the save.

Two days later, Eddie started, going six innings in a no-decision. The Yankees won 7 to 5.

At home against Boston on the 17th, Eddie won his 4th game of the season, defeating Dutch Leonard 3 to 2.

Five days later, at home against the Washington Senators, Eddie hurled a shutout, winning 7 to 0. It was his 5th and final win of the season and his last shutout in the major leagues.

At Fenway Park on July 28th, Eddie lost a close one, 3 to 2, to Carl Mays.

At the Polo Grounds on August 2nd, Eddie faced the Yankees and Bob Shawkey. It was another close game, Eddie losing 3 to 1 and falling to 5-5 on the season. The Browns were now 37-63.

In Washington, D.C., at Griffith Stadium on August 6th, Eddie toiled in one the most remarkable games of his career. He and Walter Johnson exchanged zeros until the 11th inning when the Senators finally scored a walk-off run. The loss dropped the Browns into last place. It was Eddie's last game in the major leagues.

On August 8th, Eddie was home in Gettysburg for a few days. His plan was to rejoin the team in Philadelphia. Ten days later, the *Adams County News* contained an item that Eddie was "Home for Season," having quit baseball. Eddie said he was going to focus on the garage business he and his brother Ira had just purchased a few weeks prior.

Years later, Eddie explained to Jimmy Insminger of the *North American* why he retired from the major leagues after 1917. Said Plank, "In my last game in the big leagues, I had an eleven-inning pitchers' battle with Walter Johnson. Washington beat me 1 to 0, but I was so tired at the finish, I could scarcely reach my hotel."

Fielder Jones, his manager at the time, added to the story when interviewed in January of 1918. "It is said that Eddie Plank and I had a disagreement and that Plank quit the team in August. True, Plank quit, but here are the facts: I used to tell Eddie the day before he pitched that he was to work. On one of these occasions, when it came time to warm up, Plank said he couldn't work, that his arm was sore. He went to his room after the game and the next morning called me on the phone and asked me to his room. When I opened the door, he was crying. It seems he had been to a doctor and was advised to quit baseball for the rest of the season, that his arm was in bad shape. He told me then that he thought he was through. I told him to go home and rest. The papers published a report that Plank quit the team because of a fuss with me."

The *St. Louis Post-Dispatch* confirmed Eddie's decision to retire on August 15th, however, there was speculation he was merely trying to jump ship. He had just pitched a great game and was likely trying to sign on with a contender.

Eddie finished the season 5-6 with a 1.79 ERA in 131 innings. Plagued by a sore arm most of the year, he was still effective when used gingerly.

On October 1st, Connie Mack's Athletics were in Gettysburg for an exhibition game. Eddie umpired.

On October 12th, former town teammate Frederick C. "Bill" Clay passed away in York due to a "leaking heart" at the age of 42. He had been one of Eddie's first catchers and played in the National League for the Phillies in 1902. He played sixteen seasons of professional baseball, mostly in the Tri-State League.

Three days later, the Chicago White Sox became World Series Champions, defeating the New York Giants four games to two.

On November 3rd, Eddie was a good Samaritan, recovering the car of Rev. Abner S. Dechant of Hanover along the Carlisle Road north of town. The car had been taken from in front of the Trinity Reformed Church the prior night.

In mid-November, Dr. E. H. Markley and Eddie and Ira Plank purchased a lot at the corner of York and Stratton Streets for constructing a large garage facility. Work was to begin immediately with an expected completion by April.

The year ended with Woodrow Wilson placing most U.S. railroads under the control of the Federal Government to move troops and supplies and Bob Quinn of the Browns trying to coax Eddie out of retirement.

Eddie near the end of his major league career with St. Louis.

Eddie Plank II as a tot.

Barcroft, Virginia

AUG 17 1917

Hon. Edward Plank,
    Thee BaseBall Pitcher,
        Gettysburg Pennsylvania.

Dear Sir:

    I note what U are out of game for good. I think U owe it to
the profession, from a record and statistical point of view to stay on.
Your 17 years is mighty good, but why not make 20, so we can for years
enthuse over it? Your being left handed makes the record all the more
impossible of attainment for future generations.
    I think U should hang on just as long as you can turn in
a victory so as to keep in the big league. My sentiments are voiced by
millions of bugs. Please hang on. At 42 you ar a cyclone; U must get
the spirit that wins from associations with your neighborhood, it being
famous as being place where the Stonewall Brigade could not overrun, nor
all of Lee's army.   Very truly, and sincerely,

                                            [signature]

An encouraging letter from a fan.

1918:
A MAN OF STEEL

THE JANUARY 20TH edition of the *Philadelphia Inquirer* included an article entitled "Eddie Plank Is to Pitch Again." From his home in Portland, Oregon, St. Louis Browns manager Fielder Jones discussed the matter. Said Jones, "I received a long letter and a picture of his baby with best wishes from himself and his family." Jones did not mention any instructions or wishes from Plank regarding his status, but Eddie was included on Jones' list of Browns pitchers for the upcoming season. The article went on to speculate that right-handed pitchers were inherently stronger and more durable than left-handers, comparing Plank to Mathewson and Young. "Plank is a marvel among southpaws," it said.

Two days later, on January 22, 1918, the New York Yankees traded pitchers Urban Shocker and Nick Cullop, infielder Fritz Maisel, second baseman Joe Gedeon, catcher Les Nunamaker, and an unspecified sum of cash to the St. Louis Browns for second baseman Del Pratt and Eddie Plank.

At home in Gettysburg, Eddie was bombarded with phone calls. His response was consistent to all of them, "Whatever is done on this trade is all right so far as I am concerned, but I have quit the diamond for good and will stick to business here. Baseball is a matter of history to me. Nothing done in this deal will affect my determination to stay home and attend to business."

A couple days later, Eddie spoke with the Harrisburg newspapers. Said Eddie, "I will not go to New York next season. I am through with baseball forever. That goes, I am not trying to hold anybody up, and I hope that my retirement will not upset the deal between New York and St. Louis, but if it does, I cannot help it. When I announced last summer that I was through with baseball at the end of 1917, I meant just that. Talk about doing your bit in the army, I guess I have done my bit in baseball and am entitled to a rest. I am not all in by any means. My left wing is as good as ever, but I have enough. I have my farm, my home, and enough to take care of me, so why should I work and worry any longer? If the deal is dependent on my signature for its completion, then I am sorry to say that it will be all off."

January 30th, Colonel Jacob Ruppert and the Yankees were still hopeful Eddie would sign. But, February 1st, Eddie gave an interview to the press in Gettysburg stating he was done with baseball and focused on his automobile business.

During the spring of 1918, Ira and Eddie Plank, and their partner Dr. E. H. Markley opened the planned garage business on York Street, in Gettysburg.

As World War I raged in Europe, the director of the military draft, Provost Marshall General Enoch Crowder, decreed that "by July 1, all draft-eligible men employed in 'non-essential' occupations must apply for work directly related to the war—or gamble being called into military service." Major League owners pleaded for leniency, but Secretary of War Newton D. Baker agreed with Crowder: "Life as a ballplayer was non-essential. Enlist to help stateside, or risk going to the front lines of Europe."

Eventually, the major-league owners began to be heard, and the "work or fight" deadline was delayed two months to September 1. To preserve the pennant race and World Series, the owners continued to lobby for an exclusion and won.

Though Eddie was beyond draft age at 42, the April 18th *Gettysburg Times* announced Eddie's signing with Steelton to pitch in the Schwab League, a regional baseball league represented by steel factories which had been formed in 1917 to entertain the mill hands. Said Chairman Charles Schwab: "I want some good wholesome games that will furnish amusement and entertainment for the Bethlehem Steel Company's employees, and don't bother me about details of expense." Initially, the teams were made up of factory workers, but after the work-or-fight order in 1918, plants began luring big leaguers by promising soft jobs and salaries as high as $500 a week. As the military draft proceeded through 1918, the Bethlehem Steel League benefited. Plank was signed to "pitch when wanted."

However, on April 24th, Eddie stopped in Philadelphia on his way home to Gettysburg and denied he had signed with Steelton, He said he was focused on the automobile business he owned with his brother Ira.

Regardless of what he was saying publicly, when Steelton played Lebanon Valley College on May 8th, after warming up but not pitching in the game, Eddie was "sitting on the home bench, carefully wrapped up like an Indian chief on a warpath." Continued the *Harrisburg Telegraph*: "Eddie Plank, hero, and Nestor of baseball, whose name is familiar pretty much all over the world. The mark for attention from his multitudes through a long period of years, he is just as modest as the first day he stepped into spangles and it is sure that (Steelton manager) Cockill will get some good service out of him. Eddie will shoot 'em over at the opening game Saturday and he alone is worth the price of admission."

"They tell me that Chief Bender is signed with some club in this league," laughed Eddie, "Well I hope we hook up soon."

At Steelton on Saturday, May 11th, fans were disappointed when Eddie did not pitch. Steelton beat Bethlehem 1 to 0. Manager Cockill assured the fans Eddie "would be here when the time comes."

The following Saturday, May 18th, Eddie did take the sphere and was losing 1 to 0 into the 8th when Steelton knotted it up at one. Eddie then yielded three in the bottom of the 8th and lost 4 to 3. He did have three hits in the game. He was described as "unsteady at times."

On June 1st, Eddie was back on the mound for Steelton, winning easily against Fore River 6 to 1.

The following week, on the 8th against Bethlehem, Plank was scheduled to pitch, but did not. The team lost 7 to 0.

Against Lebanon on the 15th, Eddie took the mound and shut them down 3 to 1.

The June 18th *Harrisburg Telegraph* listed the batting statistics for the Bethlehem-Steel League. Eddie was on top at .666, with four hits in six at-bats.

On June 29th, he was in Quincy, Massachusetts, defeating that team 6 to 2. Said the *Philadelphia Inquirer*, "Plank did some star fielding, stopping smashes which looked good for hits."

Steelton played two against Shoeless Joe Jackson and the Harlan team on July 4th. Steelton won the morning game 4 to 1. Eddie pitched the afternoon game, winning 2 to 0.

At Lebanon, Pennsylvania, on July 13th, Eddie won 6 to 2, pitching Steelton into 1st place. While batting, "Plank drove a hit liner towards the box which struck Miles Main (opposing pitcher) on the head, the ball landing in left field." Main was knocked out of the game after trying to pitch. Steelton had a four-run inning.

On July 17th, at the Ipatiev House in Ekaterinburg, Russia, the former Russian emperor, Nicholas II, his wife Alexandra Feodorovna, their children, Olga, Tatiana, Maria, Anastasia, and Alexei, and their retainers were executed by the Cheka on orders from the Bolshevik Party.

The next week, Eddie won his sixth straight game, defeating Sparrow's Point 5 to 0. The opponents managed only four hits.

On July 27th, at Steelton, Eddie faced Dutch Leonard, who was pitching for Fore River. Eddie threw a three-hit shutout, besting Dutch 1 to 0. Steelton was now 10-5, in 1st place.

At Bethlehem, Pennsylvania, on August 3rd, Eddie was hit hard, losing 6 to 0. This ended Eddie's seven-game winning streak.

Two Army units battled in Middletown, Pennsylvania, on August 14th. Eddie was the umpire.

On August 17th, back on the mound, Eddie lost 4 to 3 to Sparrows Point, yielding eleven hits.

Steelton was in York on August 23rd. Eddie shut them out, winning 6 to 0.

He was back to umpiring on the 28th in Gettysburg in a contest between the Kiwanis and Black Kittens at Nixon Field.

Back on the mound on Saturday the 30th, Eddie and Dutch Leonard had their rematch. This time Dutch won, and there was a tie for first between Steelton and Bethlehem with Wilmington one game back.

This summer, the "Spanish" flu spread worldwide infecting over a half-billion people and ultimately killing between 50 to 100 million people through early 1920. In total, three to five percent of the world's population did not survive the plague. Because of censorship in the U.S., Britain, France, and Germany during the war, the degree to which the virus was raging was kept under wraps. However, neutral Spain had no such restrictions and freely reported about the terrible situation resulting in it being tagged with the origin of the pandemic.

In the World Series, held September 5th to 11th, Babe Ruth's Boston Red Sox defeated the Chicago Cubs four games to two. Babe won two games on the mound.

On September 12th, shortly after his 43rd birthday, Edward Stewart Plank registered for the draft. He listed his permanent address as Carlisle Street, Gettysburg, Pennsylvania. He was self-employed, working as a farm manager and automobile dealer, located at 100 York Street, in Gettysburg. His nearest living relative was Mrs. Anna Cora Plank (his wife), also of Carlisle Street. Edward was described as tall, of slight build, with brown hair and blue eyes.

A championship game between Bethlehem and Steelton was scheduled for Saturday, September 7th at Cottage Hill, just north of York, Pennsylvania. The game was touted as "the greatest game of ball ever played in this vicinity." It was expected that Eddie would take the mound against former New York Giant star Jeff Tesreau, who had twice won twenty games in the National League. The game was held in Bethlehem a week later, Eddie winning 5 to 3, Steelton winning the championship. Eddie's record was 9-4.

On October 4th, the Steelton champions were honored by the Bethlehem Steel Company at a banquet. All the players received watches. Eddie participated in a live bird shoot and won, hitting ten of ten, the only player with a perfect score.

Fortunately for Eddie and the rest of the country, Kaiser Wilhelm II abdicated on November 9th. The "War to End All Wars" ended on November 11th.

On December 4th, President Woodrow Wilson sailed to Europe to attend the Paris Peace Conference, becoming the first sitting U.S. President to travel to Europe.

On December 18th, Plank's future in the major leagues was discussed. He was described as "unwanted by two teams" and would be caught up in a dispute between St. Louis and New York should he apply for reinstatement.

"EDDIE" PLANK

Eddie in a Steelton uniform in 1918.

EDDIE PLANK.

An earlier picture of Eddie with the A's used in a 1918 story about Steelton.

AFTER BASEBALL

VERY EARLY ON January 6th, 1919, former president Theodore Roosevelt died in his sleep from a blood clot in the lungs at Sagamore Hill, his residence at Cove Neck, New York. He was only sixty years old.

On January 16th, the 18th Amendment to the US Constitution was passed beginning the era of Prohibition.

During the winter of 1919, the New York Yankees sent Eddie Plank a contract, attempting to coax him out of retirement. On February 11th, Eddie returned the contract unsigned, stating he had retired from baseball and would attend to business in Gettysburg.

Now retired, Eddie had a lot of time on his hands. Over the next six years, he dabbled in many things, including being an unofficial (anonymous) battlefield tour guide at Gettysburg National Park, a garage owner and Buick dealer, an avid hunter and skeet shooter, and an umpire for many town ballgames. He was also a member of the Presbyterian Church, Masonic Lodge, Knights Templar of Harrisburg, Elks, and the gun club. Suffice to say, he was very popular around town, and everyone knew where he lived, and where to find Eddie Plank's Garage. The family also spent a lot of leisure time at their property along Marsh Creek, south of Gettysburg.

The garage business was very lucrative for Eddie. The business offered taxi and moving services, as well as towing and collision repairs. They even touted themselves as "first-class car washers." The Plank showroom was also a great place to find a new or used automobile. His affiliation with the auto trade also provided him opportunities to travel to Philadelphia, where he often looked in on old friends.

Brother Ira Plank was also very industrious. He was a baseball coach for Gettysburg College for many years in addition to his automotive activities. In March 1919, Ira was re-signed to be the baseball coach, a position he had held since 1913. However, by mid-April, he had decided to quit due to being very busy with the garage. This decision didn't stick, however, because he was coaching the team on May 28th as Gettysburg routed Franklin and Marshall 12-2, and June 10th, as Gettysburg routed Mt. St. Mary's 10 to 2. Ira went on to coach for many more years.

Eddie continued to be involved in local baseball, both as an umpire and occasional player. In the spring of 1919, he pitched, and won, for Biglerville in a contest against the first ward.

While he stayed in Gettysburg most of the time, it seemed as if the world came to see Eddie Plank. Over the years, many noteworthy people dropped by to visit. On Thursday, April 24th, 1919, it was reported that former teammate Rube Vickers had left town after visiting with Eddie for a day.

On May 25, 1919, Eddie was admitted as a Noble of the Mystic Shrine of the Zembo Temple of Harrisburg, a masonic order.

In June of that year, Eddie was tapped to umpire the contest between Gettysburg College and Mount St. Mary's. Said the *Gettysburg Times* about the upcoming game, "Eddie Plank, recognized as the greatest left-handed pitcher of all-time, will officiate not only because he is interested in the playground, but because of the intense rivalry existing between Gettysburg and Mt. St. Mary's, which makes it imperative for a man of his reputation to umpire."

Eddie continued his umpiring, handling games that summer between the various town wars. Plank Brother's Garage also sponsored a team that included Ira Plank at catcher and Eddie in center field.

On June 28th, the Treaty of Versailles was signed, ending World War I.

Plank's garage was in the news quite a bit towards the end of 1919. On the September 17th, there was some excitement there, as an auto thief, George Brown from Cleveland, Ohio, was arrested with a loaded revolver on his person. Apparently, the Planks had discovered the automobile they were servicing was "hot," and quietly let the authorities from York know.

That Sunday, the 21st, a "strange woman" was seen about town, near the garage. Said the *Gettysburg Times*, "On Sunday afternoon, a well-dressed woman, who was walking up and down

York street while her machine was being repaired at Plank's garage, was asked to sit down by Mrs. C. M. Wolf.

"The strange woman conversed freely about her travels in foreign countries, and after thanking Mrs. Wolf for her hospitality drove away in her machine.

"Today, Mrs. Wolf learned that her strange guest was Lillian Russell, noted actress, who was passing through Gettysburg on her way to Pittsburgh from Atlantic City."

On October 2nd, President Woodrow Wilson suffered a stroke, leaving him partially paralyzed.

From October 1st through the 9th, the World Series between the Chicago White Sox and Cincinnati Reds occurred. The Reds won, but it was widely thought the Sox had thrown the series, leading to the infamous Black Sox Scandal.

On November 11th, Mr. and Mrs. Eddie Collins dropped by, on their way back from a hunting trip to Frederick, Maryland. Unfortunately, Eddie was out hunting himself and missed his former teammate. Collins was not implicated in the Black Sox scandal.

On November 14th, in Stockholm, Sweden, Max Planck received his Nobel Prize in physics for 1918.

On Sunday, November 30th, two Buick touring cars collided on the Lincoln Highway. Both cars were towed to the Plank Brothers garage on York Street. Ira Plank said they "were the most badly smashed cars that had come to his establishment all season."

The following month, the *New York Times* reported Eddie Plank was on the reserve list of the St. Louis Browns. It was assumed he was still the property of the New York Yankees. Eddie was quoted as saying he was "through with major league baseball for all time."

On December 26th, Babe Ruth was sold by the Boston Red Sox to the New York Yankees for $125,000, the largest sum ever paid for a player up to that point.

In January, Eddie, Ira, and Dr. Markley were in Philadelphia for an auto show. Eddie was interviewed by Jimmy Insminger of the *North American* regarding why he retired from the majors. Said Eddie, "It was physical exhaustion that seized me in every hard game that caused me to retire. I had just as much stuff as I ever did, but a game of ball began to tax my strength too much. I soon realized that the wear and tear of baseball was taking my very blood out of me, and I decided to quit.

"I haven't pitched since the fall of 1917, and today my health is better than for the last five years of my baseball career. Fans will recall how nervous and fidgety I was on the hill. I have lost all that nervousness and am bigger and stronger than I was. I made no mistake to quitting and no amount of money would induce me to return. I believe I am the property of the Yanks, for the Browns traded me to New York.

"The Athletic teams from 1909 to 1914 were the strongest that ever played baseball, and I feel proud to think I belonged to it."

The year 1920 began with the Eighteenth Amendment going into effect, commencing the era of Prohibition on January 18th.

Early in 1920, teams were trying to get Eddie back on the mound. George Cockill, who was coaching the Steelton team in the Bethlehem-Steel League, had offered a contract to Eddie to pitch for the team. Eddie turned him down, saying he was too involved with his thriving garage business. When Cockill reduced his request to just a few holiday games, Plank turned it down, concerned he could not get into shape in time. "I have no more hope of pitching," he said.

On May 2nd, the first game of Negro National League baseball was played in Indianapolis, Indiana.

Eddie was back in Philadelphia in July and had a meeting with John Shibe, of the A's. He mentioned that Byron "Rube" Yarrison was a capable pitcher in the Blue Ridge League. The team traded for him immediately. Rube stopped by Gettysburg to visit friends, on his way to Philadelphia. While Yarrison had an unremarkable and brief major league career, he did win 20 games for Rocky Mount in the Virginia League the following season.

Also, that summer, Eddie returned to the mound for an exhibition game pitting courthouse officials against some town all-stars. Eddie won 8 to 3. Apparently, his control was exceptional. Ira Plank then organized an exhibition between the Independents, including pitcher Clyde Plank, and the Ira Plank's All-Stars, which included Ira at first base, and Eddie in center field. Clyde Plank, the son of Luther Plank, who had been a star pitcher in the local town league, was offered a professional contract to play minor league ball with Waynesboro in the Blue Ridge League.

On August 26th, the 19th Amendment to the US Constitution passed, giving women the right to vote.

On September 17th, the National Football League was founded.

Wednesday, September 29th, 1920, Yankees pitcher Carl Mays dropped by Gettysburg to visit with Eddie for the evening. He and Eddie were long-term friends from their days as opponents when Mays was with Boston. Mays did not discuss the recent incident regarding the accidental death of Ray Chapman (on August 17th), and no one broached the subject. He did talk about the scandal with the White Sox and offered his support for Charles Comiskey. Pitcher Eddie Cicotte had just confessed to his participation in the scheme to the grand jury the prior day.

On November 2nd, Warren G. Harding defeated Democrat James Cox to become President of the United States.

On Monday, December 20th, it was announced that "Ira and Eddie Plank, and their partner Dr. E. H. Markley, had sold their prosperous garage business to George and Charles Hemler, after many days of negotiation. George Hemler, who had been the day man at the shop the past six months, will take possession with his brother in April. The Planks will continue to sell cars through the showroom, and have leased a portion of the garage space for five years."

About the baseball world, Eddie had faded from the scene but was remembered by veteran players and sportswriters.

On April 29, 1921, the great Walter Johnson surpassed Eddie Plank's American League career wins record. That summer, the remarks of veteran Philadelphia sportswriter Cullen Cain were very favorable towards Eddie Plank. Wrote Cain, "As far as effectiveness is concerned, Eddie Plank, of Gettysburg, may be regarded as one of the five greatest pitchers in the history of baseball.

"See where a baseball authority selected the greatest pitchers of all time, some seventeen of them, without naming Eddie Plank!

By the flick of the whiplash! I can never stand for that. To my mind Plank should be named in any group of five great pitchers of the game. Of the five left-handers named by this authority, not one of them lasted as long as Plank, and only one of them, Waddell, excelled him in effectiveness. Plank started with Connie Mack in 1901 and was a star from the beginning, and then in 1914, he was just as effective as ever. In 1917, when past the age of forty, he pitched his last big league game, losing to Walter Johnson, of Washington, by a score of 1 to 0.

"Eddie Plank has probably taken part in more 1-to-0 and 2-to-1 games than any pitcher in the history of the game. Those were the scores that predominated when he was on the hill.

"Effective in the very beginning of his major-league career; effective all the way along the track of seventeen seasons, never a break or a falter or an off-year from his debut to his farewell. A 1-to-0 defeat in eleven innings in his last game. It is true that Plank was not an iron man. He did not pitch a record number of games any year, neither did he win a record number of games. But in Simon-pure effectiveness, he was as good as the best. Only Walter Johnson can rival him in the number of close games lost by low scores.

"When anyone names more than four great pitchers and omits the name of Eddie Plank, of Gettysburg, Pennsylvania, I raise my voice in protest against the injustice and ingratitude of the times."

Dr. Markley and the Planks subsequently announced their Buick dealership in an advertisement on June 6th, 1921. The garage business had been handed over to the Hemlers but continued to operate as Eddie Plank's Garage.

On August 5th, the first radio broadcast of a baseball game occurred as Harold Arlin announced the Pirates-Phillies game over Westinghouse KDKA radio from Pittsburgh.

August 26th, 1921, Eddie and Ira were in Huntington, Pennsylvania, where the local team had advertised extensively that the Planks were going to play in a game. Eddie and Ira knew nothing of this until they arrived for the game. To placate the fans, Eddie umpired.

On October 25th, the famous gunfighter Bat Masterson died in New York City.

Along the way, the Plank household was not without its events. March 21, 1922, there was an auction of the Plank farm on the Harrisburg Road. All the livestock, farm implements, and personal property were sold. The farm had been the home of Eddie's parents for decades. The auction listing declared that the owners were "giving up farming."

April 5, 1922, was a sad day in the Plant household. Eddie's mother-in-law, Ellen Myers, passed away at their home on Carlisle Street while in the care of her daughter. She was 79 years old. The funeral was held in the home on the 8th, followed by burial in New Oxford.

On May 5th, construction began on Yankee Stadium in the Bronx. It would become "The House that Ruth Built."

On May 30th, the Lincoln Memorial was dedicated in Washington, D.C.

The summer of 1922, Eddie was back umpiring the town ballgames. Saturday, August 12th, in Hanover, Eddie and Ira participated in an exhibition game pitting the Bald and Gray versus the Hanover Red Men. The Bald and Gray won 6 to 2, with Eddie pitching the first three hitless and scoreless innings.

Eddie and Ira remained avid baseball fans. On Thursday, October 4th, 1922, the Plank brothers were in New York to attend the first game of the World Series between the Giants and Yankees. Eddie had his picture taken with Bob Shawkey, Wally Schang, Joe Bush, and Frank Baker, all former Athletics.

The Giants won the game 3 to 2 with three runs in the eighth off Bullet Joe Bush. The Yankees had Babe Ruth in right field. The Giants had a player named Casey Stengel in center. Casey's boys won the series, sweeping the Yanks.

Eddie also loved to hunt and shoot and was quite good at it. He would often win or almost-win the clay pigeon shoots at the Gettysburg Rod and Gun Club.

In early November 1922, Eddie was hunting bear in Sullivan County. Five miles into the woods, he bagged a 310-pound bruin, which had to be hauled out on a sled.

During the winter of 1923, Mrs. Plank and Eddie, Jr. headed to St. Augustine, Florida, with her sister Mrs. Dick, of New Oxford. It was to be an extended visit. They returned in late February.

Early in 1923, John McGraw praised Eddie Plank and the early A's teams. Said McGraw, "I have never regarded the Chicago club of 1906-7-8 as the greatest of ball clubs. It had determination and fighting spirit, and it had smartness, but it did not have the natural strength of the Athletics of 1911 or of the 1905 New York team.

"Nobody appreciates the efforts of the famous Cubs more than myself, but in all frankness, I must say that Chance's club was not so good as the Athletics of 1911—a team that lasted until Connie Mack finally broke it up deliberately.

"In that team, Mack had practically everything that is needed for a great club. There were no weak spots that one could indicate with certainty.

"In the first place, it had wonderful pitching. Very few ball clubs were ever equipped with such pitchers as Bender, Plank, and Coombs. All of these were thinking pitchers. In addition, they had the goods physically. A club with a trio of such pitchers would be pretty hard to beat in a season or in a series anytime.

"I don't remember ever having seen a much better combination around second base than Eddie Collins and Jack Barry.

"Then, at third, there was Frank Baker. Stuffy McInnis came along soon, and there was an infield pretty nearly perfect. All of these men could hit and all knew the tricks of the game in the field.

"The Athletics had a punch at all times. Our pitchers realized that to their sorrow the first time we ran against them. On the other hand, our batters knew what they were up against when they had to face such pitchers as Plank, Coombs, and Bender.

"I have no hesitation in expressing the opinion that the Athletics of that period were one of the greatest ball clubs of all times."

On April 18th, Eddie was in Philadelphia for Opening Day of the Athletics' home schedule. The A's beat the Washington Senators 3 to 1. Slim Harriss defeated the great Walter Johnson thanks to a three-run home run by Jimmy Dykes.

Judge Kennesaw Mountain Landis and his wife dropped by Gettysburg on May 18th, 1923, to tour the battlefield. They dropped by the Plank residence to see Eddie but did not find him at home. They continued for their tour.

Eddie was back on the mound on June 11th, 1923, pitching the Gettysburg alumni against the varsity, to an 8-to-1 victory with five strong innings. He even added a base-hit. The *Gettysburg Times* described Eddie as "gray, but smiling like a happy schoolboy as he sometimes burned a fast one into the glove of his catcher."

On August 2nd, 1923, Warren Harding died and was succeeded by Calvin Coolidge as President of the United States.

During February 1924, Eddie's name was floated as the potential president of the new Adams County League. Said Eddie of the opportunity, "I will not accept the presidency of the proposed Adams County Baseball League. As yet, an offer to become head of the county association has not been made to me, but I will flatly refuse it if it is offered as I understand it will. I am willing to help form a county league, and will gladly lend any assistance in that direction, but I will not accept the presidency."

On March 7, Eddie sold the old family farm in Straban Township to Albert Keller. Keller would own it until 1939.

That spring, Eddie was listed as a coach for the Gettysburg team in the Adams County League. His business partner, E. H. Markley was the manager.

On June 2, 1924, Calvin Coolidge signed the *Indian Citizenship Act of 1924*, granting citizenship to all Native Americans born within the territorial limits of the United States.

That year, Ralph Davis, columnist for the *Pittsburgh Press* wrote an article comparing the merits of the best pitchers in baseball history, published in the *Gettysburg Times* in July. Said Davis, "Ballplayers admit that Christy Mathewson was the king pitcher of all time. He is the standard of every pitcher; the pitcher's pitcher.

"Go through the lifetime averages of pitchers and take the first 20. Placing them in order, you have Christy Mathewson, Joe McGinnity, Grover Cleveland Alexander, Walter Johnson, Jack

Chesbro, Denton Cy Young, Rube Waddell, Eddie Plank, Wilbur Cooper, Mordecai "Three Fingered" Brown, George Herman "Babe" Ruth, George Mullin, Addie Joss, Stanley Coveleski, Jim Vaughn, Vic Willis, Ed Walsh, Jeff Overall, Joe Wood, and Urban Shocker. Mathewson leads the group with a lifetime average of .695. In 13 years of pitching, he won 335 games and lost 147."

Davis then compares the best of these top hurlers in other statistical categories, and Eddie Plank is mentioned along with Mathewson, Johnson, and Alexander, but is never the top of any category.

Colliers published an article by Ty Cobb that month entitled "What Baseball Has Taught Ty Cobb," written by Dayton Stoddart. In it, Cobb referred to Plank as "the greatest pitcher he ever saw."

Said Ty, "He had everything, but most of all, he had brains. He had a good drop, control, curves—and he used to mix his fastball and drop and his curves and shoot them from three or four different positions. With Plank pitching, the batter was in the hole from the moment he stepped in the box. He used his head all the time. And after he lost his fastball, he stuck in the big leagues. How? He used to go out and practice by the hour until he developed a slow ball that was as good as any I've ever seen. I think the last game he pitched he either won or lost by only a 1-to-0 score. Think of that."

September 11th, 1924, the *Gettysburg Times* announced the paving of the Harrisburg Road from the borough limits to the former Eddie Plank farm.

On September 15th, Frank Chance, Hall of Fame former first baseman and manager, made famous as part of the "Tinker-to-Evers-to-Chance" infield, passed away in Los Angeles. He had managed the Red Sox in 1923. He was 47.

That October 1924, Eddie attended the first two World Series games in Washington.

In Game One, Art Nehf and the Giants defeated Walter Johnson 4 to 3. Billy Terry and High Pockets Kelly both homered in support of Nehf, who scattered ten hits.

Game Two was the inverse, with the Senators returning the favor 4 to 3. Goose Goslin and Bucky Harris homered off Jack Bentley, and Tom Zachary earned the win, with help from Firpo Marberry.

In November 1924, a reunion was planned for Plank and Mathewson as the highlight of a college football dinner in Altoona, prior to a clash between Gettysburg and Bucknell on the Pennsylvania Railroad field. Eddie quickly accepted the invitation. "Count on me being present with brother Ira," wrote Eddie. "We will both be delighted to see Matty again." However, Mathewson was unable to attend.

That November, Eddie sold the house on Carlisle Street to the Druid fraternity of Gettysburg College, the oldest secret organization on campus. They were not planning to move in until the following September (1925).

On November 27th, the first Macy's Thanksgiving Day Parade was held in New York City.

Late in 1924, Walter Johnson's imaginary All-American League team was published in the papers. Johnson was having breakfast with Joe Engle, a scout for Washington, while the two were in San Francisco. Engle asked him to list the all-time best American League players. Johnson provided the following:

> First base, Hal Chase
> Second base, Napolean Lajoie
> Shortstop, Tuck Tucker
> Third base, Jimmy Collins
> Outfielders, Cobb, Speaker, Ruth
> Catcher, Charles Street
> Pitchers, Rube Waddell, Eddie Plank, Addie Joss,
>   Chief Bender, Jack Chesbro, Joe Wood, and Ed
>   Walsh.
> Of course, the "Big Train" omitted himself.

On June 9, 1925, Eddie and Ira participated in the alumni game with Gettysburg College. It was hoped that Eddie would pitch at least the first inning, but he did not, umpiring instead. He would not pitch again.

During the month of July, *The State of Tennessee v. John Thomas Scopes*, commonly known as the Scopes Monkey Trial, was held in Dayton, Tennessee, challenging the Theory of Evolution. Clarence Darrow defended evolution while William Jennings Bryan defended the Christian faith. Bryan won the case, but the Tennessee Supreme Court ultimately overturned it. Bryan died less than a week after the trial ended.

This summer, columnist and former umpire Billy Evans listed his All-American team. It included:

> First base, George Sisler and Hal Chase
> Second base, Eddie Collins and Rogers Hornsby
> Shortstop, Honus Wagner and Roger Peckinpaugh
> Third base, Jimmy Collins and Frankie Frisch
> Outfielders, Ty Cobb, Fred Clarke, Tris Speaker, Edd
>   Roush, Babe Ruth, and Willie Keeler
> Catcher, Ray Schalk, Roger Bresnahan, Johnny Kling,
>   and Charles Farrell
> Pitchers, Christy Mathewson, Cy Young, Walter
>   Johnson, Addie Joss, Grover Cleveland Alexander,
>   Chief Bender, Rube Waddell, Eddie Plank, Ed
>   Walsh, and Jack Chesbro.

In August of 1925, Harry "Moose" McCormick dropped by and reminisced with Eddie about their playing days, to the delight of those present.

Plank and Markley continued their Buick dealership in the showroom on York Street. Around this time, the former Eddie Plank's Garage was renamed Gettysburg Buick Company, now under the management of Jennings and Curtis.

That October, the Plank family, including Eddie, Jr., headed to Washington to watch the World Series, attending games Three, Four, and Five. On October 7th, as the series was getting underway, the great Christy Mathewson passed away in Saranac Lake, New York, having succumbed from tuberculosis, the result of poison gas during his World War I service. "Matty" was laid to rest on October 10, in Lewisburg, Pennsylvania, near the campus of his beloved Bucknell University. He was only forty-five years old.

During the exciting seven-game marathon, between Pittsburgh and Washington, Eddie Plank was asked his opinion about

Christy Mathewson at the time. Said Eddie, "Baseball has lost the mightiest pitcher it has known up to this time.

"After our college days, we only pitched against each other in World Series contests. But, I always had the highest respect for the ability of Matty, and I keenly feel the loss as must the entire baseball world, which knew him so long, and loved him as well." Eddie recalled the two traded wins in the 1911 series.

The Senators won the third game, on the day Mathewson was laid to rest. The score was 4 to 3, giving the Senators a 2-to-1 margin.

In game 4, Walter Johnson tossed a six-hit shutout and was supported by the bat of Goose Goslin. The Senators were a win away with three to play.

Alas, it did not happen in Game 5. The Pirates came roaring back with a thirteen-hit attack, winning 6 to 3.

The series returned to Pittsburgh, and the Planks headed home. The Pirates, meanwhile, swept the remaining games 3 to 2, and 9 to 7. The great Walter Johnson was wracked for an uncharacteristic 15 hits in the final game. At 37, it was the last time the "Big Train" appeared in the Fall Classic.

Ira Plank had previously partnered with Robert F. Bell to open the Plank and Bell Ford dealership a few blocks east on York Street. In November of 1925, the dealership moved to a larger location at the corner of Liberty and York Streets.

Sometime after Christmas, 1925, Eddie, now 50 years-old, began to complain of pains in the neck and the back of his head and often appeared nervous or anxious, but he just brushed it off and kept about his routine.

Eddie had also been talking with friends about possibly running for office and taking over the old Plank homestead on the Harrisburg Road. He was considering becoming a farmer. On Saturday, February 20, 1926, Edward L. Weikert, Jr., dropped by to ask Eddie, a staunch Democrat, to sign a petition for Plank to run for the state legislature. Eddie wrote his name, place of residence, and the date, but faltered where it asked for his profession.

"Why not say retired?" asked Weikert.

"No," replied Eddie, "Sometime soon I hope to take up farming at the old place."

He then scribbled "farmer" as his occupation.

On Sunday, February 21, 1926, Eddie and his family went to Biglerville to visit his sister, Grace Spangler, who had been ill. Per those with him, he seemed in good spirits. However, early the next morning, before he had dressed for the day, he suffered a severe stroke that paralyzed his entire left side. Incredibly, the very arm that helped win over 300 major league ballgames could no longer be lifted in the air, and he could not speak.

Dr. Dalby, his attending physician, visited Plank at home on Lincoln Avenue, and said, "There is very slight hope for his recovery. Apparently, Eddie is steadily sinking, and I can't see how he can possibly recover."

Eddie's parents were not immediately notified of his condition, for fear of the impact on the frail elderly couple. But, as Eddie worsened, they were eventually told. They were devastated.

Relatives and family visiting the stricken southpaw found him alert, but unable to speak or move his left side. It was apparent that he could recognize those familiar to him, but tears welled in his eyes as he could not utter a single word.

Into the evening, those present thought the end was near, but early Tuesday morning, he was seen to rally, opening his eyes and trying to smile at those attending. However, he soon lapsed back into unconsciousness.

Through the night, his wife Anna, and ten-year-old son Eddie, Jr., were by his side. On Wednesday morning, Eddie lapsed into a coma, never to awaken again. Eddie Plank died at 3 PM on Wednesday, February 24, 1926, aged 50 years, 5 months, and 25 days. His occupation on his death certificate was listed as an "auto dealer and professional ballplayer."

Bill Sherdel, of nearby McSherrystown, had just led the St. Louis Cardinals in wins in 1925 and the National League in winning percentage with a 15-6 record. Bill, also a left-hander, had emulated Plank and had dropped by for advice over the years. Sherdel was amid a contract dispute with the club and had not headed to spring training. He was the first baseball player to visit the family, following Eddie's passing, consoling the family into the evening.

News of Eddie's sudden unexpected passing traveled quickly.

From spring training in Fort Myers, Florida, Connie Mack was stunned. "I feel like a father must feel when he's lost a son," said the "Tall Tactician," after finally finding his words. "Any words I can voice will not describe the shock I have suffered.

"It was a blow to me when I learned that Eddie had suffered a stroke. But, I had hoped he might recover from that. He was a rugged man, young enough, I was confident, to pull through and regain his health.

"Plank came to me right from college. He was with me in the days when our American League team in Philadelphia was fighting for its existence. I had to call on him to work pretty hard in those days. He never failed me; never complained.

"Eddie Plank was one of the smartest left-hand pitchers it has been my pleasure to have on my club. He was short and light, as pitchers go, but he made up for the physical defects, if such they were, by his study of the game, and his smartness when he was on the pitcher's peak.

"Plank was the master of the cross-fire delivery and that was one of his big assets. He worked hour after hour to perfect his control of that cross-fire, and it made him.

"The world has lost a fine clean sportsman when Eddie Plank died. I am certain he did not have a real enemy in the world. He was the salt of the earth. My heart goes out in sympathy to those of his family who survive him."

Thomas Shibe, president of the Athletics, echoed Mack's words and added, "A great ballplayer in his day and a lovable character; one of God's noblemen. I am grieved before the power of expression."

Former umpire Billy Evans, who wrote a syndicated column at the time, said, "Eddie Plank was one of the smartest pitchers I ever called balls and strikes for ... always a frail-looking chap and a bundle of nerves, was just the type to finally succumb to a stroke of paralysis ... Too bad Eddie Plank had to die so young. He was a square-shooter, a credit to the game, an inspiration to the collegian."

Throughout the next couple days, as the family made funeral arrangements, countless letters and telegrams arrived offering well-wishes and condolences from all over the country. Two rooms of the Plank home became filled with flowers. Anna and Eddie, Jr., were lifted by the sheer volume and sincerity of it all.

From Mr. and Mrs. Jack Coombs: "Can hardly realize that my roommate for seven years has gone to the great beyond. Mrs. Coombs and I are greatly grieved over his death. Accept our sincerest sympathy in this hour of your greatest trial. Extend to his parents, brothers, and sisters our condolences.

From Mr. and Mrs. Monte Cross: "You have our heartfelt sympathy. We feel the loss of our old playmate."

From Mr. and Mrs. Jack Barry: "Please accept our heartfelt sympathy."

From Mr. and Mrs. C. A. Chief Bender: "Our heartfelt sympathy to you all in your great sorrow. We loved him."

From Herb Pennock: "I wish to extend my deepest sympathies at this time."

From J. Franklin Home Run Baker: "So sorry and hurt to hear of your loss. You have my deepest sympathy."

From Eddie Collins, who was in spring training as a manager of the White Sox: "Words fail to express my heartfelt sorrow over the loss of a true friend and former teammate as your husband. Permit me to extend my sincerest sympathy to you and yours from Mrs. Collins and myself in this time of your bereavement."

Harry Davis was one of the first to call via telephone to offer his help in informing Eddie's friends in Philadelphia.

Saturday morning, February 27, there was a private funeral service in the Plank home attended by the family. Eddie's parents were brought from their home north of town, but Eddie's mother was too grief-stricken to continue to the church.

Eddie's body was then transferred to the Presbyterian Church on Baltimore Street in Gettysburg, where it lay in state at 1 PM, surrounded by a military guard from the Gettysburg College ROTC. For two hours, hundreds of mourners paid their respects, passing single-file through the historic church where Abraham Lincoln had visited after dedicating the national cemetery during the Civil War.

At 3 PM, church organist Miss Elizabeth van Cleve, began playing, followed by the service led by Reverend Robinson. Dr. Henry Hanson, president of Gettysburg College, followed with a eulogy. The brief service concluded with somber organ music.

A cortege escorted the casket up Baltimore Street to Evergreen Cemetery, where Eddie was then laid to eternal rest. Former Good Intent baseball coach, Robert K. Major, was one of the pallbearers.

Eddie's Shriner's certificate from 1919.

*Actress Lillian Russell who happened by the
Plank garage.*

Eddie (left) with the bear he bagged. Ira is on the right.
Jack Coombs may be 2nd from right.

The former Eddie Plank Buick dealership and garage (photo by the author).

The former Plank home in Gettysburg (photo by the author).

The former Ira Plank Ford dealership (photo by the author).

Ira Plank Ford advertisement.

Eddie relaxing at the family's camp.

Anna Cora on a beach chair.

The Planks at their camp.

The Plank family shortly before Eddie passed away.

PLANK
REMEMBERED

TUESDAY, MARCH 16TH, the work of settling Eddie Plank's estate began. His father, David, who had been named the executor, renounced this role and allowed Eddie's wife, Anna, to function in that capacity. Plank left behind an accumulation of $50,000 in assets, per the *Gettysburg Times*, the following day.

Eddie left his parents the small farm they lived on and $10,000 in cash. The remaining estate, including $20,000 in trust and the home on Carlisle Street, was left to Anna.

By the end of the month, an Eddie Plank Memorial Fund was started, conceived by Paul Roy, editor of the *Gettysburg Times*, with the support of Henry W. A. Hanson, the president of Gettysburg College. The plan was to use the funds to build a gymnasium for the college in Eddie's honor. Said Hanson, "We cannot attempt to accomplish our purpose in dedicating the $125,000 gymnasium to Eddie Plank's memory. One who played the game so fair and so square, who was an inspiration to collegian as well as the sandlot youngster, deserves every bit of recognition possible to bestow upon his memory. In keeping permanent a bound volume of the names of those who contribute to the memorial project, it will serve to encourage others to play the game of life as fair and as square as the late Eddie."

That spring and summer, Eddie Plank Days were held throughout the Cumberland Valley and across the nation, the goal was to raise funds for the gymnasium. Martinsburg, West Virginia held an event at their ballpark on May 31st. Hagerstown and Waynesboro soon followed. Other days were held in York on June 9, Hanover on June 26, Chicago in August, and Cleveland, Detroit, Washington, Boston, New York, Chambersburg, and Frederick thereafter.

Gettysburg merchant and warehouseman Grover C. Myers endorsed the "Buy a Brick" campaign and said, "I am in hearty accord with the Plank Memorial Gymnasium project. I think it is a wonderful thought and a splendid thing to put into effect. Every resident of Gettysburg and Adams County ought to contribute something to the fund. They are all aware of what the famous southpaw hurler did for Gettysburg, and to demonstrate their appreciation and to show interest such a project deserves, they ought to contribute at least a dollar if no more."

Connie Mack became chairman of the gymnasium committee. He got the commissioner, Judge Kennesaw Mountain Landis involved as associate chairman. Wrote Landis, "I am deeply interested in the success of this enterprise and will have real satisfaction in heartily cooperating." He offered his full support for the Eddie Plank Day to be held in Chicago.

Said Connie Mack, "The erection of a memorial gymnasium to the memory of Eddie Plank is a splendid thought. It is a fitting tribute to a man who devoted seventeen years of exceptional effort to raise the national pastime to the position of prominence it now holds with the American people. I am more than anxious to see the fulfillment of this project."

Other committee members included Walter Johnson, Eddie Collins, Jack Coombs, Jack Barry, Clark Griffith, Monte Cross, Tris Speaker, William F. Baker, Hyman Pearlstone, Home Run Baker, Chief Bender, Bucky Harris, John McGraw, and Ty Cobb.

After the end of the baseball season, on Thursday, September 30th, Gettysburg College closed as two hundred students planned to venture to Philadelphia for a city championship exhibition between the Athletics and the Phillies. The game had been coordinated by Connie Mack in honor of Eddie Plank. All proceeds were earmarked for the gymnasium.

Regarding the exodus of students, the *Gettysburg Times* reported: "... while a few of the students will go by train, the majority will make the journey by automobile, every available machine about the college, including some that almost seen their last days, being pressed into service to carry the local delegation to Philadelphia." Classes were expected to resume on Friday morning. Unfortunately, it rained all day and the game was postponed until the following year.

On Friday, September 23, 1927, plans for the Plank game in Philadelphia came to fruition, thanks to the efforts of Clayton Bilheimer, athletic director at Gettysburg College. The game was planned for Monday, October 3, at Shibe Park. While with Mack in his office in Philadelphia, Ty Cobb stopped by before heading out on a hunting trip. Said Ty, "The cleanest, finest, squarest player big league baseball has ever known was Eddie Plank. I am glad that I personally knew Plank, whom I had always considered the greatest southpaw the sport had ever produced."

Bilheimer arranged for Mrs. Plank and son Eddie, Jr., to be the guests of president Hanson at the event. Eddie, Jr., was asked to throw out the first pitch.

That Monday, it was overcast and rainy, keeping most of the fans away. Comedians Nick Altrock and Al Schacht performed for the crowd before the game. Eddie Plank, Jr. then threw out the first pitch. The game that followed was shortened at six innings due to a rain shower. At that point, Altrock and Schacht were inserted into the Athletics lineup, with Altrock on the mound, and Schacht catching. It was a signal to the crowd that the exhibition was over and about to be replaced by humorous antics. The ballplayers played along as the hidden ball trick and reverse base-running proceeded to the laughs of those on hand.

The Edward S. Plank Memorial Gymnasium had been completed earlier in the year.

On June 13th, 1946, Eddie Plank, along with Jessie Burkett, Frank Chance, Jack Chesbro, Clark Griffith, Tom McCarthy, Joe McGinnity, Joe Tinker, Johnny Evers, Rube Waddell, and Ed Walsh, were inducted into the baseball Hall of Fame. Eddie's plaque was engraved:

* * *

Edward S. Plank
"Gettysburg Eddie"
One of the greatest left-handed pitchers of major leagues. Never pitched for a minor-league team, going from Gettysburg College to the Philadelphia A.L. team which he served from 1901 to 1914. Member of the St. Louis F.L. team in 1915 and St. Louis of the A.L. In 1916-1917. One of few pitchers to win more than 300 games in big leagues. In eight of 17 seasons, he won 20 or more games.

* * *

The induction ceremony was held July 21, 1947, in Cooperstown, New York. Eddie's widow, Eddie, Jr., and his new wife attended, along with Mr. and Mrs. Ira Plank, Mr. and Mrs. Luther Plank, and others from the Gettysburg area.

Only Ed Walsh was present among the players who were honored. Griffith, Tinker, and Burkett were still alive, but unable to make it. Johnny Evers had just passed away in March. The others had died prior.

Many honors have followed for Eddie Plank:

1972: Voted into the Pennsylvania Sports Hall of Fame
1985: Honored on the Philadelphia Baseball Wall of Fame.
2012: Inducted into the Philadelphia Sports Hall of Fame.

In late 1939, Albert Keller transferred the farm to Joseph and Sara Keller, who owned it until November of 2003. At that point, developer Vince Cimino purchased it.

Portions of the old Plank farm along the Harrisburg Road were approved for development. Lots went up for sale in 2007, touting custom homes north of $300,000. The development is called Plank's Field. Streets were named with a baseball theme, including Home Run Circle, Double Play Drive, and Line Drive.

Thanks to Gettysburg native and doctoral student Matt Kerr, state historical markers were erected in Gettysburg and near the farm honoring Eddie Plank.

In 2009, Gettysburg Eddie's, a restaurant and sports bar at 217 Steinwehr Avenue, in Gettysburg, opened to the public. The décor respectfully honors the late southpaw. For 15 years prior, the restaurant was one of the Bill Wills' Gingerbread Man locations. Mr. Wills obtained approval from Eddie's grandson, Eddie Plank, III for use of the name and likenesses.

Eddie Plank, III, the grandson, has also been instrumental in the 19th Century Revival Baseball Team tournament in Gettysburg, which started in 2010. Players come from all around to play baseball the old-fashioned way in vintage uniforms.

As of this writing, Eddie Plank remains at the top of the wins list for all major-league pitchers in Philadelphia baseball history—which includes both the Phillies and the Athletics. He also threw more innings than any other Philadelphia hurler, and is second all-time in strikeouts, after only Steve Carlton.

All-Time Philadelphia Major League Pitching

RK	Player	Team	W	L	ERA	IP	SO
1	Plank, E	A's	284	162	2.39	3860.2	1985
2	Carlton, S	Phils	241	161	3.09	3697.1	3031
3	Roberts, R	Phils	234	199	3.46	3739.1	1871
4	Grove, L	A's	195	79	2.88	2401	1523
5	Bender, C	A's	193	102	2.32	2602	1536
6	Alexander, G	Phils	190	91	2.18	2513.2	1409
7	Rommel, E	A's	171	119	3.54	2556.1	599
8	Walbert, R	A's	134	114	4.12	2186.2	907
9	Short, C	Phils	132	127	3.38	2253	1585
10	Waddell, R	A's	131	82	1.97	1869.1	1576

For his career, Plank totaled a 326–194 record, with a 2.35 ERA, and 2,246 strikeouts. His 305 wins in the American League is the most by a left-handed pitcher. Eddie led the American League in career wins until 1921, when he was surpassed by Walter Johnson. Eddie is now 13th in wins overall, which is 3rd among left-handers after Warren Spahn and Steve Carlton. He is ranked 5th with 69 career shutouts, first among left-handers.

Eddie played in four World Series, compiling a stellar 1.32 ERA, but an unlucky 2–5 win-loss record. He pitched complete games in all six of his World Series starts.

Now, for those of you who are into more contemporary baseball statistics, aka Sabermetrics, please forgive this author for utilizing only traditional measures throughout the book. Given the time-frame Eddie Plank played, all of the sources from those days utilize the statistics popular at the time. However, a brief overview of Plank's career based on the available Sabermetrics is very instructive. For instance, his Career WAR (Wins Above Replacement) of 89.9 ranks 47th of all players in the history of the game, tied with Bob Gibson and a fraction behind Steve Carlton. His WAR for Pitchers of 86.5 ranks 16th all-time ahead of Pedro Martinez, John Clarkson, and Steve Carlton, and behind Christy Mathewson, Gaylord Perry, Warren Spahn, and Tim Keefe. He is 4th among left-handers in this category, trailing Lefty Grove, Randy Johnson, and Warren Spahn.

When analyzing Plank's ranking in Fielding Independent Pitching (FIP), Eddie is 16th all-time at 2.44, ahead of Cy

Falkenberg, Dick Rudolph, and Doc White, and behind Walter Johnson, John Ward, and Fred Glade. Among left-handers, he is 4th trailing Rube Waddell, Jack Pfiester, and Reb Russell.

Checking in on Adjusted Pitching Runs, Eddie ranks 31st all-time, ahead of Hal Newhouser, Dazzy Vance, and Old Hoss Radbourn, and trailing Roy Halladay, Kevin Brown, and Gaylord Perry. Plank ranks 8th among left-handers, trailing Lefty Gomez, Randy Johnson, Carl Hubbell, Warren Spahn, Whitey Ford, Clayton Kershaw, and Tom Glavine.

Viewing Plank from Adjusted Pitching Wins, he ranks 30th all-time, ahead of Hal Newhouser, Steve Carlton, and Ed Walsh, and behind Mariano Rivera, Tom Glavine, and Kevin Brown. He again ranks 8th among left-handers trailing Lefty Grove, Randy Johnson, Warren Spahn, Carl Hubbell, Clayton Kershaw, Whitey Ford, and Tom Glavine.

Considering Eddie's Hall of Fame enshrinement, it definitely appears it was no mistake based on the antiquated statistics. By any measure, Plank performed among the greatest of all time. According to the Jaffe WAR Score system (JAWS) comparing players to those in the Hall of Fame, Eddie ranks 23rd among starting pitchers. There are currently 62 in the Hall of Fame. He is most similar to Robin Roberts and Fergie Jenkins in score.

After he was inducted into the Hall of Fame in 2015, Randy Johnson, "The Big Unit," admitted he had checked into hotels over the years as "Eddie Plank" to avoid attention, which is difficult given his six-foot, ten-inch frame. Johnson also won more than 300 games in the big leagues as a left-hander. Tweeted Johnson:

> My last day being Eddie Plank at the Hotel, first @MLB pitcher to win 300 games. Been an amazing 3 days Thank-You pic.twitter.com/Ir5TWGyFph
> - Randy Johnson (@RJ51Photos) January 8, 2015

It seems not everyone had forgotten our Gettysburg Eddie.

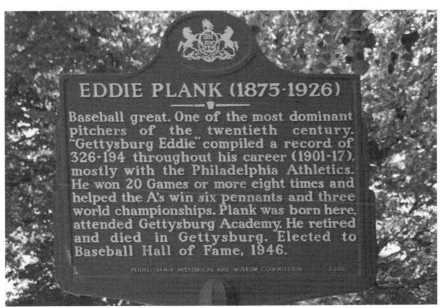

*The graves of Eddie and Anna Plank at Evergreen Cemetery,
Gettysburg, Pennsylvania.*

EDDIE PLANK (1875-1926)

Baseball great. One of the most dominant pitchers of the twentieth century. "Gettysburg Eddie" compiled a record of 326-194 throughout his career (1901-17), mostly with the Philadelphia Athletics. He won 20 Games or more eight times and helped the A's win six pennants and three world championships. Plank was born here, attended Gettysburg Academy. He retired and died in Gettysburg. Elected to Baseball Hall of Fame, 1946.

PENNSYLVANIA HISTORICAL AND MUSEUM COMMISSION   2000

Eddie Plank historical marker in Gettysburg.

CONNIE MACK AND YOUNG PLANK

The manager of the Athletics was photographed yesterday at
Shibe Park with Eddie Plank, Jr., son of the former Athletic pitcher,
during the post-season game which the A's and the Phils played
for the benefit of the Eddie Plank Memorial fund.

Connie Mack with Eddie Jr. at Eddie Plank Day in Philadelphia.

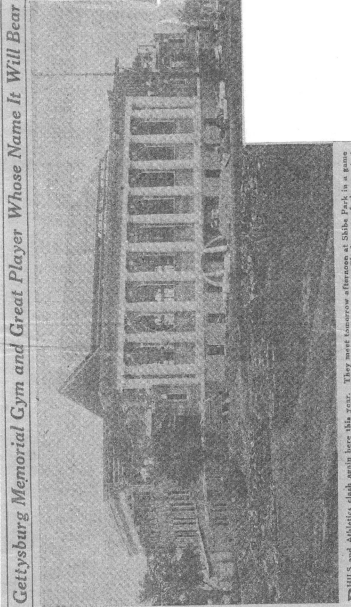

Gettysburg Memorial Gym and Great Player Whose Name It Will Bear

PHILS and Athletics clash again here this year. They meet tomorrow afternoon at Shibe Park in a game for the benefit of the Eddie Plank Memorial Gymnasium at Gettysburg. Plank, one of the greatest of all left handers, was a graduate of Gettysburg College and the gymnasium, which will be completed in November and dedicated to the popular southpaw who died this year, will cost more than $125,000. Besides the ball game, Paul L. Roy, secretary of the Memorial Committee, announces that Nick Aitrock and Al Schacht will be on hand to strut their stuff and that Walter Johnson may also be here. The Gettysburg College band will also be present.

The Eddie Plank Gymnasium at Gettysburg College.

Eddie's Hall of Fame plaque.

Family at the Hall of Fame. Eddie Jr. and Anna are in the back.
Ira is at bottom right.

Family and friends at the Hall of Fame.
Eddie Jr. is at bottom right.

Extended family at the Hall of Fame.

Anna Cora (right) at the Hall of Fame.

The logo for the Gettysburg Eddie's restaurant.

The storefront for Gettysburg Eddie's.

Entrance sign for Plank Field Estates development at the former David Plank farm (photo by the author).

Advertisement sign at Plank Field Estates (photo by the author).

One of the road signs within Plank Field Estates (photo by the author).

The likely location of the Plank ball field on the David Plank farm, now Plank Field Estates (photo by author).

SOURCES

Books, Magazines, Journals, Files:

Adams County Historical Society. Plank family and Eddie Plank files viewed at Gettysburg, Pennsylvania.

Allen, Lee, and Tom Meany. *Kings of the Diamond*. New York: G. P. Putnam's Sons, 1965.

Cleveland, Linda K. "From Family Farm to Baseball Hall of Fame: Edward 'Eddie' Stewart Plank 1875-1926, Family History and Stories Added". Unpublished, December 2013. (provided by Edward Plank, III)

Eddie Plank files at the National Baseball Hall of Fame and Museum in Cooperstown, New York.

Enders, Eric. *100 Years of the World Series*. New York: Barnes & Noble Books, 2003.

Gulden, Dave. "The Forgotten Games of Eddie Plank." *The National Pastime*. 24 (2004), 41-47.

Hoie, Bob, and Carlos Bauer, compilers. L. Robert Davids, Bob McConnell, Ray Nemec, John Benesch Jr., and Bill Weiss, eds. *The Historical Register: The Major & Minor League Records of Baseball's Greatest Players*. San Diego and San Marino: Baseball Press Books, 1998.

Honig, Donald. *The Greatest Pitchers of All Time*. New York: Crown Publishers, Inc., 1988.

James, Bill. *The New Bill James Historical Baseball Abstract*. New York: The Free Press, 2001.

James, Bill, and Rob Neyer. *The Neyer/James Guide to Pitchers: An Historical Compendium of Pitching, Pitchers, and Pitches*. New York and London: Simon & Schuster, 2004.

Jordan, David M. *The Athletics of Philadelphia: Connie Mack's White Elephants, 1901-1954*. Jefferson, NC: McFarland & Co., 1999.

Kashatus, William C. *The Philadelphia Athletics*. Charleston, SC: Arcadia Publishing, 2002.

Kulick, Bruce. *To Everything a Season: Shibe Park and Urban Philadelphia, 1909-1976*. Princeton, NJ: Princeton University Press, 1991.

Leventhal, Josh. *The World Series: An Illustrated Encyclopedia of the Fall Classic*. New York: Black Dog & Leventhal Publishers, 2001.

Macht, Normal L. *Connie Mack and the Early Years of Baseball*. Lincoln, NE: University of Nebraska Press, 2007.

Mack, Connie. *My 66 Years in the Big Leagues*. Mineola, NY: Dover Publications, 2009.

MacKay, Joe. *The Great Shutout Pitchers: Twenty Profiles of a Vanishing Breed*. Jefferson, North Carolina, and London: McFarland, 2004.

Meany, Tom. *Baseball's Greatest Pitchers*. New York: A. S. Barnes and Company, 1951.

Neft, David S., and Richard M. Cohen. *The World Series: Complete Play-by-Play of Every Game 1903-1989*. New York: St. Martin's Press, 1990.

Palmer, Pete, and Gary Gillette, eds. *The Baseball Encyclopedia*. New York: Barnes & Noble Books, 2004.

Plank, Edward, Jr. "The Life and Baseball Career of Eddie Plank". Unpublished, circa 1936. (provided by Edward Plank, III)

Purdy, Dennis. *The Team by Team Encyclopedia of Major League Baseball.* New York: Workman Publishing, 2006.

Smith, Ira. *Baseball's Famous Pitchers: Capers Cut and Records Made by Fifty-three Pitching Greats.* New York: A. S. Barnes and Company, 1954.

Spatz, Lyle. *Yankees Coming, Yankees Going: New York Yankee Player Transactions, 1903 Through 1999.* Jefferson, North Carolina, and London: McFarland, 2000.

Taylor, Ted. *The Ultimate Philadelphia Athletics Reference Book, 1901-1954.* Xlibris Corporation, 2010.

Thorn, John, Phil Birnbaum, Bill Deane, et al. *Total Baseball: The Ultimate Baseball Encyclopedia. 8th ed.* Wilmington, Delaware: Sport Media Publishing Inc., 2004.

Threston, Christopher. *The Integration of Baseball in Philadelphia.* Jefferson, NC: McFarland & Co., 2003.

Westcott, Rich. *Winningest Pitchers: Baseball's 300-Game Winners.* Philadelphia: Temple University Press, 2002.

Westcott, Rich. *Shibe Park – Connie Mack Stadium.* Charleston, SC: Arcadia Publishing, 2012.

Wilbert, Warren N. *What Makes an Elite Pitcher? Young, Mathewson, Johnson, Alexander, Grove, Spahn, Seaver, Clemens, and Maddux.* Jefferson, North Carolina, and London: McFarland, 2003.

Online Resources:

Ancestry.com – for census, birth, marriage, death, military services and numerous other records.

Baseball-Reference.com – for most box scores, game records, career statistics, and post-season information.

FindaGrave.com – for burial information, vital statistics and obituaries.

Gettysburg College Archives – provided access to the Gettysburgian college newspaper accounts of the baseball team's games.

Newspapers.com – including primarily the Philadelphia Inquirer, Philadelphia Times, Gettysburg Times, Gettysburg Compiler, Harrisburg Telegraph, St. Louis Post-Dispatch and others. Hundreds of newspaper articles were accessed—too numerous to mention here. Most are cited in the text and can be found by searching for the newspaper for the day after the events occurred.

SABR.org – access to Eddie Plank's biography and the biography of several other players mentioned, including Doc Powers. Also, access to the *Sporting News* archives.

Wikipedia.com – for general historical information regarding baseball, the United States, and world history.

Interviews:

Eddie Plank, III – was interviewed on the phone and in-person numerous times from early 2017 through early 2018. Eddie also provided files containing personal stories, photos, and ephemera related to his family history.

INDEX

Made in the USA
Columbia, SC
07 July 2019